PRAISE FOR

THE GIRL IN THE GUN CLUB

"What kind of marks do fourteen years in the United States Marine Corps leave on a young woman? The short answer: a lot more and a lot deeper than fourteen years anywhere else. Tracy Salzgeber serves up a super-concentrated juicy slice of the diverse humanity who choose to become Marines. And she delivers it in tales cut with the precision of a diamond-bladed microtome. Dark, dry, wry, absurd, and ineluctably weird, this is the work of a natural storyteller produced under what any Marine will tell you are highly unnatural circumstances. Check your preconceptions at the door. This is a military memoir unlike any you have ever encountered."

—**Alan Axelrod**, author of *Miracle at Belleau Wood:*
The Birth of the Modern U.S. Marine Corps

"A solid page-turner. Tracy has moral fortitude to tackle some of the most difficult subjects in military life. *The Girl in the Gun Club* is a stunning tapestry of military life."

—**Galen D. Peterson**, author of *Strike Hard*
and Expect No Mercy

"A rare glimpse inside the Marines. Tracy Salzgeber gives as good as she gets in this rollicking account of her years as a female Marine. Thick skinned, tough talking, and determined, she earns her *wasta*."

—**Rona Simmons**, author of *A Gathering of Men*

"Eye-opening, visceral view of the Marines from a unique perspective that is truly addictive. There were many moments where I thought, *WOW, every leader should set down their latest fad leadership handbook and read this!* This book drives home so many great points and in truly tangible and useable ways. Excellent! I want more!"

—**Keith Weinzerl**, director at Seattle-based tech firm

"A honest, hysterical, and gripping look at what it is to be a female Marine. Salzgeber does a great job making you feel like you are in her boots."

—**James E.**, Desert Storm veteran, US Army

The Girl in the Gun Club: My Time as One of the Few Good Men

by Tracy Salzgeber

© Copyright 2022 Tracy Salzgeber

ISBN 978-1-64663-598-6

Published by

 köehlerbooks™

3705 Shore Drive
Virginia Beach, VA 23455
800-435-4811
www.koehlerbooks.com

THE GIRL IN THE GUN CLUB
MY TIME AS ONE OF THE FEW GOOD MEN

TRACY SALZGEBER

VIRGINIA BEACH
CAPE CHARLES

TABLE OF CONTENTS

PART EIGHT
Camp Lejeune, North Carolina Part II

PART NINE
The Pentagon, Washington DC

AUTHOR'S NOTE

I have changed names, places, dates, and other details in these stories to protect the guilty. And the innocent. And the bystanders. And the entirely unaffiliated who may or may not have even been aware this was all going on.

I decided to write this book after a disturbing phone call I got in 2017. A friend from my time on active duty asked me to speak to his teenage daughter, who had decided she wanted to join the Marines. At first, I was delighted with the idea and agreed. When she called me, I gushed about all the positives and avoided focusing on the negatives. I could tell that she had something on her mind, though, and was working up the nerve to ask.

Finally, as we were winding down, she just went for it.

"Everyone says that if I join the Marine Corps, I'm going to get beaten and raped. Is it true?"

I was floored. I knew my branch had a reputation for being rough, but I didn't think we were perceived like *that*. Not in the twenty-first century. We hung up, and I sat down to have a long think. Then I wrote this book.

Hopefully, the next phone call will go better.

NOVEMBER BRAVO

There are a few things you should know before we start.

First, we were bored.

Second, the Marine Corps is one of those hallowed institutions that sprang forth from the American Revolutionary War. From the very beginning, Marines earned a reputation for being tough, fierce, and deadly. The Marine Corps is also the smallest service branch within the Department of Defense, although the Marines are technically an offshoot[1] of the Navy. At this time of writing, in 2020, there are approximately 182,000 Marines on active duty. That makes us rare.

According to the DoD's own statements, active military personnel account for 0.4 percent of the American population, United States Marines make up 14 percent of those, and female Marines are 8 percent of the USMC. For the fourteen years I was on active duty, I was one of the 8 percent of the 14 percent of the 0.4 percent of American men and women who ever wear what recruiters like to call the "nation's cloth." (Most of the time, that cloth was cammies.)

Third, we were *really* bored.

One thing I knew by now was that grunts are famously superstitious. They may look and act like barely literate meatheads, but I haven't met one yet who did not, deep down in his grungy, dirty soul, believe in things like luck and being watched over by a guardian angel/God (or gods)/a relative who had passed on. Additionally, for as long as there has been

---

1 We're pretty salty about this. Best not to bring it up.

history, women have been associated with witchcraft. In every culture I've ever learned about, someone somewhere eventually made a connection between women and the occult.

It's an enduring stereotype, and I knew a thing or two about it, thanks to my decidedly nonstandard upbringing. So, I played to it. Not in the teenage-goth-kid way that arouses irritation in most right-thinking human beings, but in my own way.

I was the staff non-fire NCO on the range at Stone Bay in North Carolina early in 2010. My job was to shepherd 110 Marines from H&S (Headquarters and Support) Battalion through their annual rifle-qualification week on the range. Our day usually started at 0400 and went until 1800 or later every single day.

Swarms of Marines from other units were there as well. SSgt Vasquez, another staff sergeant from an infantry battalion, had roughly ninety-eight Marines, all infantrymen, to get through the armory each morning and afternoon for weapons withdrawal and turn-in. The process of pulling weapons or returning them to the armory represented a solid hour or more of verifying paperwork and serial numbers as each Marine handed the armorer a rifle-issue card that detailed the exact rifle they were permitted to pull from the armory, along with their military ID. Failure to produce either card would result in bureaucratic chaos with serious consequences, like the armory just refusing to issue any weapons to the unit until the oversight was corrected. That, in turn, would lead to the entire unit missing a day of shooting, and *that* would cause heads to roll, starting with the staff non-fire who had failed to make sure that a hundred Marines all consistently showed up on time, without forgetting either card, each and every day for one week at oh-my-God in the morning.

As a result of this, the order in which units lined up to draw weapons became a critical matter. If your group was at the front of the line, you had time to get food and a smoke after pulling weapons. If your group was the last in the queue, you had time to find the idiots who showed up fifteen minutes late because whatever-the-fuck excuse and prevent your group from getting kicked off the range. The order for units to be served by the armory was announced the day prior so that the staff non-fires could manage their assigned groups appropriately.

Because Vasquez and I were both non-fires (meaning we didn't actually do any shooting, just watched others while they shot and made sure they weren't about to shoot something or somebody they should not), we mostly just sat on a bench, watching our troops and being bored out of our skulls for hours in the heat of North Carolina's early summer. Rifle-range duty was full of dirt, grease, the smell of spent gunpowder, mud, grass, sweat, and swamp-creature levels of humidity. Incessant tobacco use added another layer to the grime, as Marines chain-smoked their boredom and stress away. In between shooting relays, Marines stood on a concrete walkway between the firing lines and smoked, talked, and compared how they were doing that day.

The Marines who actually ran the range, grunts to a man, kept these messy and distracted shooters away from the piles of live ammunition stacked on a red wooden table behind the mobile wooden shed where instructions were barked via megaphone-like speakers to hundreds of Marines, most of whom had earplugs in. It was loud, and it was uncomfortable, but it made up for it by being unbearably dull.

So, I told SSgt Vasquez one day that I was a gypsy. To be honest, this was a bit of a stretch. I grew up in a staunchly Southern Baptist family who would have graphically demonstrated their horror at my interest in things like tarot cards and palm reading. But Baptists, especially Southern Baptists, while not superficial, do have a bright surface and, below it, a quieter, darker stratum. At least, that was the case with the Southern Baptist women I knew, who whispered to each other that sometimes prayer and medicine did not quite satisfy the moment.

Sometimes a woman felt the need to give fate and destiny a small push. Anyone who has studied the Bible knows that passages discuss gifts of prophecy and such; if you are a good Christian, then exercising certain gifts is, in theory, no longer "witchcraft" but instead evidence of your blessed status.

Just as a fish feels the currents of the water, a gifted person might feel the shape the world is taking and see the most likely outcomes—that is, predict the future. This isn't as crazy as it sounds. People predict their future every day: *Today, I will go to work. I will get there without being killed in traffic. I will get paid for my labor.* These are easy, common predictions. As a Marine, there were a great many of those I could predict. I'd get bored, I'd be sleepy, I'd be out here on the rifle range today far longer than I had any desire to be.

These predictions weren't going to pass any time, though. I mean, no one cared to hear me predict that lunch would be short and unsatisfying.

We were really, really bored.

"Hey, Vasquez, did I mention that I can tell the future?"

SSgt Vasquez snorted. "Whatever."

"No, really. I'm a gypsy. I can read tarot cards and palms and shit. My people are legendary for it." I squinted toward the firing line as I spoke, keeping my eyes on the shooters.

Vasquez's face lit up.

"What? Like the kind of gypsy that steals kids and casts curses?"

"Yep, that's me. You have any idea how hard it is to get a security clearance when your mom caught twenty-three kidnapping charges?" We both laughed. "For real, though, want me to tell your fortune?"

"No! Besides, I don't believe you. Don't curse me or some shit for saying that."

I giggled. "Okay."

A few minutes passed and then, "Prove it."

"How?"

"I dunno, think of something. You're the all-seeing one."

I laughed and said, "Fine. I'll tell you how many of your Marines are going to fail to qualify on the range today. If I'm right, you gotta let my platoon go in front of yours at the armory."

"Deal. I gotta see this shit."

I focused and blurted out the first number that popped into my head. "Seventeen."

Vasquez nudged the other staff non-fire next to him, who had been listening in on the conversation. "You heard her, right? She said seventeen."

The other non-fire nodded and smirked. At least we now had something to look forward to at the end of the shooting part of the day.

"Where'd you learn how to do this?" Vasquez inquired.

"It's passed down in my family. My mom is really gifted at it. She talks to angels and stuff. It's creepy sometimes." I tried not to yawn.

"It's not in a book or something? I've seen those books before. All satanic stuff. Do you sacrifice animals and things?"

"For fuck sake, no. You don't involve blood in magic unless you want really bad outcomes."

Vasquez waited for me to laugh. When I kept silent, his eyes got wide.

"You do MAGIC? That's not real!"

"Believe what you want. So long as you're behind me at the armory at the end of the day."

I stood and stretched as the firing finished on the 200-yard line.

"I'm going to get smokes. Need anything from the store?" A small vehicle-driven store was parked on the side of the road nearby with a line of Marines getting sandwiches and other small things before they had to shoot again.

"Naw, I'm good."

I nodded and walked off, hurrying to complete my purchase before we all moved to the 300-yard line.

Hours later, Marines wrapped up calculating their scores and began reporting to the non-fires. Most reported their status as "qual'd," meaning they'd shot a high enough score that they were "qualified" as basic marksmen or better. If they failed to meet or exceed that threshold, we called them "unks," short for "unqualified" and therefore required to try again the next day or else suffer the indignity of being non-recommended—or "non-rec'd"—for promotion. (Don't try to make the rules of written English apply here. Marine-speak doesn't care about such trifles.) It was typical to have a handful of unks at day's end—although the fewer, the better.

As SSgt Vasquez got the results, he sorted who had qualified and who hadn't into separate formations. Infantrymen were especially sensitive to failure to qualify, as shooting their rifle *was* their entire MOS (military occupation specialty). He had fifteen Marines in the unqualified pool.

He turned back to me and smirked. "Hey, not too bad. Fifteen is pretty close!"

I smiled back, willing to accept I'd lost the bet but gotten close enough to maybe earn a little wasta.[2]

I had yet to concede defeat when two more bedraggled grunts staggered up to the group. SSgt Vasquez turned and asked if they were qual'd or not. They admitted, with shame on their faces, that they had failed.

Seventeen. *Yes! Front-of-the-line privileges, here I come!*

Inside, I was thrilled. Being first at the armory meant I might actually get home before I died of sleep deprivation. But I had to keep up appearances as an all-knowing psychic, so I stood there looking professionally smug instead.

Vasquez was absolutely astonished. After he dismissed the platoon to the armory, he went around telling everyone, sharing his disbelief with the other skeptics.

"Yo, Salz predicted my unks! *Whaaat,* that's some witchcraft shit!"

---

2   *Wasta* is an Arabic word that was in common usage during my service. To us it meant something like reputation, respect, and status if all three were combined into one word.

Other people laughed, a few teased me for my good luck, and then Vasquez upped the ante.

"Tell me how many are going to fail tomorrow! If you get that right, then I'll believe you!"

I shrugged and said, "Two."

I was certainly going to blow it this time; no one gets that lucky twice.

The next day, two failed, and now even I wasn't sure how I was doing this. It didn't take long for gossip to spread.

As I accompanied my gaggle of Marines to the armory for turn-in, others caught up with me to ask if I would read their palm. I laughed and asked them to wash it off first. I'd squint for a minute or so and then make statements about their love lives or their past before they joined. A few Marines wandered off looking bemused; a couple gasped in delight and spread the rumor of my burgeoning powers even further. I wondered if I was taking it all a little too far.

Marines are surprisingly bad at figuring out cause and effect, so the chief warrant officer (CWO) whose platoon Vasquez was leading, decided to come over to my hangout by the range shed later and, without warning, picked me up by the neck.

"Stop making my Marines fail!"

I wiggled until he put me down, and everyone howled with laughter. It was hilarious, but I could tell the CWO didn't find this funny. He rationally knew it was the rounds on target (or rather, a lack thereof) that were making the Marines fail, but if there was any chance I was hexing infantrymen, it simply must be discouraged.

I stood off to the side under a small copse of trees as my Marines happily went through the turn-in line, handing off their rifles and sighing with relief that they could now leave the range area without getting tackled by the MPs. Another staff sergeant made conversation with me about the palm readings.

SSgt Boyar was a giant Black man from the islands. I've no idea which islands because he always just said "the islands," and I was afraid to ask which ones for fear of unwittingly insulting him. He asked for a palm reading, and I obliged, pointing to different lines as I went along. After I finished, he scowled at his hand and then shrugged.

"It's interesting, but I don't really believe in that stuff. That's all noise." He rocked back and forth on his heels, crossing his arms over his chest. People did that when I made them uncomfortable, which I felt bad about more often than I'd ever admit.

"Don't mock the gods!" I admonished him. "They don't take kindly to that, and no one is out of their reach!" It sounded silly when I said it out loud; however, I had a burgeoning mythos to protect. Besides, anyone who might be shot at one day by enthusiastic enemies needs every friend he or she can get.

But just as I finished speaking, there was a cracking noise, and then something plummeted from high up in the tree behind us and crashed to the soft earth: a rotted branch that had chosen that very moment to break off. It split upon impact with the ground a couple of feet behind SSgt Boyar.

He jumped, and I shot him a smug look. It occurred to me that the two events, our conversation and the branch's submission to gravity, looked a bit shady. "Told you so."

SSgt Boyar looked from the busted wood to my face and then back again, eyes wide with shock. Then a shiver ran through his torso, and he briskly walked off.

"Can't fuck with that, uh-uh," he called back over his shoulder. "Nope, that's too weird. I'm out, Salz!"

It was funny, but now I'd lost my conversation partner. I stood there by myself, waiting the final few minutes until all the rifles were turned in and, at long last, I could leave for the day.

I drove home very, very carefully.

PART ONE:

A STRANGE GYPSYIN A STRANGE LAND

I.

IN THE BEGINNING WAS THE WORD

I was born in a hospital in Kansas City, Missouri, on May 1, 1980. I was extremely premature, about eight weeks, but my mother's health was collapsing from stress, and the doctors were positive that carrying me to term would kill me, her, or the two of us. I was four pounds and change, and my mother was advised against naming me because the likelihood of survival was low. After two weeks in the NICU, the doctors decided I was going to live after all, and I was named Tracy Elaine Miller.

My father, a veteran of the United States Air Force, was a Kansas City police officer. Mom was a housewife whose first years in that position were spent with my father in Taiwan, where he was stationed at the time. There, "housewife" seemed more exciting, and Mom talked about Taiwan throughout her life. In grade school, I did class projects about Taiwan because I knew my mother would be happy when she helped me draw my posters and such.

The happy times changed shortly before my birth, in the form of an acrimonious separation (is there any other kind?) amid accusations of infidelity and misconduct. Years later, all Mom told me was that they could not get along, and that was why we moved every year or two to different cities and states.

I was enrolled in the local school each time and got caught up with the lessons. The one thing that bothered me was that I had no ties to any of the communities in which I lived. I always just showed up, new and weird, while the other kids seemed to be in their natural habitat. Thanks to the interminable car rides that made up most of my childhood, I read books a LOT. There was nothing else to do. We were generally strapped for cash, and my mother worked jobs like gas station attendant or food worker, so books and a small black-and-white television were it. My stepfather taught me things like how to tie fishing flies or reload ammunition. He took me mining for fire opals in Idaho, mining for garnets in Montana, and helped me search for obsidian in New Mexico. None of these experiences made it easy to talk to other kids my age.

This meant that I got restless in class pretty easy. In Florida, I loved the lessons and did countless projects on things like the Hopi Pueblo Indians of the Southwest, but I was never focused, let alone driven. My fifth-grade teacher did not take offense at my inattention, though. She did something else, which changed things dramatically for me. She identified me for testing to see if I qualified for the school's advanced program. I wasn't sure what that meant, but the tests the school psychologist gave me were pretty fun, and I got pulled out of class to do them, so I was happy to be tested for as long as they wanted.

One day, I was on the playground, playing with that awful ball-on-a-string thingy that every playground had and no one knew what to do with. It was tied to a pole that was grounded in a tire, and you just hit the ball and watched it fly around the pole until the string was completely wrapped up, and then unwound it and did it again.

A girl with red hair and a disapproving expression came over and gave me the eye of a critic. I was used to it. Always the new kid, I couldn't make friends until I'd been weighed and measured by whichever children were the ruling committee. That was just life.

"I hear you're testing for gifted," she sniffed.

I nodded but kept playing with the ball. It was the safest way to avoid giving accidental offense. She tossed her hair and then slapped the ball when it passed her. I stood back, waiting submissively for her to say what was on her mind.

"I tested for that, you know. They ask you what 'espionage' is. Do you know what that is?"

I shook my head. I thought it was something to do with spies, but I figured she wasn't really interested in my input.

"It's the buying and selling of government secrets. That's what it is."

She seemed satisfied that I had not known and therefore could be safely written off. She flounced off to where the other girls were playing.

I stood waiting for a moment, embarrassed but with no idea why, and then went back to my ball. Well, maybe I wouldn't do well on the test. But astronauts had to be smart, or they wouldn't be allowed in space. *I should probably remember what "espionage" is.*

Later, the school psychologist sat me in her nice, quiet office. I was delighted to have one-on-one attention from an adult. With two working parents and no siblings, I never had anyone's undivided attention, so that was gratifying, and I really wanted to please. She went down a list of questions, then sighed and asked me, "Do you know what espionage is?"

I nodded and regurgitated the answer fresh from the playground. She smiled, placed a tick mark next to the question, and then we did some puzzles.

My mother was very anxious about the test, and I didn't know why. I thought she wanted me to be smart and do well in school, so when she acted cold or angry about it, I was very confused. As we lay in our tent one night (we weren't living in a house yet, just sleeping in a tent in a family member's yard), she finally let it out.

"You'll get a big head, and you'll think too much of yourself! I don't want to deal with that."

I cried. I didn't think I had anything to be proud of anyway. We didn't even have a house, and all my clothes had either been sewn by my relatives or bought at the Goodwill. How would being smart give *me* a big head? At most, maybe I wouldn't feel like a constant outcast.

Weeks later, they told Mom I had passed. She wouldn't tell me my score, just looked down at me and coldly announced that I 'd barely made it and had no reason to be proud of myself.

Honestly, by that point I didn't care. *She* could think what she liked, but *I* got to leave class once a week with the other kids who qualified and go to a separate school, where they let me spend the whole day studying anything I wanted. The kids there all treated me like one of them, and they were nice. They didn't think I was weird. The lunch there was pretty good, too.

The only part that was odd to me was that all the kids in the program from my school were boys, except one other girl and myself. I started to think maybe I had more in common with boys. That notion shaped a lot of my behavior for the rest of my adolescence. If I couldn't be one of the pretty, normal girls, I'd be a tomboy. As I saw it, there weren't any other options.

I passed the rest of my schooldays attending different public schools up and down the Florida coast. My stepfather often went wherever work was available for a machinist, and that led us all over. When I reached high school in Vero Beach, I convinced my parents to finally marry and buy a house and settle down. While I was still the weird kid with the weird parents, I at least had a social circle, and I was in a few school activities like the Masterminds team and some writing clubs. A friend and I wrote our own magazine and published it with saved-up lunch money, handing it out for free around school. That was when I learned how to handle criticism. Nobody can criticize a writer like their peers.

I graduated with my class in 1998 and got a job in town as office manager for a substance-abuse clinic that did court-ordered counseling for people. It was boring, but at least it was an office job and it let me work on computers. After a few months of that, I edged into my first adult existential crisis. One day, I was sitting in the clinic office. It was quiet. The counselors had no appointments that day, so they had all left, and I was just manning the phones, alone, taking any appointments that called in and balancing the books.

It suddenly hit me. This was it.

Someone once told me that some people spend their whole lives in places they never meant to stay. They just keep doing the same thing, day after day, waiting for change. After a life of moving every year or two, constantly being uprooted and experiencing new things, greater challenges, and learning more, suddenly it all . . . stopped. No more teachers or grades. College was out of the question. My family had no money to support that, and what I earned barely paid my share of the rent on a place I shared with three other people.

I needed something major to happen. The alternative loomed in my vision, stretching out far in front of me: years and years of . . . this.

I had never before experienced anxiety like this—a great, crushing wave cresting over me. My heart pounded. I got up and paced around the office, trying to breathe while pondering the sudden, sharp feeling that I was disappointing *myself*, and horribly. This is what I'd grow up to be? Left behind in a small town, working a low-paying job, and just accepting that not going to college meant my life pretty much stopped here?

This was NOT the dream I'd had. Okay, maybe being an astronaut was off the table because of my grades. That was a basic concession to reality. But it never occurred to me that once I left high school, the world stopped caring about how or if my life ever went any further.

I'd always been capable of making things happen. When my mother became unable to work anymore because of a heart condition, I helped her start a pet-sitting business. Her business grew and provided for her and my stepfather for decades. As for me, I had written my own resume at thirteen and went out seeking a job cleaning machine shops for money so I could afford snacks or a new shirt. I had made and sold jewelry, collected cans for recycling, babysat, cleaned houses, mowed lawns, and held yard sales—anything to fund my ambitions.

I decided I had to come up with something fast. My eighteenth birthday was a fading memory, and my nineteenth was rushing up with alarming momentum. Time would not wait for me. No one was going to teach me a skill, not for free, and I had no money to pay for an education. I had to figure out what I could parlay into a real future.

What did I have besides my youth and my body?

I gasped and fumbled in my purse. What had Nick said, when I saw him in class before we graduated?

Nick and I were passing acquaintances who sat next to each other in economics during our senior year. We talked about all sorts of bizarre shit while we avoided doing classwork. I asked if he was going to college, and he grinned at me, saying, "No. I'm going to be a killer."

I laughed, but then he handed me a Marine Corps recruiter's business card.

"I'm going to the Marines."

I kept the business card because, at the time, I had a thing for collecting the weirdest or rarest cards I got. I liked to look through them and reminisce about all the strange and strangely wonderful people I had met. Now I thought about that card and dug it out of my purse: *Staff Sergeant Dennis Basaragh, Marine Corps Recruiter.*

I recalled my classmates. Mindy had said she was joining the Army after high school. My best friend, Andrea, she'd gone off to West Point. *Maybe . . . maybe I could try something like that, too? I'm not in high school anymore, but still, I could call him, right?*

If he turned me down or said I didn't qualify, well, I had nothing to lose. No one else wanted me. I didn't think Marines even had females in their ranks. But it would be cool to try it.

I picked up the phone receiver and dialed the number on the card.

"Good afternoon, sir or ma'am, this is SSgt Basaragh, Marine Corps Recruiting. How can I help you?" It all came out like one rapid-fire, thoroughly rehearsed sentence that, repeated so often, was automatic.

"Uh, hi! Um. My name is Tracy and, uh, I had a friend who joined the Marines, and I was wondering what the requirements are? Like, do you take girls?"

There was a pause. I could feel him switch gears as his voice warmed up.

"Well, that depends. We do have some screening requirements that need to be met, but if you'd like to learn more, I'd be happy to meet up with you for lunch sometime, and we can talk about what you are looking for."

I felt an unfamiliar lightness in my chest at the offer. Someone was willing to talk to me! I could maybe take a step forward, into a future. I told myself not to get my hopes up; just the invitation to sit and talk was more than I thought I'd get. My fear was that he'd simply say no, sorry, and hang up.

I stammered that I'd very much like to meet.

He asked me a few questions about my age (eighteen), my health (fine), and my police record (none). He also asked me what had made me interested in calling him. I had no response planned, so I just told him the truth. I had no idea what to do with myself now that I'd graduated, and I needed something for a future.

He seemed satisfied with that.

We met the next afternoon at a diner near my office, and he bought me lunch. Since I was always counting my small change, this gesture was more appreciated than he probably knew.

SSgt Basaragh was tall, fit, African American, not quite thirty, and he possessed a smooth, commanding manner that made it easy to go with his flow. His approach was light, and he cracked jokes, but there was a serious, driven undertone that suggested he could become intimidating very quickly if needed.

I answered his questions, and then it was his turn to answer mine, but I didn't know what I could or should ask. He stepped into the silence by asking what kind of job I was interested in.

"I don't know," I stammered. "Aren't all Marines infantry? Isn't that, like, the only thing?"

His face was a picture of dismay. Clearly, I was one of those kids who only knew about the Marines from movies.

"No, there are a lot of other jobs in the Marines. Currently, we do not accept women in the infantry, but we do accept you for roles like intel analyst, linguist, admin, and a few others."

I jumped at the mention of linguist. That sounded amazing! I had only studied French and Spanish, but learning a second language fluently would be a dream come true. Unfortunately, school seats for crypto-linguists (as they were called) were already filled for the year, SSgt Basaragh said. I would need to pick something else, and he suggested I try for something in the field of computers, provided I got the test scores to qualify.

Oh yes, please! Tests! I liked those. I knew where I was with tests.

Two tests were required for that field. First came the ASVAB, which every service member has to take, regardless of their eventual job field. If I scored high enough on that test, especially in the GT and EL categories (I had no idea what these were; I just knew I needed a high number in them), then I'd take another test for electronics aptitude. That one involved number patterns, like Fibonacci's sequence, and figuring out the relationships that created the patterns. I loved the whole idea and agreed to shoot for that.

Then he told me about the places where Marines get stationed: Camp Lejeune in North Carolina, Camp Pendleton in California, and Okinawa, Japan.

I choked. Japan!? I hadn't traveled internationally in my whole life, apart from crossing through Canada on the way to Alaska. After studying Taiwan, I dreamed of seeing the rest of Asia, and now this man was telling me I could go to Japan if I joined?

My mind was made up right then and there. If there was a way, I was damn well going to try. We agreed to work together toward my enlistment, although SSgt Basaragh warned me that I had to be willing to accept the next available seat in boot camp. There were not as many openings for females as there were for males, and shipping out needed to happen when the opportunity was available.

After some back-and-forth, SSgt Basaragh scheduled the ASVAB test for me at a local testing center. I went straight there after work and took the exam. It was much different from any of the tests I had taken in high school, such as the SAT. The ASVAB asked me about mechanical things and electronic circuits. But I plunged ahead anyway, having no idea what kind of score was good or how it was graded. On the little sample ASVAB I had taken at the recruiting office, I scored a sixty-one, which SSgt Basaragh said was good enough but not impressive. That stung my pride, so I devoted more brain power to the real deal.

I finished up, and my recruiter took me back to the office to go over the results. I had improved dramatically, scoring ninety-four, although he got a huge and utterly unrestrained laugh from my score on mechanics.

"You can't tell a toaster from a carburetor, can you?" he asked.

SSgt Basaragh scheduled the appointment into the Military Entrance Processing Station (MEPS) for my health exam. I came out fine, and then, after some other tests, I swore into the program for shipping out to basic. From start to finish, it took two weeks to get me into Parris Island. The speed with which everything happened was breathtaking, certainly the most exciting thing that had happened for me since graduation. I was terrified, but I was also not going to give up what I saw as my one shot to matter in the world.

I had no idea where this would take me. For once, Mom was proud and supportive, and besides, I didn't care, as long as it took me away from Vero Beach.

2.

THE PARRIS ISLAND
PENAL COLONY

Before I went to boot camp, I was scared stiff, my mind filled with images from *Full Metal Jacket* and thoughts of getting beat up. If I had known how understated my fears were, I probably wouldn't have gone. The Air Force recruiter never returned my phone calls, and while I don't regret it now, in boot camp I wished to God I had called the Air Force one more time.

The whole process of enlisting was very beguiling. It takes a week, which is too long in the recruiter's estimation because that gives you six days to change your mind. Many recruiters later told me that girls are sent out to boot camp quicker than boys because girls will change their minds at the behest of their boyfriends or their parents much faster.

The part of the process that sent shivers down my spine and made me taste aluminum in my throat was the oath. I said it a total of three times in my military career, and each time, it gave me butterflies.

> I, Tracy Miller, do solemnly swear that I will support and defend the Constitution of the United States against all enemies, foreign and domestic; that I will bear true faith and allegiance to the same; and that I will obey the orders of the President of the United States and the orders of the officers appointed over me, according to regulations and the Uniform Code of Military Justice. So help me God.[3]

The flight to South Carolina was filled with would-be Marines, and we all voiced our speculations and third-hand knowledge of what would happen once we got there. By the time we landed, the tension was humming. As we stepped off the plane at midnight, my throat constricted, and my stomach flipped. A short Marine was waiting for us, and he had everyone who had stepped off before me sitting in two rows with their hands on their knees, staring straight ahead silently. He appeared quite unfriendly with his hateful scowl, sharp haircut, and pressed-out uniform.

He looked at me and said, "You! Get over there now, sit down, and keep your mouth SHUT."

I jumped and then scurried over to the seat. There we waited in nervous silence until he gave us the command to stand and hurry out to the buses.

The bus ride to the base was creepy, as being in unfamiliar territory in the middle of the night usually is. As we got situated on the bus, the Marine stepped on behind us and made a disturbing announcement.

"I suggest you keep your stinking mouths shut and get some sleep, because this might be the last nap you get for a while."

This struck me as ironic; we were all so scared we couldn't have slept without chemical sedation.

Two hours later, we got to the base and saw the guard at the gate. It felt like I was going to jail. The man was in cammies with a shaved head and an M16 over one shoulder, standing in the pale fluorescent light of the guard shack. He looked at the Marine on our bus and waved us through. Before the bus proceeded, the Marine turned and addressed us once again.

"All right, LISTEN UP! Every one of you will put your nasty face to your knees and then lock your hands behind your head. Do it now! If I see one—ONE—of your ugly eyeballs trying to look around, you will just stand by!"

---

3   Title 10, US Code; Act of 5 May 1960 replacing the wording first adopted in 1789, with amendment effective 5 October 1962

I put my face down before he finished talking, the adrenaline coursing through my body and making me shake. *Oh God, oh God, oh God,* I thought. What the hell did he mean by "stand by"?

The bus drove for what seemed like hours again. Then it stopped. I heard footsteps as someone got off the bus. I peeked out from under my elbow. Everyone else was still seated, so I covered my eyes again. Then a loud and terrifying voice started yelling from the front of the bus. It was another man's voice.

"LISTEN UP, YOOHOOS! Welcome to my island. From this point forward, you do not move until told to move. You answer with *yes sir* or *yes ma'am* every person who speaks to you, and then you KEEP YOUR MOUTH SHUT. DO YOU UNDERSTAND?"

We voiced our acknowledgment in unison: "Yes sir!"

The man growled and said, "What, all I got are a bunch of stinkin' GIRLS on this bus? I SAID, *DO YOU UNDERSTAND?*"

This time we yelled as loud as we could, but with our knees in our faces, our voices were muffled. He seemed satisfied, though, and launched into his first set of orders—the ones we had seen in every recruiting video.

"When I say move, all of you MALES will grab your belongings in the most expeditious manner possible and GET OFF MY BUS. You will immediately line yourselves up on the yellow footprints and stand AT ATTENTION. DO NOT talk to anyone. NO ONE cares what you have to say anymore. DO YOU UNDERSTAND?"

The guys all sounded off in the affirmative.

"Good. Now: GET OFF MY BUS!"

The sound of so many leaping to their feet and frantically grabbing bags was alarming. I soothed myself that they would not treat us women like this. This was for the men. The invisible speaker yelled for them to move faster. After about ten minutes, everything was silent. Then I heard the man say softly to the bus driver, "You can go." The door of the bus closed, and we started to sit up and look around.

"WHO THE HELL SAID TO SIT UP AND EYEBALL THE AREA?"

Oops! The other Marine was still on the bus. The bus started to roll again, and we ducked back down and went quiet. What was waiting for us? My heart raced, and I thought I was going to throw up. The bus came to halt, and the door opened, followed by footsteps and a soft, feminine voice greeting the bus driver. A woman had stepped aboard.

The scene that had played out when the men got off the bus replayed exactly one octave higher. When she gave the order to get off the bus, I scrambled to get my bags and get away from this woman. She looked to be in her forties, wearing green woolen trousers and a khaki, short-sleeved shirt. She had many ribbons on her chest, and rank-stripe thingies (what I later learned was the symbol for staff sergeant) on her sleeves, but what stood out most right then was that she looked meaner than any human being I had ever met. Her eyes were cold, and her voice was piercing. She had a little black name tag that said "Whitewolf." It suited her. But her most notable feature was the campaign cover—the Smokey-the-Bear hat—on her head. It was the universal symbol of a drill instructor.

She slapped the back of a bus seat and shrieked at us to hurry up because we were currently moving as slow as a bunch of stinking civilians. I bailed out of the bus, jumped onto the first set of yellow footprints I could find, dropped everything, and stared straight ahead.

Fuck me. What have I gotten myself into?

I spent that first night filling out forms and being issued gear, which between the drill instructors and the supply Marines was the most stressful event of my life.

Many of the opening rituals of boot camp are sacred to those who have been through them, so I will not describe too much more, but we did not sleep the first three days, and most of it ran together in my head. When we were finally allowed to shower and go to bed, I think I heard every girl in the squad bay crying into her pillow.

3.

NO LOOKING BACK; YOU'RE NOT GOING THAT WAY

One of our morning rituals as soon as we were awakened—the DI always woke the platoon with some unnervingly unpleasant noise or sudden burst of light—was to "get on line." We scrambled out of our racks and stood directly in front our footlockers in a line down both sides of the squad bay. The "guide," or recruit in charge of the rest, would yell, "Platoon 4025! Count off!"

We went down the line as quickly as possible, yelling out our designated number, and then the guide would yell to the drill instructor, "Good morning, ma'am! The guide for platoon 4025 reports the count on deck is ninety recruits ready to train, there are ninety rifles secured properly, and all money/valuables have been accounted for!"

The details may have varied slightly from one platoon to another, but the format never changed. As we proceeded through training and girls were dropped back for whatever reason, the count changed to reflect the loss. I made it a personal goal to always be part of that count. Anything else spelled doom.

As new recruits, we women were separated not only physically but geographically from any contact with men. We were ensconced in our own little world, the 4th Recruit Training Battalion. Our building had everything: a beauty shop (for the drill instructors; we recruits did not get to use that particular facility), a chow hall, a parade deck, a PT field, a medical clinic. You name it, and they had built it into our fortress.

Every Marine in the 4th Recruit Training Battalion was a woman, with the exception of a few cooks and the chaplain. All of our drill instructors and chain of command were women.

We focused solely on our training, which consisted of four things: classes on military subjects, drill, learning from our DIs (take that how you will), and physical training. Physical training seems like the single most important thing in the Marine Corps and the one area that can be really difficult for some women. You might be dumb as a rock, but if you can run and push (do push-ups and other upper-body calisthenics), you will be fine through boot camp.

When we went out to physical training at 0500 in the morning, our brother platoons would be out there. We tried to sound off as loud and proud as we could, but it came off ridiculous next to our male counterparts, who had subwoofer bass in their voices.

We would then set out on a run course. The length of the run varied from a mile to three, depending on what stage of training we were in. Our initial strength test consisted of doing a minimum of fifty-five sit-ups, a flexed-arm hang (hang from a bar with arms flexed until your elbows straighten out) of at least fifteen seconds, and a mile-and-a-half run in fifteen minutes or less. I dreaded this because I smoked a lot and never liked running. I could just barely hang for the fifteen seconds. I managed ninety-eight sit-ups, and then, finally, all the recruits lined up for the run. As the drill instructor explained the run route while doing her best to sound as though she hated us (and it was remarkably believable), I thought about the consequences of failing this. Fail any portion of the test, and you would be in boot camp at least a month longer than everyone else while they focused on getting you up to speed. Pass, and you went on to training and graduated (hopefully) in three months.

On your mark, get set, go!

I took off running and settled into my rhythm, keeping my breathing under control and pushing as hard as I could. By the half-mile mark, some girls were walking. Some guys were walking too. By the three-quarter mark, many people were walking. I felt better already. Maybe I was not as bad as I thought.

I started shouting encouragement to the ones walking: "Come on! Just try a little longer. You'll get there!" They did not look grateful. I shut my mouth and kept running before I got into trouble.

As I rounded the one-and-a-quarter-mile mark, my stomach started feeling queasy. I did not want to see what would happen if I got sick, so I sprinted the last length and got in. My time was thirteen minutes and forty-five seconds. It was no championship race time, but it was good enough for me! We lost half our platoon that day due to failures, and rounded out Platoon 4025, November Company, 4th Recruit Training Battalion at fifty-nine recruits. Our brother platoons had eighty-nine apiece.

Every run from then on was different. Male drill instructors would dash behind their herd of recruits much like German shepherds alongside a pack of sheep, barking orders at their recruits not to let "a girl" pass them on the run. They would accuse them of whining like a woman, weak and helpless. They would say anything to goad the male recruits on. My cheeks reddened at some of the remarks. I felt like an object of ridicule, as if I were stupid for even trying to become a Marine.

Our drill instructors ran with us, too. They would charge up behind us, growling and snarling, mocking, threatening, and yelling. In all reality, they were chasing us. Nothing makes you put out on a run like the fear that slowing down will get you killed.

"You gonna let some stinking, stupid man pass you by, recruit? What the hell, you gonna let them see you can't hack it? You gonna make all your sisters out here look bad because you can't stinkin' run? It's too hard? You gonna fall down and die? Just quit right now, 'cruit. I'd love to drop you out of my platoon. You are not even worthy to try to gain the title *Marine*," and on and on it went for three miles.

Nothing ever changed in boot camp; they always talked to us like that. After a while, you tuned it out, but not too much. Ignoring a drill instructor brought the same if not more catastrophe than disobeying one. They convinced you that they were a hair's breadth from ripping your throat out and you were dangerously close to closing that gap.

Recruits May and Hernandez were in my platoon and were both pro runners of a sort. May ran fast because she played college soccer, so she passed most of the males to finish three miles in 21:39. Hernandez blew past every man out there, even the DIs, to finish her three-mile run in 19:45. Our drill instructors hid their smug grins from our view, but they rubbed Hernandez's success in the face of our brother platoons every chance they got. A woman had beaten them. A little Hispanic girl had put all those big, bad, future infantrymen in their place.

The glares our brothers shot us, their snickers and their anger, were felt across the PT field, as their DIs let it be known that punishment would be forthcoming for their lazy, weak, soft- bodied incompetence on this run.

They were not war fighters. They were stinkin' civilians.

It was important to never show the slightest sign of feminine weakness in front of the instructors. Do a proper push-up. Keep up on the run. Do not whine when the forced march starts to hurt. I thought, *Just stay with it*. Right.

Later in my career, when it was an officer leading my formation runs and he decided the right pace was about a seven-minute mile, staying with it was not always an option. I mean, you cannot expect everyone to run with the same ability. That is absurd. I figured, *Hey, I'll just try as hard as I can, and they will be satisfied with that.*

Poor, dumb girl that I was, I found out that the Marine Corps does not accept your best. To hell with *your* best. It is *their* best they want. In my drill instructor's opinion, it was not lack of ability on my part; it was foul laziness that prevented my achieving their standards. My personal cowardice concerning pain kept me from running like the wind. If I were a better human being, I could run well.

The thing is, when someone pushes you that hard, sets their expectations that high, and accepts nothing less, you do find yourself capable of things you never imagined before. Your head gets inspired a lot more than your body, however, and I soon experienced pain with my running. I am not talking about sore shins here. When I lay down to do crunches and my partner grabbed my legs to hold them, I screamed.

It turns out they don't allow screaming in boot camp. You'd better "save the drama for yo' mama," as we were told repeatedly. I ignored the pain until I could no longer make it up the stairs to our barracks after PT. My drill instructor decided she'd had enough of my weak ass and sent me to Medical for an evaluation of my condition.

I had been to Medical several times. "Doc" always said it was shin splints. I found out later it was a bone fracture. They would give me Motrin for the pain, which I never took. It was widely believed that if you went to Medical disemboweled, the corpsman would look at you and say, "Take these Motrin and drink more water."

If it was just pain, I would get through it. If there was something wrong, I wanted it fixed, not masked. Just my luck, I got a Navy doc who thought he was hard as a coffin nail and needed to prove it.

I sat down in the examination room and put my leg up on a chair. Dr. Larsen came in and sat across from me. His eyes were cold, and his face had disgust all over it. Inwardly, I cringed. He was high ranking, pretty close to being a colonel. Drill instructors had trained me to fear and avoid officers because they were so far above me on the food chain that my very existence was a nauseating insult to them.

After a long silence, almost-colonel Doc leaned forward and grasped my shin. I winced but fought hard to keep my bearing. His hands felt cruel and calloused. He looked at my face to see if he intimidated me. I must have looked unafraid because he decided I needed more convincing of his toughness.

"So, what's your problem, 'cruit?" he sneered. "Go ahead, tell me where it hurts."

"This recruit's shins hurt, sir, very badly."

I sat stock-still and looked straight ahead at the wall behind him.

"Well, it's boot camp! It's supposed to hurt!" he yelled.

I thought that the comment was extremely unfair. It is not as though he had ever been through Marine Corps boot camp, and I was not sure Navy Officer Candidate School really compared. Fear rose in my stomach. He was going to tell my DIs that I was a nasty little malingerer, and I would be in severe trouble. I had to convince him I was sincere.

"Sir, this recruit can't make it up the stairs to her barracks, sir."

I tried hard to look as innocent as possible so he might believe me.

"Oh yeah? Really? Well, fine. We'll just drop you back in training. I bet you'd enjoy a nice little stay at the medical recovery platoon, eh?"

He growled and pulled the trouser leg of my pants up. He looked at my shin. Then he dug his fingers into the tibia. I gasped as pain shot through my leg, and I jerked in my seat. He smiled and continued digging his fingers in my shinbone all the way down to my ankle. Tears leaked from the corners of my eyes, and I bit my lip hard, refusing to cry out. The old man looked smug and let go of my leg. I was terrified now. He stood and turned to the corpsman behind him.

"Fine, she wants to play injured, get her some crutches and do up the papers. This one needs to go to MRP."

He walked over to a sink, washed his hands as though touching me had soiled him, and then went back into his office. I sat mortified. He had sentenced me to precisely three more months of boot camp. When you are dropped from training, you no longer progress toward graduation; you sit suspended in boot camp until you heal, and then they return you to another platoon, a couple weeks behind where you had been in training. I only had three weeks until graduation at this point. The embarrassment of having to tell my family that I would not be graduating on time was too much. I could not let this happen! MRP was the closest thing I could imagine to hell.

The corpsman felt bad for me; I saw it in his eyes. He smiled sadly but briefly. He would not get himself in trouble by being nice to me. He helped me out to the waiting room.

I hobbled back to the squad bay on my new crutches, my mind now racing. I had to get past this. No. I had to find a way to heal quickly—or something.

I went through the door to my squad bay and saw that everyone else had gone to evening chow. The only ones there were two girls guarding our gear. Recruit Zinnerman came over to me. She looked like a real Marine, in my opinion. She had short blonde hair and appeared positively skinny inside those huge, wrinkled cammies.

"What's wrong, Miller?" She looked very concerned. I had never been afraid like this. I started crying. Just broke down. She hugged me, and I cried on her shoulder.

"Z, they're gonna drop me! They . . . think . . . that I—I'm not gonna finish," I sobbed. She looked sad for me, too. We were all afraid of MRP.

"Can you still run? Can you make the last run? They won't drop you if you finish that."

Z looked hopeful. I looked at the papers in my hand—the ones telling the senior drill instructor, SSgt Whitman, to drop me out of her platoon. If I did not give her these, she would not kick me out of training. Medical would never call to ensure their orders had been carried out. They couldn't care less. But then I would have to find it in myself to run, to pass the three-mile portion of the physical fitness test (PFT) in under thirty-one minutes.

I completed the final run in 28:11.

4.

WE ALL GO A LITTLE MAD SOMETIMES

I f you have ever thought of going insane, the military is the place to do it. It really brings it out of a person. Of course, I was not perfectly normal when I joined; very few women I have met joined because their life was all sunshine and rainbows.

As we returned to our squad bay one afternoon after chow, all the recruits scrambled to "get on line" and stand at attention for the count. The count was done every single time we moved between points. Accountability is a huge deal in the Marines.

Recruit Nurse and I got to our bunks and stood side by side in front of our footlockers, staring off at the other side of the bay at attention. As a recruit, I got very good at observing the world through my peripheral vision. Once everyone was in their spots, the guide would yell for us to count off, get the number, and away we'd go into the afternoon's fun and games.

Um, except Recruit Winters, a tall, gangly white girl with short red hair. She was not on line. In fact, while the entire platoon was standing at attention, waiting for the drill instructors, Recruit Winters had . . . taken a seat. On the floor. She was smiling, sitting crisscross applesauce like a child.

None of us had any idea why this was so, but we stayed perfectly still. We wanted to see what the drill instructors would say. Winters was inviting trouble, but this looked like the kind of trouble we wouldn't get group-thrashed for. Or maybe it was. Who knows?

Recruits started whispering to Winters, "Get on line! What are you doing?!" Winters just kept smiling and ignored us. Her bunkmate muttered, "What the fuck *are* you doing, Winters?" No one was going to try harder than that. We weren't *all* crazy. Get caught talking and moving around when the DIs came in, and you were screwed.

Mere moments later, Drill Instructor Sgt Kramer came on deck. Sgt Kramer had the temper of an angry leopard with indigestion, so most of us jumped when she so much as looked at us. As she strode toward the guide to get the count, she did a double take at seeing Winters sitting peacefully on the floor by the metal double doors. For a fraction of a second, her bearing broke, and she looked just as baffled and confused as the rest of the platoon. Then her features hardened.

"What are you stinkin' doing, recruit? GET ON LINE!"

"No," she answered quietly, still smiling.

It was then that I noticed Winters wasn't wearing her black boots. She was in the white running shoes we were all issued. *What the hell is going on?* Maybe she was on light duty? Recruits that were hurt in certain ways wore the running shoes sometimes, with Medical's permission.

Regardless, if I had been standing still before, it was practically spastic dancing compared to the lack of movement we all achieved as we froze. Did she just tell a drill instructor *NO*?

Sgt Kramer also looked taken aback at this direct affront to her authority. She tried again, stepping toward Winters. "Recruit Winters, GET ON LINE NOW!" she snarled, putting all her ferocity into each word.

Winters turned her head and looked directly at the drill instructor.

"My name," she replied softly, "is Ashley."

Holy shit. I felt the situation slip into something more dangerous and far more uncomfortable. From the corner of my eye, I saw Sgt Kramer's own face contort in shock and outrage.

"WHAT DID YOU JUST SAY TO ME, RECRUIT?? GET ON LINE!"

Suddenly Winters leapt to her feet and screamed, "MY NAME! IS! ASHLEY!!!"

Then she bolted out the double doors. Just took off running for her life. Not even taking time to blink, Sgt Kramer yelled and sprinted out the door after her. Five other drill instructors, including our sister platoon next door's drill instructors, seemed to appear from thin air and join the chase instantaneously. This was a code-red, all-hands-on-deck, full-blown emergency now. Doors slammed as they all pursued Ashley to wherever she thought she'd get on a swamp island. Dead silence reigned in the squad bay now.

Not one single girl so much as coughed. We stayed locked in perfect obedience, not moving, not going to the head, not doing a single fucking thing. This was really, really bad. Shock, surprise, and fear paralyzed us. One hour later, our drill instructors returned, sweating and clearly freaked out. We never found out what really happened; Ashley was never seen again for the rest of training, and no one spoke of her, as if her name alone were a curse. But the platoon scribes—recruits who did paperwork and such for the drill instructors—whispered that she'd been apprehended by the DIs and handed over to the military police for assault. That sounded so insane I couldn't even imagine it. *Hit* a drill instructor? Hell, I was scared to brush against them on accident. But that was all that was ever known or suspected.

Well.

Bye, Ashley.

5.

ONE BIG FAMILY

I f you are accustomed to a large family, the military is probably not that big of a transition for you. But when you are an only child like me, the sudden and complete lack of privacy can drive you into frenzies. It is not just in boot camp that privacy is taken from you; your life, from day one till you leave the barracks, is shared with everyone, whether you want to share or not.

Part of basic training is getting used to taking a shower with hard soap, no hot water, and eighty other girls. Every one of us was trying to cover up and hurry. Above all else, we wanted to avoid the drill instructor standing in our way, *in the shower, still in uniform*, yelling for us to hurry up and wash our nasty bodies. When we got comfortable being naked in front of each other, some of us would walk out of the shower without bothering to put the towel on. That led to more yelling and verbal abuse because of our immodesty.

Later on, you realize there are no right answers in boot camp. You just pray the DI is too busy to kill you right then.

Do not touch your face. Do not look around. Do not talk. At all. Ever. Do not put your clothes on without being told to. Do not put your shoes on without being told to. Take initiative and do what you think is right, without waiting to be told. Push-ups—do it now. Move. What the hell are you doing? I said sit-ups: do it now. Move! Your name is Recruit, understand? Go to bed, wake up, get on line, run faster, quit whining— geezus, you're never gonna make it, Recruit. Look at you; you let everyone see how bad you are hurting. What are you scared of? Of course it will hurt, but you should not fear pain. Pain is a lesson. Learn from it. Try to say your lines without screwing up—it ain't that damn hard. "Good morning, ma'am. Recruit Miller requests permission to go to the bath—uh, I mean, make a head call." Did you forget to request permission to even speak first, Recruit? Good, you'll pay later.

If the previous paragraph has left you confused, it's even worse to be on the receiving end of the monologue. The orders often contradict themselves. It is done deliberately to bring the stress level up in the platoon. When you are stressed, you do not think so well. Pretty soon, the only way to cope with rapid-fire commands that you have no reasonable hope of successfully obeying is to either ignore some of them (bad idea, unless you are tough, and even then you might want to think on how tough, exactly) or simply respond to them one at a time as fast as possible and accept the inevitable contradiction as part of the game. I tried both routines, with minimal success. I was snarling under my breath and ready to cry with irritation through most of the "games" we played.

What in the hell was this supposed to teach us? How to think and control yourself under intense pressure, of course. What seems like sadism is the only way to condition a recruit for something like combat.

6.

IN THE SHIT

One of my high school English teachers told the class a story about a man who was captured by Indians during a raid in the Old West. The man decided that to survive, he would have to become a horse—mentally, at least—because he knew that Indians never killed horses. Accordingly, he was always quiet, obedient, and worked hard for his captors. In time, they let him go.

While my situation was not nearly as dire, it felt so at the time, and something strange happened to me. I stopped thinking.

I no longer thought about what I was being told to do. I just reacted to orders and forgot them as soon as the next order came. I performed every ritual of boot-camp culture with the same precision devout Catholics exercise in their ceremonies. I could stand perfectly still for hours, without talking or looking around. I accepted whatever happened to me as inevitable and was therefore unburdened by the stress of frustration.

I was not the only recruit who used a fatalistic attitude this way, either.

We were in the field one night, close to the end of training. The platoon was settling into our sea huts—wooden recreations of our squad bays, but without racks or offices—and I was sitting on the floor, leaning against my pack. We'd been given dreary reading materials to study, with things like the history of the Marine Corps and different weapons specs and such. It was dry and dull, but I knew very well from my childhood how to sit quietly and read. So that's what I did.

It was closing in on lights-out, and girls rushed back and forth from the port-o-potties as they completed whatever hygiene they could manage.

As in ladies' rooms all over the world, we had been strictly warned not to dispose of any tampons or pads in the portable toilets. In truth, we had been warned more strictly than we would have been anywhere else in the world. The drill instructors were, shall I say, forceful, going so far as to threaten that anyone found to have ignored the do-not-jettison order would be forced to reach into the toxic, raw sewage and fish "it" out.

Recruit Leeson had been assigned the rack adjacent to mine throughout training, and knowing her was an experience. She talked openly about her sex life prior to enlisting. She was twenty-three, whereas I was mere meters north of my nineteenth birthday. She'd gone to college and dropped out, had tattoos (I didn't and don't), and seemed very relaxed about the insanity around us.

That night, she stood from her pack and said, "Hey, Miller, I'm going to the head. Will you come with?"

It was normal to go everywhere and do everything in pairs, so I agreed. When it was my turn, she'd do the same for me. I closed my book, grabbed my rifle, and we began the trek through the dark to the toilets, which could be found readily by smell. One hundred women using four toilets that didn't flush left a lingering (and kind of traumatizing) aroma.

I stood off to one side, holding my rifle and Recruit Leeson's rifle, as we were not permitted to take them in the head with us. No one had live ammo, but the principle was the same. I plugged my nose and waited, watching more and more Marines queue up as we ran down the clock until bedtime.

Then I heard a very small splash. Followed by a very big scream.

"God DAMN it." Recruit Leeson's muffled curse brought me back to reality.

"Leeson? You okay?" I asked, not wanting to imagine what kind of tragedy had befallen her in a port-o-shitter.

There was the sound of a deep breath (who the fuck takes a deep breath in one of those things?) and then a squelching, squishing, watery noise. I discovered in that instant that a sound can make you sick.

The door creaked open, revealing Recruit Leeson holding her arm straight out from her body. It dripped. Something was clutched in her hand. She looked far away, expressionless. It was the infamous "thousand-yard stare" described by combat-hardened Marines who, as they put it, had been "in the shit."

Oh, fuck no. "Leeson, you fucking *did not* do what I think you did!"

"It fell in. I had to, or they'd make us all do it."

She was in a state of shock. Me? Revulsion overtook me pretty quickly, and I scrambled backwards to go find Drill Instructor Sergeant Kramer.

When I managed to locate her and get through a narration of what I was pretty sure had just happened, even she looked sick. Now, drill instructors *never* look sick, but DI Sgt Kramer was deeply shocked and a little green. (How appropriate.)

She followed me to where Recruit Leeson stood motionless, like a robot with dead batteries, holding some nightmarish collection of goo and dripping to the elbow. After struggling not to retch, DI Sgt Kramer ordered Recruit Leeson to march—FAR OUT IN FRONT OF HER—toward the medical tent, to be sanitized and possibly receive a battery of shots.

Before advancing, she turned to snap at me: "Stand here, and do NOT let this happen again." I didn't ask how she expected me to do that. I just agreed and stayed rooted to the spot.

It was easy to obey because I had just received a lesson in unquestioning obedience truly worthy of a Marine.

Most every recruit by the end of boot camp would follow their DI into hell itself. By the final phase of basic training, recruits are perfectly capable of killing. Thirteen weeks of indoctrination will dissolve your sense of reason to slush. You are a part of your platoon, and that's an extension of yourself. Anyone who even thinks of taking a short cut by walking through the formed-up ranks will get snarled at and driven off for invading the body. This is the goal of boot camp. There are other goals, like making you disciplined and respectful and teaching you how to wear the uniform correctly and shoot an M16 with a moderate level of accuracy. Marines, however, are best known for their vicious and tenacious presentation in battle. This fundamental element of a Marine is achieved in boot camp, and in recent years, female training has become nearly identical to the male training. When we graduate, we are of the same mentality as our brothers: "Ma'am! Discipline is instant willing obedience to orders, respect for authority, and self-reliance!"

One concept we had difficulty with during training was the idea of group punishment. The thought goes like this: In combat, one Marine screws up, and your whole fire team is killed. There is no mercy in a combat situation; you do not always die because you were the one who made a mistake. Now, as a civilian, hopefully by the age of eighteen you have come to the level of maturity where you are willing take responsibility for your own actions. As a Marine, you learn to take responsibility for your team's actions.

At first, we were all baffled by this. We wondered how they could hold us responsible for the actions of other recruits. Eventually, one recruit would take control of the others to keep us out of trouble.

The recruits with natural leadership ability stand out during boot camp. When the drill instructor comes out of the "DI hut" (where the drill instructors sleep, change clothes, and eat) and sees that not everyone made it into their cammies on time (there is usually a two-minute time limit), the leader does all the pushing while the rest of us stand at attention and watch. Your mind climbs the walls when this happens. Seeing someone being forced to suffer because of you—and the DI forces you to watch—can make you feel like the lowest human being on earth. Then you are invited to come up and suffer right along with the leader, who is sometimes reduced to tears and other times holds out like a champion. The invitation forces you face-to-face with your own cowardice. You do not want to go up there and suffer humiliation and pain. Yet there, on the quarterdeck, lying in a pool of their own sweat, is another person who is being thrashed for your inability to dress yourself on time.

The first couple of times I was in this situation, I did not respond to the offer to come and "get some" myself. Then I felt so ashamed of my fear that later I volunteered often to "push." We all developed this way, and we were willing to go to the quarterdeck, part of the squad bay that is clear of furniture so you can do exercises, to pay for our mistakes, others' mistakes—hell, just to break the boredom of training.

The quarterdeck was not the most fearsome arena, however. The real thrash sessions were held in the "Pit," a large sandbox filled twelve inches deep with loose, sugary sand. In the humid, sticky, July afternoons, our fed-up drill instructors would take us out there and unleash hell.

In one case, a recruit was caught stealing food from the mess hall. While we sweated in the Pit, the larcenous recruit stood at attention and watched. As I panted and sputtered to get sand out of my mouth and tried to do another push-up while a drill instructor stood over me, snarling at and mocking me, I looked to my left. Next to me, Recruit Collazo had sand stuck to every part of her. Her tan T-shirt was caked with sand—her face, her elbows, everything. Her long, dark hair had come loose in the ruckus, and wisps of it were in her eyes. She looked like an anthropomorphic sugar cookie.

She looked over at me then, and without anyone else noticing, she winked.

I froze.

Then she smirked and continued trying to do more push-ups. It was so insane to be smiling that my own mouth curved into a grin.

Holy shit, we're a pair of sugar cookies baking in the South Carolina sun.

I started giggling and couldn't stop. I laughed with each futile attempt to appease our drill instructors and was pretty sure that unless SSgt Lawton actually kicked me in the ribs (she didn't), I wasn't going to stop laughing. Of course, it would cost me later, but it felt good to know that I still had my spirit. I knew I could make it.

As our training came to a close, our senior drill instructor came into our classroom during a break and said she was holding one last Pit call, for the recruits who still owed her. You would never have guessed that this was a form of punishment from the way we all jumped from our seats, tore off our cammie blouses, and raced out to the sandbox, positively delighted. When we came back in ten minutes later, sweating and panting, shaking sand from our clothes, we were smiling at one another and muttering about how much that had worn us out. There was nothing to fear from constructive pain. Never be afraid to pay for your mistakes.

★ ★ ★

Competition between the sexes did not have the desired effect of making us anathema to one another. By the third month of boot camp, I had forgotten a lot of things about men due to their overall absence. So it came as a shock when, while I was sitting on my foot locker, spit-shining my boots one afternoon, a very strange and pleasant smell hit my nose.

I paused. *What is* that? It was musky, but in a deep and appealing way. It was completely foreign to our living environment. Forgetting all about my boots, I looked around the squad bay and sniffed the air again. *Is that . . . cologne?*

Glancing around to see where it might be coming from, I saw other girls had also put down their various tasks and looked as confused as I was. Parris Island is many things, but sweet smelling it is not. I looked up to my bunkmate, Recruit Nurse.

"Do you smell that?" I whispered. "What is it?"

Recruit Nurse rolled her eyes at me and continued making her rack. She was from New York City and thought of me as a silly stoner from Florida.

Where I spoke slowly, Nurse rushed every sentence to its conclusion. Where I was always about one minute behind events, she had gone to a merchant marine academy for high school and already understood what was happening.

"It's the Marine who just walked in, Miller. He went into the DI hut." She nodded toward the far end of the squad bay. "I think he's a lance corporal, but I couldn't see."

I saw the Marine emerge, carrying a clipboard and headed for the exit. He was probably sixty feet or more away from me. But we could *all* smell him, and many of us now remembered why hating men wasn't going to work out for us.

Later, on the rifle range, our platoon was broken into groups, and we were assigned a primary marksmanship instructor for each squad. PMIs were almost always young grunts and therefore, at the time, all male. As we struggled to learn how to zero-in on targets, line up our sights, and other minutiae of putting rounds downrange, we occasionally treated ourselves to calling for help. The PMI would arrive and crouch next to us to see how we had our weapons set up, and we'd enjoy some attention from the opposite sex, if that's how nature took us. Not our proudest moment, but hey, we took our pleasures where we found them.

As boot camp finally wound down, I could hardly believe it was ending. I wanted to leave and regain my personal freedoms, but I could not fathom what would follow act I.

One *little* detail about life before basic training came back to us with some difficulty: we struggled to recall how to wear makeup. When we'd first arrived on Parris Island, the right and privilege of painting our faces and wearing powder or foundation, even a touch of mascara, had been roundly forbidden. After three months of not applying it, we were ill prepared for the lifting of the ban shortly before graduation.

How much eye shadow is too much? How the hell should I know? I haven't seen a TV commercial or magazine in ages. I stared in the mirror and tried to use muscle memory, but the result was laughably bad. When I glanced around me, our platoon looked less and less like Marines and more like soon-to-be graduates from a school for clowns.

To be fair, none of us really cared. The freedom to wear it again was delicious; the actual makeup was a side note. For most of my Marine

Corps career, I chose to forgo makeup entirely anyway. It was heavy, my face felt sticky, and it never looked good for more than an hour or so after putting it on. Besides, the guys weren't allowed to apply purple sparkle dust on their eyelids, so I'd be better off not having any on mine. Fair's fair.

The day before we graduated, we were allowed four or five hours with our families. As we marched in to be presented to our parents, I had no idea I would feel like I did. I believed that the basic-training experience had put me through the full gamut of human emotions, but there was one more in store for me: pride.

As I stood with my platoon and listened to the drill instructors tell our families about all the things we had been through, I felt the change inside me. I was no longer a rebellious teenager trying to prove my adulthood. I had proved more than anyone had thought I could. I had endured, and now I belonged. I was a Marine.

When they dismissed us to go to our parents' side, there was an awkward moment. We looked around and smiled nervously. Then chaos broke out as girls went running over to mothers and fathers, hugging boyfriends and siblings. My own mother and father were there, and they were positively beaming. I walked up to them and wanted to cry. I smiled and blinked a lot instead. They hugged me and admired my uniform.

I told them how eager I was to get outside and walk around. I had been denied even the smallest freedoms for so long that just being able to talk felt like a high privilege. We ate lunch, and I showed them the squad bay that had been my home. I thought of introducing them to my DIs, but then decided I was still far too intimidated to try that. We talked about my trip home tomorrow. I was so excited about graduation that I did not dare think about it, lest I jinx myself somehow. Too soon, sunset came, and Mom and Dad left for their hotel. I returned to my squad bay. We recruits spent the evening packing and chattering. Tomorrow morning could not come fast enough.

Before the sun rose, we woke quietly and went to chow as Marines. We ate our breakfast and then hurried back to the squad bay. Our DIs showed up and inspected our uniforms one last time. Then we got into formation and prepared to march to the parade deck, giddy, frightened, elated.

It is a tradition, along the final march on Parris Island from 4th Battalion to the graduation ceremony, for graduating female recruits to sing the "Lady Leatherneck Song," which goes something like,

We're Women Marines and we march with pride.
We march shoulder to shoulder and side by side.
On our left. Our left. Our left. Our left.
Hi lee. Hi low. Your left your right your left your right you better know.
Cuz it's your left foot, ladies. Your left your right your left.
Your left foot, ladies. Your left foot strikes the deck.
We march to the chow hall. We march everywhere.
We march shoulder to shoulder to show we care.
On our left. Our left. Our left. Our left.
Hi lee. Hi low. Your left your right your left your right you better know.

I do not know how long this has been a practice, but we all looked forward to it. The sound of that melody meant you had made it; you were a Marine now. You had better not get caught singing it until you were certain to graduate because only *Marines* rated to sing that song. When, after thirteen weeks, it was finally our turn, we sang with all we had, and everyone in 4th Battalion heard us. We let the entire battalion, all the girls who were still in training, know that Platoon 4025 was going home.

The graduation went smoothly, with all the ceremony and pomp the Marines are so fond of. As our DIs turned to face the platoon one last time, they said the word we had waited thirteen long weeks to hear: "DISMISSED!"

"Aye-aye, ma'am!" we shouted out in perfect unison.

As one, we turned our backs and then fled to our families as quickly as possible. We were free, and it was over . . . for ten days.

PART TWO:

SAN DIEGO, CALIFORNIA

7.

THE FIRST DUTY STATION

"It's a love-hate relationship; I love her, she hates me."—Unknown

I t was September 2000, in San Diego, California. I was stationed at the Marine Corps Recruit Training Depot as a network technician, repairing computers, patching up email problems, and placating officers. I was a lance corporal and, like most others of my rank, did not have brains enough to keep my mouth shut and do what I was told. Disgruntled, as almost all young enlisted people are, I was devoutly praying for the end of my current contract.

Every Friday, the Depot was awash with privates who had just graduated from boot camp and their families. Young men (women went through training only in South Carolina) walked about with small entourages of parents, siblings, and grandparents. Some guys had their girlfriends with them, young girls in awe of their new Marine boyfriends. It was a great day for them. For the permanent personnel on-base, it was a pain in the ass.

I stalked angrily out the door from the Drill Instructor School, where I had witnessed one of the worst computer hardware atrocities I could have imagined in my short IT career. I cursed DIs, the whole computer-illiterate lot of them. My camouflage utilities were crisply starched and stifling in the hot afternoon. My black boots were spit-shined, reflecting the glaring sun back into my eyes. I had pulled my dark hair back in the severe bun that regulations preferred. I strode toward the bright, construction-yellow golf cart that made up my only form of transportation around the base, my small toolkit in hand.

Hopping up on the metal seat, I tossed the kit on the bench next to me and tugged the tiny aluminum key out of my pocket to shove into the ignition. I needed to return to the shop to get more RJ-45 connectors so I could fix a cable on the computer. One of the drill instructors figured he could fix the last connector and had mutilated it beyond hope. I grumbled as the small electric motor turned on. Just as my foot started to lower on the accelerator, a voice startled me.

"Excuse me, young lady."

I turned to look at the man who had walked up to my cart. He had soft wrinkles and merry blue eyes, with short-cropped white hair and a thick mustache. He smiled at me. I was scowling at him. Beside him, clutching his hand, was a little girl. She was maybe five years old, with dark hair and large dark eyes, chewing three of her fingers and staring shyly up at me from the protection of the old man's side. They were both dressed casually, which I envied as sweat rolled down my back under my uniform. I breathed out my irritation slowly enough to disguise it and smiled back.

"Yes sir, what can I do for you?"

I was trying very hard to be polite even though I felt like chewing glass and spitting nails. My time working in the restaurant business had taught me some valuable lessons in bearing, which came in handy during my military tenure.

"Could you tell my little granddaughter here what it is like to be a woman Marine?"

I stared, uncomprehending.

Tell her what it was like? The endless stream of bullshit from a bunch of pigheaded, testosterone-engorged monkeys, the constant pit in my stomach at not being able to run fast enough, work hard enough, or behave well enough to get by without criticism, and my overall disenchantment with the leadership ability of my noncommissioned officers all sprang to mind.

My inner censor told me that kind of conversation was not fit for a child, so I looked down into her eyes and tried to think of something nice to say about being in the Marines.

I drew a blank.

Finally, I smiled and said, "Oh, it's one of the most interesting careers I could have imagined."

"Do you like it?"

The man looked at me encouragingly, so I felt obligated to say something more.

"Some days yes, some days no. It's a lot like any other job, except nothing else I know of requires you to do so much running." Dancing around the fires of my integrity, trying not to burn myself, I thought, *Well, I might like it—someday.* I laughed aloud.

The little girl did not look any more comfortable with this subject than I was. She said nothing and stared at me with mistrust.

"Do you want to be in the military when you grow up?" I asked.

She hid behind her grandfather's leg. The man laughed and said, "Well, thank you for talking, and thank you for serving your country."

He took the girl's hand, and they walked off across the parking lot. I sat in my scooter, thinking. I thought about how sick to my stomach I felt at night when I knew other Marines thought us females were a joke, or an amusement, or maybe a big problem that the Marine Corps should rid itself of. I was torn painfully between leaving the Marines at the end of my term and giving the guys back their gun club or staying and telling them to stick it up their collective orifice. I thought seriously about whether I was strong enough to endure this for more than four years. I felt ashamed for feeling this way when other people saw me as a strong woman serving her country in the toughest branch of the military open to women. It did not feel noble to be terrified of being branded a slut or a dyke by the young guys around me, although that threat was always imminent.

I told myself I was stupid and should be grateful that someone thought I was doing something good. I slammed on the accelerator and tried to get the little cart back to my shop quickly. This was not a subject I cared to think on any longer.

8.

IN BUDWEISER VERITAS

"Always do sober what you said you would do drunk.
That will teach you to keep your mouth shut."—Ernest Hemingway

One of my NCOs, Sergeant Hanson, and I were sent to Norfolk, Virginia, to attend the Defense Messaging Systems Course in June 2000. We spent two months learning the ins and outs of this new software. As we both came from the same shop and I was the junior Marine, Sergeant Hanson took responsibility for me. He made sure I had a room, knew where the course was, and that I was getting food. Virginia Beach was nearby, and the only thing to do at night was go to the clubs. Much to my surprise, he reduced himself to hanging out at eighteen-and-up clubs in our off time so I could tag along. Sometimes he even discouraged the young men who tried to make my acquaintance in these clubs. This was quite a change from his attitude toward me at work, where he basically ignored me and all the other junior Marines to the point of oblivion.

But I always felt slighted by my NCOs; I didn't trust them, and I thought they were assholes. Getting me in trouble seemed to be their mission in life. My attitude was the petulant resentment of a younger sibling toward older brothers who were a bit coarse, to put it mildly.

One night, after we came back from a place where I had snuck a few beers on the dance floor, all of us, including a couple other Marines attending the same course, returned to our hotel and hung out in Sgt Hanson's room. We were all in states of intoxication running from "tipsy" to "hammered." I may have been the one most adequately filling the "hammered" slot. Beer bottles lay scattered across the room, and we sprawled on the various furniture, staring at the small TV on the dresser and finishing off the remaining beer in the mini-fridge.

Sgt Hanson was flipping through the channels and stopped on a documentary about females going through Marine Corps basic training. Within minutes, everyone started making fun of the girls on the television, mocking their soft voices and lack of upper-body strength.

(Imitating a child's voice) "Oh my God, I sprained my ankle!"

The guys giggled.

"I chipped a nail!" Corporal Nelson's squeaky, faux-female voice was grating.

"I bet by the end they're all crying and at least two are pregnant!"

This witty remark caused all the guys to laugh together, their derision hitting me like acid.

"Bruh, look at how she runs, oh my God. She'd be dead at the first sign of trouble."

That's unfair, I thought, as my brain stewed in its juices. *You're a fucking data dink, not an infantryman. You'd die the second there wasn't electricity*. I hiccupped but otherwise kept my mouth shut. Furious as I was becoming, I wasn't sure how to approach this situation.

I sat in a haze of drunkenness and started feeling as though they were ridiculing *me*. The remarks were now personal. As I became angrier and increasingly hurt by their remarks, I felt obligated to say something. The part of my mind that always gets me in over my head sneered, *You gonna sit there and take this?*

I stood and glared at them all, seething.

"Hey, Sergeant. Hey. Why don't you ssshut up! Why don't you *all shut up!*"

I weaved a bit as I struggled to keep my balance. I locked eyes with Sergeant Hanson.

Telling someone two ranks above you to shut up is not done in the Marine Corps. He looked at me in dismay, mentally performed the same calculus I had, and scowled. I was drunk underage, in a hotel room, disrespecting my leadership. But the blame for the situation would almost certainly fall on him for allowing it, so writing me up wasn't an option. But his shock was clear, as if the couch had started yelling at him to lose weight. Furniture doesn't complain directly to the user, and non-NCOs aren't supposed to complain to the NCOs.

That didn't mean he was powerless. His friends' eyes darted back and forth between us, waiting for him to say something. Finally, he just laughed at me and waved his hand, gesturing for me to sit back down.

"Look, just face it, Miller. Those girls aren't really gonna be Marines. They're just doing this to prove something to their boyfriends or their daddy. They couldn't actually go into combat. I wouldn't want them in a foxhole with me, I tell ya that. This is just more politically correct garbage being forced on the Marine Corps."

He took a sip of beer and turned back toward the television, considering the matter handled.

"What the hell do you know?" I shouted. Voice modulation is not my best skill when I am drunk. "You don't give any female Marines a chance! You just—you just ridicule them and sneer at them!"

I staggered a little and then regained my composure. I leveled a finger at him.

"Anyway, you're a shitty NCO!"

Dead silence. Cpl Howard stood and backed away from the bed, holding his hands up. I'd probably just ensured I'd be left out of any future gatherings. *Well, fuck them.* I didn't care, not right then.

Cpl Howard tried to defuse things.

"Calm down, now. C'mon, guys. It's just a TV show—nothing to argue over."

But my remarks had stung, and Sgt Hanson rose to confront this accusation. He started shouting at me, slurring his own words a little bit.

"Oh yeah, like you would know! I wouldn't give a female a chance because I don't want to get killed, that's why! What are you gonna do when someone starts shooting? Run for cover and cry, that's what! Girls are always falling out of runs, complaining and whining, worried about their looks. I bet you wouldn't last a day in a combat zone! Ha, women Marines! Whatever, they're just walking mattresses to keep morale up is more like it."

"Shut up. You don't know shit! You don't know anything! You're supposed to know your Marines and take care of them. That's what an NCO does! You don't know anything! I know who your girlfriend is, I know where you hang out, I know what kind of beer you drink, where you are from, even what religion you are! What do you know about me, Sergeant? Huh? Nothing! You barely know what I do at work, let alone what kind of person I am!"

I was shrieking and crying at the same time. Cpl Howard looked frantically for a way out of this situation.

"And now . . . now I sit here and listen to what you really think of women Marines. How am I supposed to feel as your subordinate, knowing you think I'm a fucking joke? Huh? Now I know you think higher of my male counterparts than me, based on my gender! I hate you!"

I sobbed with all the impotent anger inside me and stormed out of the hotel room. I glanced back just long enough to see Sgt Hanson looking almost as angry as I was. He opened his mouth to shout some further imprecations as the door closed behind me, but I couldn't hear him because I didn't want to.

Looking back, I don't think I was being entirely fair to him. He *had* tried to look after me, but my hurt feelings overrode everything else. I staggered to the vending machine at the end of the hall, fumbling in my pocket for some change, and shoved in miscellaneous coins until my options lit up. Still crying, I just jammed a couple buttons until something came out. It was a pack of Hostess Zingers. I ripped open the cellophane and shoved two of them into my mouth, one right after another. Then I sank to the floor and chewed slowly, still crying. *Damn, I might be white-girl wasted. This blows.*

Here I was, angry at being stereotyped—and then eating junk food because I felt unhappy. What the hell had I done with my life? Maybe I had no business here. Maybe the Marines really were just for guys.

No! Why should I let them drive me off with their ignorance? How was anyone ever going to prove them wrong if we all got out when the criticism broke us down? Hell no; I was staying!

But I suck at pull-ups.

Is that what makes you good, pull-ups? Running? As far as I could tell, the skills all Marines needed to be "a good Marine" were cleaning, looking fit, and having a high threshold for bullshit. Well, my grandmother had that in spades, so fuck them!

No sooner did I think this than I started to doubt my cause. *Why should I suffer to prove something to people who are not going to change their minds?* It is useless for sheep to a pass a law for vegetarianism when the wolves remain of a different opinion. I remember that quote from somewhere (I think it was William Randolph Inge).

Cpl Howard approached me where I sat on the floor by the vending machine and leaned down, looking at my face. I tried to hide my tear-stained cheeks and vigorously rubbed my eyes. Suddenly I felt like a pig. I quickly threw the leftover food in the trash can next to me. He smiled and extended his hand.

"Here. You need some help getting to your room?"

I sniffled and nodded. He picked me up and supported me by one arm into the elevator and back to my floor. My face burned from all the crying, and I felt ashamed. Cpl Howard was significantly bigger than I was and probably could have carried me on one shoulder. He looked like a football player. Here I was, a Marine, and I was leaning on his arm like some drunken sorority girl. *Great way to prove them wrong, Tracy.*

He opened the door to my room, put the key in my back pocket, and laid me on the bed. When he turned and said good night over his shoulder as he headed back out the door, I felt like cursing him out too, just because he was a male Marine who now probably thought ill of me. Instead, I mumbled good night and fell asleep in my clothes on top of the covers.

Sgt Hanson never mentioned the incident, and I was profoundly grateful he did not punish me for my disrespect, which had been ample. I don't know if my drunken tirade made any difference to him or if he wrote me off as a dolt. But he did make what seemed to me a more noticeable effort to be involved in the lives of his junior Marines, and he never said anything disparaging about female Marines again—at least, not where I could hear him. I was happy to have someone I could rely on, even though my cheeks still colored with embarrassment when I thought about that night. To get drunk and scream at people is not a good problem-solving strategy, but it made me feel better this one time. It's such a Marine way of dealing with shit.

9.

THE FIRST FEMALE RECRUIT IN MCRD SAN DIEGO

Chow hall duty is not fun. Because the chow hall in MCRD San Diego, like many other stateside dining facilities, was short-staffed due to cutbacks in the number of cooks the Marine Corps trained in 1999, there was a duty roster where each shop on-base would surrender privates, PFCs, and LCpls, as required, for two weeks of mandatory service as chow hall personnel. When the data shop came up on the roster, I volunteered to go.

It was not that I really loved being at work by 0500 every day in my scratchy service charlies or staying until nearly 1900 every night, including weekends. I just really hated being one of two junior Marines in a shop with eight NCOs. Getting away from that for a couple weeks sounded like a fair trade to me, especially when it meant front-of-the-line food privileges. Besides, most of the dirty work in the chow hall was performed by third-phase recruits who were near graduation. After all the exciting business of the rifle range was over and the Crucible was just ahead, the recruit platoons had what was known as a "mess and maintenance week," in which they worked all over the base, doing necessary tasks to clean up, fix up, straighten up, or otherwise serve the command.[4]

I reported to the chow hall that served the permanent personnel on-base, as opposed to the recruit chow hall, where I also took chow duty from

---

4   There is a VERY STRICT policy that recruits and junior Marines may NOT be asked to perform any personal services for senior Marines. They can do something for the base or the unit, but they are not to be treated as slaves or body servants.

time to time. This one was a very nice facility with carpeting, red leather-upholstered booths for Marines to take their meals, lamp lighting set at strategic points in the dining area, and a very clean and well-presented food line that served such entrees as baked chicken with lemon, rice, steamed vegetables, and chocolate cake for dessert that was moist and fresh. The food was served by incredibly polite and disciplined recruits in crisp, all-white coveralls who kept their bearing as they greeted each customer and served them. A drill instructor or two lounged nearby to ensure that customer service didn't slip. The Marine cooks made sure the meals were up to snuff and otherwise just supervised the rest of us. There were even potted plants and two large-screen televisions playing different channels so Marines could look at something besides each other while they ate.

This chow hall served every VIP, civilian, and Marine on-base, which meant that the line for breakfast really got moving by 0500. There was even a cart wheeled out to the courtyard in front of the building so that hungry Marines who had just come from PT could get chow without having to change clothes or violate dress codes. My assignment for the first week was to stand behind a podium inside the entrance and collect money from those Marines who were not issued chow hall cards. It was a struggle sometimes to take money, count out correct change, make sure the sign-in sheet on the stand had been filled in correctly by the payee, and everything stayed accounted for while I stifled yawns and repeated the greeting of the day over and over for two hours. By the time breakfast hours ended, I was already hurting. This was probably when my critical coffee addiction started.

One morning, I overslept in the barracks. I arrived by 0515 in uniform and ready to rock, but that fifteen minutes of obvious lapse in duty was going to cost me (as it should have).

After I got caught up and finished accounting for the cash, I reported to the office of the head cook, MSgt Williams. He was a stout Black man with broad shoulders and a perpetual smirk that could mean many things. His deep-red cook's coat was immaculate every day, and the gold chevrons, which only cooks wore, sparkled on his collar. I knew I was due an ass-chewing at the very least, but MSgt Williams had something much more fun (for everyone else but me) in mind.

I banged on the hatch of MSgt Williams's office.

"Lance Corporal Miller reporting as ordered!" I announced with all the humility of an underling who knows they're in the shit.

"Come." Master Sergeant didn't look up from the computer. I stood front and center of his small desk, at attention and waiting for the dressing down to commence. When he finished what he was doing, he leaned back in his chair and finally looked up at me.

"Where the fuck were you this morning, Lance Corporal?"

"I overslept, Master Sergeant." At a time like this, why lie?

"Unsat. Very unsat." He glared at me. I held my breath, hoping that this calm demeanor was not a prelude to paperwork. Ass-chewings didn't follow you around the Marine Corps in your record book, but paperwork most certainly did. My shop would hear about that, and then I'd have even more happy fun times to look forward to.

"Here's what we're going to do. Since you can't seem to be on time, like a Marine, you're going to go back out there in the chow hall and help the recruits clean until lunchtime."

"Yes, Master Sergeant." I always said the entire rank of the person when I spoke. MCRD San Diego was hot on proper military protocols, and it would not do to slur the rank of someone placed so far above me in their eyes. I started to turn to leave.

"Wait! I'm not done, Lance Corporal."

Shit. I returned to attention.

"You're going to change into the white coveralls, wear a white paper hat, and you're going to report in to the guide for the platoon. Ask him what work he has for you, and do whatever he assigns you. Understood? Let's see if you can show him the respect you clearly didn't show me this morning."

MSgt Williams looked especially pleased with himself.

"Aye, Master Sergeant." *Fuuuuuuu—*

"Dismissed."

I turned and left.

The punishment was meant to be mortifying. As a lance corporal with boot camp barely a year behind me, being a recruit for even a couple hours was like getting demoted to the sub-basement level of a civilian job. However, there was one unusual twist to it.

Marine Corps Recruit Training Depot, San Diego, California, was an all-male boot camp. No female Marines were ever trained there, to my knowledge, without exception. But here I was, about to dress up identical to the chow hall recruits and role-play as one of them, reporting to the guide as if I were just another member of their platoon. The drill instructors were going to lose their fucking minds.

Most recruits knew who I was by now. They'd seen me standing in my uniform at the front of the chow hall, greeting other Marines, for the past week. My orders from MSgt Williams were clear, though. For the rest of the morning, I was now Recruit Miller instead of LCpl Miller. I exited the office and went looking for where the recruits changed coveralls in between meal servings to remain clean and presentable. Finding the back area that doubled as a dry-goods locker, I opened the door and waved to the guys crammed in an area that was maybe three hundred square feet total.

Several recruits were in the process of changing. Under the coveralls, they wore green T-shirts and olive shorts (the normal PT uniform). I squished in, already changed into my green PT uniform, and asked the recruit next to me, now as an equal, if he'd toss me a clean pair of coveralls. When I got no response, I looked up from my bag and saw them all staring at me in utter horror. No one wanted to speak or move because recruits speaking to Marines in any manner that could be construed as disrespectful would invite the wrath of the drill instructors, even if said drill instructors weren't present at the moment. Recruits disrespecting a *female* and a Marine at the same time would likely incur the same outcome as pissing on a drill instructor's leg. Being caught in a closed room with a female who wanted them to hand her clothes was too far beyond the pale for even Lovecraft's imagination to deal with.

After some silence, I tried to explain that I was ordered to do this, and it was okay. When that didn't win any converts, I decided to lie. I told the young men, to a mixture of consternation and bafflement, that I had been late for chow duty this morning, so Master Sergeant had busted me all the way down to recruit again. I now had to re-finish boot camp with their platoon to regain my lost rank. Therefore, I concluded, I'd really be grateful if they could hand me a paper hat and some coveralls so I could get on with things.

A recruit named Gonzalez (recruits don't ever use their first names, not even among themselves, not even in private) was the first to snap out of it. He shrugged, like having a chick in the platoon wasn't the craziest thing he'd seen so far, and went to grab the items I had asked for. He might not understand what the hell was happening, but he knew he had been given something like an order from someone who'd been a Marine five minutes ago, and *that* he could deal with.

After Gonzalez broke the ice, the rest of the recruits unfroze. They were still leery of me, expecting my existence to be some cruel trick by the drill instructors. These young men hadn't been allowed anywhere near a female for over two months. Even the smell of my perfume was probably too much. It'd be just like the DIs to set up this situation and then crush anyone who handled it with anything less than perfect professionalism.

After suiting up, I asked Gonzalez who the guide was so I could report in. The other recruits came alive; they really wanted to see what happened. Boot camp is notoriously short on entertainment, and this was sure to be notable at the very least. Everyone offered to take me to him, which was great because, let's face it, recruits all looked the same to me by this point.

My new friends and I found the guide in the dessert-bar area, industriously cleaning the ice cream machine. He was easy to spot, being over six feet tall, gangly, and with the odd mix of dark-brown hair and bright-blue eyes. After pointing him out, my entourage dissipated into the scenery, watching events unfold while simultaneously doing their own tasks. No one wanted to be in the blast radius when the DIs caught up with me, but neither did they want to miss the show.

Remembering the proper customs and courtesies from my own experiences, I marched up to the guide, came to attention, and in a loud, clear voice announced, "Recruit Miller reporting to the guide of platoon 2046 as ordered! This recruit[5] requests the guide to give her tasks to complete!"

The guide could not have looked more shocked if I had busted out a risqué striptease involving goats. Like the previous recruits, he froze for a moment. Feeling that more was expected of him, he sputtered, "Ma'am? This recruit doesn't understand, uh . . . ?"

I broke my bearing for a moment. "I got busted back down to recruit for being late to work this morning. So now I'm in your platoon. Please give me something to clean before I get in even more trouble."

The guide continued to stare, waiting for sense to reassert itself. When that didn't change anything, he took a big gulp of air. "How does ma'am feel about washing the windows?"

He cringed the tiniest bit. Giving orders to a Marine when he was just a recruit was such a violation of the natural order of things that he almost refused to do it. I wanted to laugh, but smiling at him would once again run afoul of the drill instructors, so that was a no-go. They wouldn't

---

5   Another rule of etiquette in boot camp is that you do not refer to yourself in first person, ever. It's always "this recruit."

punish me for it, but he'd get destroyed later that night at the barracks for letting himself be distracted.

"Windows sound great! Where do I start?"

Two hours later, after cleaning windows with a few other recruits who finally felt comfortable enough to talk to me, I'd gotten most of them to believe this was really happening. I was really going to finish boot camp all over again with them as the first female recruit to graduate from MCRD San Diego. I'm not sure they all bought it, but they seemed amused when I asked what phase they were on, whether they had already done the gas chamber, and wondered out loud about where I'd shower and sleep over the next few weeks. Then I was summoned to the head cook's office once more via the intercom system. I disposed of my cleaning supplies and reported to MSgt Williams. He dismissed me back to the barracks to change and get ready for the lunchtime service, and I complied.

I returned in my service charlies and took up my post at the cash podium, straightening the sign-in sheets and making sure all my pens actually worked and didn't run. As I counted out the cash box, the guide came by my podium. He brought me a strawberry milkshake.

"Glad to see you got promoted again, ma'am."

He flashed a brief smile and then darted off to avoid any suspicion of misbehavior. I looked at the milkshake and smiled. Yes, MSgt Williams, I learned my lesson.

10.

TEMPUS FUCK IT

As I was leaving MCRD, San Diego, to go to my next duty station in Okinawa, certain traditions had to be observed. Without fail, a shop is expected to send off a Marine with at least some sort of luncheon, and maybe, if you have been a decent worker, a plaque is made to commemorate your time with the unit. This was my first duty station, so I was new to the tradition but excited about it.

I had just gotten married in a small ceremony while on leave in Florida, and my new husband was already stationed in Okinawa. We were sweethearts from our time together in Twentynine Palms, California, where communications school was held, and when the orders to Okinawa fell from the sky, we decided that maybe we'd both be better off as a team. My orders were to 7th Comm Battalion—or 7th Crime, as it was otherwise known, thanks to a string of misconduct issues that gave the unit a bad reputation on the island. I wasn't looking forward to being locked down in a barely functional barracks with a bunch of pissed-off Marines, so getting married held even more attraction.

There were two types of orders to Okinawa: "accompanied" orders, which were three years long and permitted spouses and dependents to accompany the Marine to the island, and "unaccompanied" orders, which were only one year long and were the basic orders everyone else got. The rights of the accompanied Marines were much broader. They could live in houses as opposed to the barracks, own cars, and get better pay. Unaccompanied Marines were basically at the disposal of the receiving unit and had no say in where they lived or how much they worked. My orders were "unaccompanied," as were Jens's, but we thought that maybe once I arrived, we could convert to "accompanied" status and improve the quality of our lives.

On my last day in the shop, I was invited to lunch with all my NCOs and my civilian supervisor, a GS-12 named Mike Peissner.[6] Our shop only had two non-NCOs, myself and LCpl LeMasters, with whom my relationship was rocky. Other than us, there were nearly ten NCOs at any given time, so being the lowest-ranking, least-privileged members of the team had been rough going at points. I'd shown up as a very naïve young woman of nineteen, and now I was departing at the wise old age of twenty-one. It was May 2001, and I was over the moon to be going to Japan.

When I showed up in civilian clothes at the restaurant off-base, I was excited about my new adventure. Strict rules about uniforms off-base meant that all of us were in regular clothes, and it felt a lot more like lunch with equals than my status normally allowed. It was a bright, airy café, and I was seated at one end of a long table. Mr. Peissner, being our boss—technically—was seated at the head of the table. He was a large, jolly white man with a mustache and glasses, and he had a reputation for occasionally saying things that sounded wrong without a major dollop of context.

We all ordered food, with my meal being picked up by the team, and then we chatted and made small talk. It was pleasant, although my mind was already on other things, like packing the last of my belongings that night, checking out of my barracks room (an involved process that required passing an inspection before I could leave), and the other minutiae of leaving the country. After everyone had gotten at least their lunch eaten, Mike Peissner tapped his glass with a fork and called us all to order. He stood and smiled brightly, ready to make a speech.

No one had ever given a speech about me before, so I was suddenly very nervous. Thinking people are talking about you behind your back is anxiety provoking, but somehow having someone talk about you while you sit there looking manically cheerful is worse.

"When Salz came to our shop, I wasn't sure she knew anything about IT," Mike began, warming to his subject.

"Still doesn't!" piped up Cpl Buress, always ready to keep me from overestimating myself. There was an awkward laugh, but Mike pressed on.

---

6   Not his real name . . . I don't think.

"She did really well when I sent her out on trouble calls, though, and I have to tell you, Salz, you did so well at times that I forgot you were a girl!"

Everyone started laughing, but I saw Sgt Nellis and Sgt Hanson (the same one I'd drunkenly screamed at before) cover their faces in embarrassment while other diners stared in horror. I burst out giggling because, as always, Mike's remark sounded terrible without context.

Because MCRD San Diego was an all-male training center, there were nuances that normal workplaces didn't have. Inside every recruit barracks was a large office called the "DI hut," where drill instructors did all their administrative business, and each barracks also had a company office, where the really senior staff like the company commander and the company first sergeant handled their paperwork. Every single office was equipped with at least one computer and a printer, and drill instructors were loathed for their ability to break shit. At one point, I watched in horror as a first sergeant closed-fist punched a printer to pieces and then demanded to know why it wasn't working. I gulped and said maybe it was a bad power supply at first, but now it was probably a bad everything.

Whenever a trouble call popped up in the queue to go fix an asset at the barracks, the issue of my femaleness arose. On the one hand, I was supposed to be a Marine like any other and treated as interchangeable with my male counterparts, at least in theory. On the other hand, sending a teenage girl to an all-male recruit barracks to fix things presented issues. The training schedule could leave recruits in any kind of condition or dress, depending on the time of day, and my schedule to go around base and fix things didn't always line up. Additionally, access to the offices and equipment occasionally required me to detour through recruit-only areas. Therefore, I'd have to sometimes disrupt things in order to fulfill my duties.

Despite what others may have thought, the drill instructors didn't mind my presence at all. DIs never passed up a chance to lose their minds on recruits, and a female walking by was the kind of distraction they longed for. Back in my shop, as trouble tickets piled up, a grudge grew against letting me out of responsibilities just because the building in question was all male. So Mike sometimes assigned me work that most definitely fell crosswise with the etiquette and protocol of boot camp, and his compliment was meant to say that he'd never figured my gender into those assignments.

But of course, it *sounded* like he was saying girls can't be good at computer stuff, and he'd mortified our surrounding guests. Remarks like that were always dreaded in case the woman in question took offense and took that offense all the way up the chain of command for discrimination. That kind of accusation ended careers, or so I had heard. Everyone would wait for my reaction before they decided how they felt about it.

Shortly after that, Mike concluded his remarks and passed off hosting the get-together to Sgt Nellis, who stood and presented me with a modest plaque bearing my dates of arrival to and departure from the unit, along with a network-interface card bolted to the wood. It was tasteful, and I really appreciated it.

PART THREE:

OKINAWA, JAPAN

II.

WELCOME TO OKITRAZ

When I touched down in Okinawa, it was still peacetime, so the Marine Corps had seized on the moment to train Marines in a new kind of hand-to-hand combat training. The unarmed combat training we received in boot camp equipped us to *almost* fend off a mayfly, so this was a definite improvement. Kind of.

I am not going to lie: I have never been within overnight-delivery distance of combat. I like to think I would be brave, but my moderate sense of self-preservation screams that it's a worthwhile effort to avoid flying bullets altogether. The notion that someone out there hates you enough to try to kill you is enough to keep you awake at night. How do you overcome this fear? Short of encouraging Marines to go through life picking fights with people[7] just to harden themselves to fighting, the Corps developed the Marine Corps Martial Arts Program (MCMAP).

Like most other Marines, I laughed off the notion of a martial arts program, thinking nothing they could teach us about hand-to-hand combat would be worthwhile. In the spirit of voluntary participation that runs rampant in the Corps, however, it became mandatory immediately, and I soon found myself getting ready to learn the beginning level: tan belt. The program was only in its second year. In the afternoon, about fifteen or so Marines wearing boots, cammie trousers, and green T-shirts gathered in a field by the base gym.

---

7   Not saying we don't do that anyway, encouragement not required.

The first part of class focused on stretching and injury prevention, followed by a warm-up. Part of the warm-up routine for the program was called "body hardening."

Body hardening is every bit as painful as it sounds and went something like this: Marines were teamed up with a partner (theoretically with a nod to size and weight but most times not) and then took turns "hardening" each other. First, we would slam our forearms together to try to toughen the nerves on the inner parts. Then we hit the outer parts of our forearms together to deaden the nerve there. Next came the stomach, which to me sounded like some frat-party game. We took turns punching each other in the stomach—not especially hard, but enough to know that someone had hit us. Then we worked on the legs. We would face each other and kick the inside and outside of each thigh with the top of the foot. After this was done, the instructor started on the actual techniques.

Body hardening was a great opportunity for me to prove I was already hard. There were a few problems, though. First, my male partners were extremely reluctant to hit me. Second, I seriously doubted I could have taken a full-force punch from some of these guys. Cpl Pray, for instance, was big enough to pass for a linebacker. He also had a chiseled face that showed no mercy and frozen, pale eyes that did not register pain—his own or that which he inflicted on his victims . . . err, partners. One of his partners barely made it through the second set of twenty body-hardening repetitions. When Cpl Pray came around to kick his thigh the final time, the boy fell to the ground and stayed there until the instructor came over and ended their practice.

When it was my turn as his partner, though, his face clouded with confusion as he tried to figure out where he could hit me that wasn't soft and inappropriate. The distance between my chest and my pelvis wasn't wide enough for him to comfortably throw blows, although I made up for that by giving him acres of hip and leg area to kick with gusto. When we were done kicking each other, I felt so sore I knew the bruises would last for at least a week.

The instructor then moved to teaching ground-fighting techniques. This is still one of my favorite activities, and I promoted this heavily as a way of keeping morale up and tension low in a platoon. Ground fighting is the Marine Corps' way of saying "LET'S WRESTLE." We went over to a grassy field and made a large circle. Two Marines chosen by the instructor would sit back-to-back inside the circle. The instructor came out, put his hand on their shoulders, and stated the rules for all to hear:

"This fight will go no longer than two minutes. At no time are you allowed to stand any higher than your knees. There will be no eye gouging, no groin shots, no hair pulling [not that the zero-to-three-inch hair on the guys was particularly inviting for this], no biting, no closed-fist punching, and no fish-hooking. If I say stop, you will get the hell away from each other immediately. If your opponent taps out, the fight ends. All commands will come from my voice, and I will start and stop the fight. Understand?"

The two men nodded, both looking a little nervous. I became nervous just looking at them. I was the only female in this class, which translated to one thing in my head: I was going to get my butt kicked. The instructor smiled and then pulled his hand off the combatants' shoulders.

"Fight!"

The two leapt around to face each other, grabbing clumsily for an immediate choke hold. They backed away on their knees and eyed their opponent, looking for an easy opening.

"I said *fight*, not stare at each other like you might want to date!" the instructor snarled.

The two looked slightly abashed, suspended until one went for it. He lunged and climbed on top of his opponent's back. He slid his arms down to the man's neck and then pulled up hard, choking his partner forthwith. His airway constricted, the victim deflated quickly and, after a few seconds of futile struggling, summoned the strength to tap out.

The instructor blew his whistle, and in less than a minute, the first match was over. We all cheered and then moved to let them into our circle.

I found myself slightly exhilarated by the performance. The thought of getting in the circle myself sent adrenaline coursing through my veins. The instructor must have interpreted what I was feeling as fear because he smiled at me and said, "Okay, Salz, get out here. Who do you think you can fight?"

I crawled to the center of our circle and took my seat. I looked around and saw one guy who was skinny everywhere except his gut. He looked weak and flabby to me.

I pointed. "*Him*, Sergeant."

Grant was his name, I found out later. The other guys all laughed and jeered, and Grant crawled into the circle, squinting his entire face in the sheer embarrassment of fighting a girl.

He got back-to-back with me. I took a deep breath, barely hearing the instructor as he recited the rules again. I was still new to this unit, and these guys were taking my measure. I was so hyped up that I almost missed the command: "Fight!"

I turned with panicky swiftness and grabbed around Grant's throat with every part of me that would fit under his chin. He gasped and pushed me onto the ground, his head shoved into my chest. I clung to his neck as if it were a life preserver. It seemed to me I could win if I just did not lose his neck.

But he tugged his head free and got on top of me. I pushed against his upper body to keep him off and, kicking a leg up, tried to hook his neck again. I was flexible enough to get it up there, and I jerked him off me. He tumbled backwards. The guys cheered.

I rolled over, racing to think. I knew I would tire out quickly as the adrenaline ebbed. I had to win this fast before I lost my hormonal advantage. Grant lunged at me again, and I rolled to the side, grasping his throat again. Now I rolled him over on top of me and pulled his neck with all my might, yanking his head back and sideways. I wrapped my legs around his torso and pulled the rest of him back and down, increasing the strain on his throat. He gurgled and gasped but did not tap. Frowning, I tightened my hold, putting everything I had into it. He still didn't give. I began twisting his head around, hoping the pain would convince him to tap. He groaned, clawing at my arms. I was breathing hard but also starting to get bored with choking him. I had to think of something to make him end this. I began to wonder if I had the strength to break his neck after all . . .

And that is when the instructor yelled, "*Tap!*" and pushed us apart.

I let Grant go and just lay there, gasping, covered in itchy grass and sweat. Grant rolled off and looked back at me with anger. Seems I had just made an enemy. I did not care. I had won.

I crawled back to my place in the circle. No one congratulated me, however. They just mocked Grant for getting beat by a girl. Still, I felt the exhilaration of triumph.

"Well, not bad for your first match, Salz. Let's see how you do in your second."

The instructor turned his back to me. I paused and looked around. *Oh, shit. Another match?*

Most of the men were ignoring me again, waiting for their name to be called. The instructor called two more and began their match. I watched them, looking for pointers. This was going to be a hard afternoon.

For my second match, I was up against a Marine named LaCrua. I applied a pressure point to his inner thigh that made him yelp, but he was nevertheless happy to choke me out. I tapped quickly and declined a rematch. Maybe it was because he won, but LaCrua had a very different attitude about the whole ordeal, and later we would be friends.

One for two. That was my introduction to Marine Corps martial arts ground fighting. I later fought women in the ring in addition to men, and it got downright dirty. One of the more memorable fights was with Gunny Schnepp. She was a couple of inches shorter than I, blonde, a few years older, and willing to be as hardcore as the next girl. When we got in the circle, she had no qualms about going for my two-foot-long braid and using it to her advantage. If the instructor hadn't called foul, I might have lost that match.

When later I talked to female Marines like the master gunnery sergeant who worked in our ComSec Vault, I realized how far females had come in the Corps. She told me how she had received makeup classes and tea-party lessons in boot camp some thirty years ago. She laughed about how the final trial before graduation was entertaining their company officers at a mock social function. I stared at her in wonder, comparing her experience with mine. She stared back, marveling at how much more young ladies have to expect from themselves in today's Marine Corps. It was an insightful conversation. I could never imagine her rolling around like a tomboy, wrestling and learning hand-to-hand combat.

12.

SHIT GETS REAL FOR THE WHOLE UNITED STATES

When I joined, it surprised me to learn that Marine recruiters were turning women away. Ladies came into their office every other day, whereas men, who were eligible to fill empty combat billets, had to be practically shanghaied, especially in the slow seasons. After September 11, 2001, this all changed. Young people of both genders felt an irresistible impulse to defend their country. For once, instead of desperately scrambling to get waivers for less-than-qualified candidates, recruiters had the luxury of picking and choosing. The Recruit Training Depots were overstocked with fresh faces.

It was late night in Barracks 473 on Camp Foster. A barracks is a lot like a college dorm, with a common room called a lounge on each floor. They usually doubled us up, two to a room. However, I was fortunate to have a room to myself. I was trying to sleep in my bed, praying for quiet and forgiveness, when a loud, obnoxious fist began pummeling my door. I cursed and kicked off the covers. I was wearing the PT gear issued at boot camp as my pajamas, which consisted of the world's smallest pair of silky green shorts and a T-shirt. It was cold in that small barracks room. My bare feet froze on contact with the tile floor, and I had to force myself to take another step toward the door. The knocking continued, then evolved into hammering, demanding my attention immediately.

"Wake up, dammit!"

"All right. Hold on a minute, geezus!"

I ripped open the door and glared at the duty NCO.

"What?"

"Get to the lounge. There's been an attack on the Pentagon. Hurry up."

He moved to the next room to bang on another door.

"Huh? The Pentagon? Fuck off, are you serious?"

First, I could not even imagine who would (or could) attack mainland USA; then I could not figure out why they had woken me up in Japan of all places because of it. It was not as though we were close enough to risk being attacked ourselves, right? What could *we,* sitting as we were in the ass end of Japan, do about it anyway?

"No fucking joke, all right? Get to the lounge." He resumed hammering my neighbor's door. Grumbling to myself, I slipped on my shower shoes and tromped down the hall, shutting my door behind me.

The lounge was already full of Marines in various stages of dress, from uniforms to pajamas. The large lounge TV was on, and I saw a skyscraper burning on the screen. The image looked like it might be of New York. It definitely wasn't the Pentagon.

"What the hell happened there?" I asked the girl leaning against the wall next to me. She looked more tired than I felt—and slightly bored.

"A plane flew into the World Trade Center."

"Oh."

She yawned. I wanted to laugh with relief. I had never been to New York City, and I knew that this certainly involved many tragic deaths, but this was no full-blown onslaught against the USA. It was probably just a lost Cessna aircraft, a drunk pilot cruising into the wrong airspace in his three-seater. This, in my opinion, was something that was bound to happen. If you build something that tall, eventually . . .

I nudged my neighbor again.

"Wait, what the fuck? They didn't close the airspace around the towers?"

She peered at the TV at the other end of the lounge. "Huh?"

I pointed. "See the tiny plane in the background? I grew up near Piper Aircraft in Vero Beach.[8] They close airspaces when there's been an accident. But there's a plane *right there.* That's really weird."

"I can't see shit. I left my glasses in my room." She squinted.

Then it happened.

I watched in stunned silence, listening to an increasingly hysterical reporter describe the event I was witnessing in slow motion. A second

---

8 Where the terrorists who were flying these planes trained, as it would later turn out.

plane—a 767, as it turned out, just like the first one—circled around and slammed with earthshaking impact into the second tower. My mind reeled. *Two* planes. This was no cosmic coincidence. But what could it be? *My God.*

I sank onto a nearby ratty couch and felt my stomach twist. I was nauseated with fear—no, not fear. Dread. Growing up in America, there is plenty to fear but little to dread, and you do not feel like anyone could ever seriously threaten your country. I mean, there's giant oceans on each side and NAFTA to the top and bottom. I couldn't imagine, at the age of twenty-one, why other people would hate us enough to do something like this.[9]

That was bad enough. But behind the dread, the nausea, was my realization of what this meant for me, as a Marine. I knew, with goose bumps rising on every part of me, that this meant we were going to war. No idea against whom or exactly when—only that, as a country, we would demand that someone pay for this. My time in the Marines was not going to be a ho-hum, peacetime tour anymore. Those people in those towers, the people in those ill-fated airplanes, were just the start of the casualty count. There would be hell to pay for someone. That someone included us.

When you sign a contract with the military, there are no hidden clauses, just people who don't really think through what they're getting into. You are agreeing, in essence, to give your life willingly if circumstances dictate at any point in the next four years. You are agreeing to fight America's enemies, whoever they are and wherever you are told to fight them. This is no lighthearted agreement, yet when we make it, we feel sure that it will never actually place us in this situation: "Hey, man, I just joined for the college money and to see the world."

Now, as I listened to reports pouring out of the TV—a plane crashing into the Pentagon, another plane augering into the earth of Pennsylvania—I stared in numb silence at the two smoldering towers, which soon, one after the other, imploded groundward in massive, opaque clouds of dust and smoke, swallowing up who knew how many thousands of human beings.

The gravity of our situation and my commitment hit me, and I wanted to run over to my naval messaging shop across the street to see the real intel as it came in. I imagined the machine that alerted us to important message traffic blowing up with the volume of messages flowing in from

---

9   Later on, when I did my master's in international relations, I figured out what a foreign policy is.

commanders and generals, ordering all personnel to report immediately back to base: *Lockdown. We are under attack. Highest level of defensive posture possible ASAP, ASAP, ASAP.*

But my orders were to remain in the barracks. It was morning in New York—an incredibly clear, supernaturally blue September morning—but it was late night in Okinawa, and none of us went back to sleep. We gathered in each other's rooms, playing cards, talking, and talking some more, comforting those who were frantic to call family members in New York. The lines into and out of Okinawa could not support the sudden rush of international phone traffic. Few Marines got through to the people they urgently wanted to reach. Phone cards sold out, and none of us were allowed out to buy more. The base locked down, and life as we knew it stopped with bone-jarring abruptness.

Most of us stayed like this for two weeks. My shop was mission critical, so we were back at work the next day, only now we were working twelve hours on, twelve hours off, no rest days, thanks to the deluge of messages. The cooks brought food to us from the chow hall in seven-ton vehicles. That same night, a major typhoon chose to crash into the tiny island. It sat on us for a week, ensuring that the weather was even more dreadful than our moods.

Marines tend to subscribe to the ethos of smashing, killing, and breaking anything that bothers them. We smelled blood; we wanted to fight. We wanted anything but to sit where we were, feeling helpless. I was luckier than most. I was able to go back to work.

It was my job to sift and sort through messages that came in from everywhere and direct them accordingly, notifying the right people if important ones came down the pipes. I had considered the work dull and of very little value to anyone, really. Not anymore. My work suddenly seemed anything but boring. I stayed in a windowless vault for a dozen hours at a stretch, processing message after message, many filled with terrifying speculation about who had done this and what might happen next. My shift over, I went across the street to the barracks, showered, and slept, only to return for another twelve hours. At least I had the comfort, if you can call it that, of knowing as much if not more than most of my fellow Americans. I had CNN, but I also had an endless torrent of incoming firsthand news.

It dawned on me only slowly, after more than a few twelve-hour watches, that no one in charge knew who, why, or how any more than I did. Sometimes, it is better not knowing.

13.

AIN'T NO PARTY LIKE A TYPHOON PARTY

O kinawa Marines have a unique experience we all share regardless of when we were physically stationed on the island. No, it's not the buy-me-drinky bars, or the unholy level of humidity. It's not accidentally eating a banana spider while on a trail run (just start chewing as fast as you can, and everything will be okay). It's not even the unique and historic richness of doing "acclime," or acclimatization PT, when first arriving (or else you might *actually* die on the very first battalion run).

It's the typhoon party.

Okinawa is settled at just the right spot in the Pacific Ocean to catch as many as six to eight typhoons each year. Usually, one or two score direct hits, and everyone goes into lockdown to ride it out. Okinawans build their communities for these very events, so they are usually quite relaxed and unconcerned. However, many Marines have never seen a hurricane. Those of us who came from places like Florida, Texas, and Louisiana all got a pretty good laugh at watching our brethren from Nevada, Montana, and Idaho lose their minds as the winds picked up and the rain started coming down sideways. And if those Marines were poorly suited to a typhoon, the buildings we all lived in are worse.

Almost as soon as the clouds gets dark and the winds really get going, the power goes out in the barracks. I'm talking pitch-black, void-of-the-cosmos dark while the howling and whipping weather makes a horror-movie score for the ages. Because the buildings were designed by at least one person who'd heard of severe weather, while each individual room has a window, the hallways and metal exit doors are solid. No windows, no light from the outside, nothing.

As the typhoons draw closer to the island, the bases raised the threat level. Like DEFCON, typhoon conditions (TC) start at 5—meaning someone somewhere saw a typhoon maybe possibly hypothetically forming—and work their way to imminent disaster in TC 1. TC 5 through 3 are pretty much business as usual with caution elevated appropriately. The winds kick up a bit, but everyone is still expected to go to work, PT, and so on. TC 2 has some formal definition, I'm sure, but what it meant to us was "GO BUY ALL THE ALCOHOL NOW NOW NOW BEFORE THE STORE RUNS OUT."

There were limits on how much alcohol each individual Marine could purchase based on rank. Per a single day, E-5 and below were allowed a single six-pack of beer, E-6 up could buy two to three packs, and officers could drown themselves in hard liquor if the fancy took them. Regardless of whether or not you consumed alcohol, though, you went and bought it immediately. If you drank, then congratulations; you were now somewhat stocked. If you did not drink, you collected money from those who did and, after concluding your max purchase, were awarded a small premium for your acquisition services.

Commanding officers issued policy letters and administered scoldings to their entire units at regular intervals about refraining from drinking during typhoons because if the storm suddenly vanished into the ether, the Marines were technically right back on normal duty.

No one paid attention.

The liquor store panic was because once TC 1 (IT'S COMING RIGHT FOR US!) was declared, all the package stores (read: liquor stores) closed, and the sale of alcohol was no longer permitted by order.

TC 1 has sublevels to it, and the one that foretold the end of electricity in the barracks was TC 1E (for "emergency"). Once TC 1E was declared by Kadena AFB, who were usually the ones calling these weather conditions, no one was allowed outside. No going to work, no going to the gym (that is quite a blow for some Marines), and no going to the shops. Everyone locked down in place to ride out the storm.

I was visiting my husband in his barracks room on Camp Schwab, where we often hung out while our paperwork to get housing was being processed. It wasn't exactly permitted, but no one complained, and I kept myself unobtrusive while I was there. I had come to Schwab earlier in the day because I saw the typhoon warnings rising, and I'd already maxed out my beer purchase on Camp Foster. My friend Mike and my spouse had commandeered a Nissan Skyline with blown power steering and picked me up.

Before TC 1E was declared, the barracks lost power. It was already 2000 in the evening, so the change was pretty stark. Only sickly orange lights from the street outside illuminated the room. We lit a couple of candles that we absolutely were not permitted to possess or burn in the barracks, grabbed some beers from the ice box, and went for a hallway stroll to visit the other inmates. Shortly after the pitch darkness of the power outage dropped like an axe, the howls and shouts and laughter began. No need to wait for winds to reach a hundred miles an hour to get soused. Anonymous voices shouted from each room, strange glows emanated from a newly discovered box of glow sticks, and no one could see who anyone was. It didn't matter anyway; there's no rank in typhoon party.

As I wandered in the black abyss of the hallway, one Recon Marine narrowly avoided crashing straight into me as he buzzed past, hooting and waving his arms about because he had tied his poncho liner to each wrist and both ankles. He was headed outside to see if the winds were strong enough to lift him up. After about thirty minutes, someone decided to stab a couple glow sticks and spray them on the walls and ceiling in the hallway. That made sense, honestly, because if the Marines were going to be forced to clean that hallway for an interminable number of hours every single week, they might as well get some enjoyment out of it. Besides, the overall effect was pretty cool to look at, like a Jackson Pollock version of outer space.

Someone at the far end of the hall, near where mama-san kept her own room that served as a tailor and laundress shop for the young men with no button-reaffixing skills, started playing guitar and singing at the top of his voice:

> *Wasting away again in Okinawa-ville!*
> *Looking for my lost bottle of Beam.*
> *Some people claim that there's an officer to blame . . .*
> *But I know . . . it's all Gunny's fault.*

Every single room door was open. When the power went out, the air-conditioning died. Even at night, Okinawa was not freaking playing about the heat. The winds grew more severe, and the large metal storm doors rattled and banged, adding to the growing cacophony. An hour or so into the evening, Recon Marines were down to their UDT shorts (basically booty shorts made from khaki material) and shower shoes (flip-flops), chatting in the hallway, and drinking by the pale-green glowstick light.

This was all very unusual, from my point of view. Camp Foster Marines were a little more domesticated than Recon Marines. We hung out and drank, sure, but very few of us went up on the roof during a typhoon to see if we could fly. What was remarkable was the relaxed, totally normal attitudes the guys all had while doing completely not normal things. Someone had on glow-in-the-dark plastic glasses, a cone-shaped straw hat, a T-shirt sprayed with glow-stick juice, and a long wooden staff. He went up and down the hall, pretending to bless revelers with his beer bottle in hand, murmuring gibberish. A wrestling match was already going down in the common-area lounge. The Navy corpsman had his bag on and drifted between rooms where his arrival was celebrated with offerings of alcohol, all the Marines knowing that his ministrations would likely be required by dawn. Many a Marine has dodged alcohol-related disciplinary charges thanks to an IV drip of saline solution before morning formation.

After three or four beers, it was time to finally break the seal (yeah, yeah, girl bladder, whatever). I guided myself back toward Jens's room in search of the toilet. Each barracks room here was blessed with a head of its own, so I expected to enjoy a modest amount of privacy as I peed in total darkness. Bloody stupid thing to worry about in a blackout, really.

Hoping I had located the right room (they all looked the same in the dark), I walked in the head and was about to shut the door when I heard a rustling of the shower curtain behind me. Thinking I might've just gone to the wrong bathroom and someone was taking a shower in the middle of a blackout (weirder things would happen), I paused to listen for the water turning on. Maybe I was just hearing things.

Dead silence. *O-kay. Fine, fuck it. I've peed in worse situations. Whoever's room this is, they'll forgive me, I'm sure.* I started to unbutton my pants, leaving the door slightly ajar to get a tiny bit of light. Then I heard a very soft, slightly high-pitched giggle come from the shower.

I froze. *What. The. Fuck. I'm so not about to get murdered in a bathroom in the barracks of 3rd Recon, am I?*

I heard my own heartbeat in my ears as I stared wide eyed at the closed shower curtain. *Is someone fucking with me?* My friends weren't above such pranks, that was for damn sure. Maybe Herzbog? Macon, the cocaine cowboy? Letting adrenaline do the work of courage, I grabbed the shower curtain and snapped it open, prepared to bravely make the highest, loudest scream of my life.

Of course, I couldn't see a goddamn thing except a very faint outline of a man crouching in the tub. He screamed, like an actual terrified scream, and lunged out of the shower in a panic, trying to flee the bathroom as fast as he could, knocking me backwards into the sink. I screamed too, but less because I'd just been shrieked at by total stranger and more because that fucking bastard dropped something very heavy on my bare toes as he shoved past me. He vanished into the hallway, never to be identified or seen again. Cursing with all my might, I knelt down to examine my wounds, my need to urinate totally forgotten as I rubbed my toes and felt for damage. The pain had been so sharp I wondered if he'd stepped on me while wearing boots. When no injury seemed apparent to my questing fingers, I tried to locate the cause. After feeling around on the floor, I found the item responsible for my sudden crippling toe pain. I squinted at it.

It was a full-size can of baked beans. Still closed. He'd been cuddling a can of baked beans. In the shower. In the dark. Giggling.

I stared off in the darkness for a moment, hoping that something might start making sense. Nope. *That one's going in the vault*, I thought. I put the can on the sink, hurriedly used the toilet, and then limped back out into the hallway. I didn't tell anyone about it because I wasn't really sure what to tell.

A friend led me back to the correct room for fresh drinks, and then we stood in the doorway. A couple of really drunk Recon guys had found mop buckets, filled them with soapy water, and were converting the tile hallway into a slip-n-slide. We watched several Marines throw themselves merrily down the slick course, oblivious of any possible injuries, and complete the slide by crashing into the metal storm doors, much to the loud mirth of all the onlookers. Long after midnight, I started to get tired, but the party went all night, so there was no sleeping. By the time the typhoon had abated, these incredibly bruised and hungover Marines had already started cleaning the hallways. Around ten that morning I was finally able to grab a pillow and blanket and hide under the bottom rack in the room to get some sleep.

They really should put this shit on a recruiting poster, I thought as I drifted off.

14.

OF SWORDS AND SARCASM: THE BALLAD OF CORPORAL JACKSON

In Okinawa, I had my first encounter with the NCO courses, aka the Corporals Course and the Sergeants Course. They were considered professional requirements upon ascension to NCO ranks, and most Marines were forced to attend them shortly after being promoted. No one actually wanted to go to these classes except for the hypermotivated future drill instructors and lifers.[10] Weeks of drill and PT? In Okinawan heat and humidity? No, thank you, I'll stick to my air-conditioned server room.

Both courses were a couple weeks long. There were classes on military codes and laws, history, traditions, and warfare. I dodged assignment to the classes for as long as I could get away with doing so, but a mere five months after promotion to corporal, my OIC decided enough was enough. I had to go.

Upon arriving at the schoolhouse a few blocks from my shop, I realized I didn't know anyone taking the course with me. I'd have to *shudder* meet new people. I know the slogan is "alone and unafraid," but I really wasn't looking forward to this. There were more than fifty corporals in my class, and I secretly suspected at least forty-five of them to be far better Marines than I could ever be. My goal was to graduate with as little humiliation as possible.

Then I met Cpl Jackson.

Cpl Jackson was an admin Marine who worked in Base G-1 for Camp Butler. She was diminutive, dark of hair and skin, and easy with charm.

---

10   A Marine who intends to serve as long as they can possibly get away with.

Cpl Jackson and I were assigned to the same squad and therefore shared a row of desks in the classroom. When I slunk into class, Cpl Jackson was seated next me. Yawning and grouchy, I didn't say anything to her. Despite any indications to the contrary, I hated meeting people and always felt like I'd say something stupid. I preferred to just stare at paper, reading or drawing, waiting for all this group stuff to stop happening to me. Corporals Course was no different.

Without appearing to notice my mood, Cpl Jackson turned to watch me get settled and subjected me to a critical stare. I averted my eyes, trying to seem unaware of being looked at. Finally, she broke the ice.

"Your hair," she announced, "is a mess."

"I know," I mumbled. I have wiry, naturally curly, unruly hair, which requires a lot of effort to even form a decent ponytail. Flyaways were my constant companion, even when plastered to my head with hairspray. I hated it, but shaving my head wasn't allowed. As a child, no one had ever done my hair or taught me the ways of feminine appearance, and in high school, I just shaved half my head and dyed what hair was left green. Now I slouched lower in my chair.

"I can fix it. My hair is the same way. You want me to?"

Her expression was indifferent, as if she didn't care one way or the other, but I was taken aback. Most other females just bitched me out for not looking poster ready and then stomped off, satisfied that they had demonstrated their devotion to Marine regs and put an inferior in her place. Cpl Jackson was offering to help me out instead.

"Sure, but . . . I don't know what to do with it."

Cpl Jackson considered my bun and then reached up, removed my hairpins, and started unwinding the hair. Class hadn't started yet, so we had a few minutes. After she liberated the tangled mess, she began braiding my hair with startling quickness, face fixed in the expression of a professional. When she reached the parts I was especially bad at, she pulled some tricks of grouping the hair *here* with hair *there*, reaching my damaged ends in minutes and then standing to rewind it and pin it into a neat bun. She tucked in a piece or two that was making a break for it, reached into her backpack, pulled out some spray, touched me up a bit, and then, satisfied, returned to her seat.

"There. That's better."

She handed me a compact mirror, and I regarded her work. The improvement was astonishing. I no longer looked like I'd been playing with electrical sockets. Now I was all slicked down and decent—in a word, unremarkable.

"Thank . . . thank you." I flashed a grateful smile and went back to my papers. Cpl Jackson just nodded and put her supplies away. The instructor had arrived, and our first class was about to begin.

The war in Afghanistan had started about six months earlier, and our brothers in the United States were the tip of the spear in that theater. Even though we were in Japan, we all followed the conflict and angled for a chance to deploy. A real combat deployment could gain you the kind of credibility that earned a Marine respect for years among his (or her) peers. No one had been to combat since the first Gulf War, and we were all thirsty to earn our stripes. But Cpl Jackson was admin,[11] and I was data. Aside from our biology, our MOSs weren't highly desired for the current conflict at that time. We hoped that the grunts wouldn't end things[12] before any of us had a shot to see what it was like.

The class this morning would cover what ongoing operations looked like, from a theoretical standpoint. Our instructor was Cpl Lake, whose claim to fame in the battalion was as the Marine who ran a 14:11 three-mile. He was beyond fast. For that reason, no one seemed to mind that he was also extremely slow on the uptake at times. I can't even remember what his MOS was. Running seemed to be it.

"Good morning, Marines." Cpl Lake spoke barely loud enough to be heard in the back row. He fumbled in his books as he set them on the podium, trying to find the notes. We chorused back the greeting of the day and then sat in sullen silence while he found the lesson plan. Looking up, he cleared his throat and tried to get things moving.

"Um, anyone here been to Afghanistan?" he mumbled.

Of *course* no one here had been to Afghanistan! We were all new corporals in Okinawa! The war had started six months ago! There was no possible way anyone here had ever depl—

Cpl Jackson's hand shot straight up, startling me. No. Way. She'd been to *Afghanistan?!?!* Now I really felt inadequate.

Cpl Lake looked as stupefied as I was. He called on her.

"You've been there? Really?"

"Yep," she replied, confident and assured.

---

11   The Marines who handle all the myriad paperwork required for anything to happen in the Corps.

12   Turns out we needn't have worried; a decade is a long enough time for anyone.

Cpl Lake seemed awed. "What was it like?"

Without missing a beat, Cpl Jackson replied, "Fightin'. Straight fightin'. E'erbody fightin'."

Her face and tone were completely serious. I put my fist to my mouth to cover my grin. Cpl Lake took a moment or two to catch up and then deflated.

"Oh."

Now the Marines around Jackson started to smirk and laugh. Cpl Lake tried to get back on course again. "Well, um, today's class is about . . ."

The day went on, and Cpl Jackson kept up the earnest appearance. I took notes about articles in the Uniform Code of Military Justice and how to look up Marine Corps orders regarding leading physical training and weight standards. These things were important but not exactly enthralling. As classes droned on, Cpl Jackson and I got to know each other.

"Where do you work?" I inquired, choosing the smallest of talk to start with.

Jackson rolled her eyes. "CPAC.[13] It's nothing but leave requests and PT scores all day, every day." She stretched and grabbed her water bottle. Every single Marine in Oki had to have water with them at all times, but the rule was kind of unnecessary; those who flouted it were all in the hospital. Oki cares not if you can handle 100-degree heat coupled with 100 percent humidity. Oki destroys the weak. *Hydrate or die* isn't just a slogan there.

"Need water?"

"Yep."

I grabbed my own bottle and tagged along into the hallway, searching for the water fountain.

"What do you do?"

"I'm in the local control center. We handle naval message traffic. Every time I try to read one of those, I think I'm having a stroke." I was only half kidding. One of our senior corporals in the shop actually had three strokes in one week and was being processed out. We blamed it on messaging formats. They are truly unreadable without training.

Jackson knew what they were. While we filled our containers, she chatted about having to decode them when the messages touting new Marine Corps orders or changes to existing ones came down. Marine Corps orders are not *orders*, exactly. They are rules, guidelines, and yes,

---

13   Centralized admin for the whole base.

from time to time, specific commands given from on high to the particular commands or occasionally the Corps as a whole. Admin dealt with them as much as we in the LCC did, so we bonded a bit over that and kept the banter up once we were seated back in class.

On the third day of class, GySgt Wilson came in to give us young corporals a rundown on the law of war. "Law of war" sounded interesting. The class was just after lunch, usually when we were all struggling not to fall asleep, but this time I noticed we were all more perked up.

GySgt Wilson came swaggering into our classroom and immediately made his presence known by yelling.

"GOOD AFTERNOON, MARINES!" he boomed.

"GOOD AFTERNOON, GUNNERY SERGEANT!" we replied.

"GOOD! Good. You're all awake! Now, before I start, let me make clear that Marines are professionals, and professionals don't swear." Despite the looks of disbelief he received, he pressed on. "So, as we go, if you catch me swearing, call it out. Roger?"

"Aye-aye, Gunny!"

None of us had any intention of obeying that order. We probably wouldn't notice.

"Outstanding. Let's get started."

Unlike other instructors, GySgt Wilson didn't have papers. He didn't have notes or slides or anything. He paced ferociously back and forth, hypnotizing the class with the motion while he talked, and gently but repeatedly punched his left hand with his right fist. It seemed like a movement born of a desire to stop himself from excessive gesturing, but it just enhanced his appearance of being someone who preferred hitting things to talking.

"Now, today we're discussing the law of war. This is going to cover how we as Marines conduct ourselves in combat operations, oo-rah?"

"Rah." We privately loathed all the motivation.

"I may be a gunnery sergeant, but I'm a fucking—excuse me— grunt. Let's start by talking about an incident that happened on my first deployment. I was in charge of the guard, the sentries surrounding our position. I made sure LCpl Schmuckatelli[14] was on duty and prepared, oo-rah? Well, it was the time for evening changeover. So I escorted the new duty to relieve the others at each post."

---

14   Generic name for any given Marine

He paced toward the windows.

"Now, WHY is that a dangerous time?"

Cpl Cristian raised his hand. GySgt Wilson freed his right hand and gestured to him.

"Yes, Marine?"

"Gunnery Sergeant, because everyone's tired? Or not paying attention?"

"Negative, Devil Dog. The reason is because there are twice as many Marines at each post!"

He paused and gave us a long stare.

"Why is that dangerous?"

Another corporal raised their hand.

"Gunnery Sergeant, because . . . because they're focused on changeover?"

"Negative again. The reason is because that's twice as many targets vulnerable to the enemy." GySgt Wilson bounded back from the opposite wall and began his trek to the windows once more. "If there's normally three Marines on post, changeover will have six or more! If those bast—. . . pieces of—. . . *bad guys* want to take a shot at Marines, that's a good f-ing time, you understand. Take out six Marines instead of three? Maybe that's worth going to Paradise for."

He grimaced but kept going.

"We were doing changeover at the front gate that day. While I was verifying the logbook, we heard a kid start yelling. There's kids everywhere, but this one sounded like he wanted our attention. He's running toward the gate, maybe nine years old. We all turn to look at him, and guess freaking what?"

Was this rhetorical? Did he want us to guess?

"He was holding a pineapple bomb. Running toward the front gate with a pineapple bomb."

Now we'd stopped breathing.

"So, what do you freaking do? What are your options?"

I raised my hand. "Gunnery Sergeant, you . . . shoot him?"

GySgt Wilson looked at me hard.

"You think you have what it takes to shoot a nine-year-old boy, Corporal?"

I gulped. "I mean, if he's a threat to the lives of my Marines . . ."

"No, you fucking don't."

I didn't dare correct him.

GySgt Wilson now stood still. Somehow, this was worse than the pacing.

"That's the kind of shit you have to be ready to deal with if you deploy. You had better pay attention to my class because you have no idea what's out there, and lives may depend on it."

Now he turned and went to the laptop set up in the front of the class. Quietly, he began looking for his files to start the class in earnest.

We waited.

Finally, he turned on the projector and began going over the material. "Marine Corps Order 3300.4a states, 'The "Basic Principles" of the law of war are the following: (1) Marines fight only enemy combatants. (2) Marines do not harm enemy combatants who surrender. (3) Marines do not torture or kill enemy prisoners of war or detainees.' Write that down."

GySgt Wilson turned back from his slide to look at the classroom. We all began to jot down notes, but I couldn't wait any longer. I raised my hand, nearly lifting myself out of my seat.

"GySgt Wilson?"

"Marine?" He locked eyes on me again.

"What happened next?"

"What happened with whom?"

"The boy? With the bomb?"

"Oh." GySgt Wilson waved his hand. "That? I pulled my pistol and ran out to the kid so he couldn't get in range of the guard shack. Stopped him with my gun in his face, and he started crying." GySgt Wilson started to get back to the slide, but I wasn't satisfied yet.

"But WHY did he have the bomb? Weren't you scared?" I didn't know why, but I really needed to know how that was resolved.

Now GySgt Wilson glared at me for the interruption.

"He didn't know what it was. He just thought we would trade him food for it. Took a while for that to be sorted out because he was blubbering in Arabic. Okay? We good now? Can I teach my class, Corporal?"

"Aye, Gunnery Sergeant." I shifted in my seat. I knew everyone in the room had wanted to know just as much as I did, so the rebuke didn't faze me. More important, I resolved that I should probably learn some Arabic. GySgt Wilson was right. I didn't want to shoot kids in the head at all.

GySgt Wilson was the high point of the lectures, but then we reached the first dreaded exercise of the course: drill. All of us had been through basic drill in boot camp, but in Corporals Course we had to learn how to do the fancy, impressive parts using the NCO sword.

Sword drill is its own beast and requires strength in the wrist. After chow, we were each issued a sword, and we stood outside in the sun, scattered across a huge, rectangular, concrete parade deck. In our own private spots and at our own pace, we came to attention, holding a drill card at arm's length, then practiced calling out the commands listed on the card and moving the sword appropriately for each command. Dozens of corporals shouting and then repeating commands again and again as they tried to get the sword tip smoothly from the ground to their shoulder without stabbing themselves in the eye was a sight to make a drill master weep in despair.

I was as frustrated as everyone else was, stating commands in a regular speaking voice so that no one would look at me.

"Order . . . arms!"

I tried to move the sword with only a flick of my wrist and watched as it wobbled a few inches off the ground and otherwise did nothing. *Ugh! This is awful!*

Then a clear, loud voice sounded off from the far right side of the parade deck.

"ORDER! ARMS! PREEEESENT! ARMS! FORWAAARD MIZZIZZARCH!"

There she was. With impressive voice projection, Cpl Jackson proceeded like a small, orderly locomotive, marching with firm, loud steps in a direct line like a toy soldier. Around the deck, people broke their bearing to giggle. Cpl Jackson wasn't done, though. She continued to sound off at maximum volume without an iota of self-consciousness, executing the moves listed at random.

"YUT! YUT! MOTIVATION! SIX TO THE FRONT AND THREE TO THE REAR! FORTY INCHES BACK TO CHEST! YUT CHUTT CHUTTA YUT YUT MOTIVATE IWO JIMA!"

She barked each word on the beat in perfect time with her footfalls. All of us stared as she went off, delighted and amused. Cpl Jackson couldn't have cared less about being the center of attention. What was really fantastic was that our chief instructor, SSgt Campbell, was also watching. SSgt Campbell was a former DI and had returned to the fleet only a year ago from Parris Island. As he watched Cpl Jackson verbally and physically motivate her whole self across the parade deck through sheer drill power, he looked dumbfounded. Loud and silly though she might be, she was executing the moves with precision and, without question, intensity. No one could argue she wasn't giving it her all. By the time she hit the other side and stopped to review her card, everyone else had come to a complete standstill. She scanned the card, and then it finally seemed to dawn on her that we were all waiting for her next performance.

She glanced around and said, in a much more normal volume, "I think I've got it."

Silence reigned for a moment longer.

Then SSgt Campbell spoke up: "Yes, I think you do, Marine."

When we eventually graduated and returned to our shops, I started to miss the serious-not-serious way Jackson had approached the Marine Corps. It was an example I was happy to emulate.

15.

EQUALITY MEANS EQUALITY

As much as I'd like to pretend otherwise, some rather coarse things pertained solely to being a female Marine. In civilian life, Americans shout, "Equality!" from the rooftops but struggle with the unequal reality on the ground. Marines do pretty much the same thing, but because it *is* the Marine Corps we're talking about, the method of dealing with it is rather more in-your-face.

One approach was used in boot camp. Our female drill instructors told all of us eager girls that if we thought we were going to graduate and be equals with the males, we needed to rethink that. Drill Instructor Sergeant Carter[15] told us bluntly one day, "There are only three things you can be as a female Marine: a bitch, a slut, or a dyke. Figure out which one you are because the men will do it if you don't."

That felt like being slapped with a brick. Were those my only options? What a disappointment! I could've been at least one of those back home in Florida without all this running and waking up early.

To be fair, it was my experience that the men had their own trials of what kind of Marine they would be. They'd either be a badass who was socially inept, a shitbird,[16] or a meathead. Just as Marines fall all around and outside those categories, lots of females do as well. But making categories and rules is a very Marine Corps thing to do, so why throw out

---

15   Proper form is to use her entire title at all times, and no part of it is negotiable.
16   Someone who failed to even meet the bare-minimum standards and always caused trouble.

a system that works (at least, for some people)?

Another product of the Marine equality ideology was the "Don't Be a Slut" speech. (Side note: if that's not okay, why was "slut" on the menu in boot camp?) The speech was not as malicious in intent as it sounds to outsiders, and it's such a pervasive feature of the professional military landscape that it has even been carried over to the movies.

This is how the process typically unfolded: When a new girl arrived in the unit, all idealism went out the window, and introducing the ground rules became an immediate necessity. It wasn't that the newbie was out to wreck the "good order and discipline" of the unit. But like freshmen going to a university party, her likely maturity level and that of her peers could lead to some poor conduct that might disrupt unit cohesion. If you were trying to instill a deep sense of professionalism and self-control in people who for the most part were just beginning to kick the tires of adulthood and still surging with all those excitable adolescent hormones, it should be addressed head-on, with as little tact as possible, just like Chesty Puller would've done.

Of course, I'd only heard the speech a couple times when I landed in Okinawa, and by the time I achieved the rank of corporal, I found my own way around it by being safely married off and therefore considered less of a potential threat. However, as a Marine, tradition was important, so when I stepped into a leadership role, I tried to find a way to handle the speech. After all, a good portion of the reason it was given just to females was that if I had to tell every male Marine not to be a slut when they landed, I'd never get any work done. There were far fewer females, so it was much easier to just tell them to take responsibility for everyone's behavior. It was not right or fair; it just was.

I was the platoon sergeant of my shop, although not through any great virtue of my own. The other NCOs had been picked off by misfortune and misconduct until I was the last one standing. Even though I was only a corporal, there was no one else to do it, and the staff NCOs weren't keen on personally supervising twenty to thirty non-NCOs in a twenty-four-hour shop. Therefore, I assumed the mantle of den mother, for lack of a better metaphor.

Part of my duties included handling new joins when they arrived from the United States. Company office would call me up and tell me that ten to fifteen new Marines had arrived at the in-processing station for Okinawa, and I needed to pick them up and get them to my shop on a specific date and time. Then I'd receive an email detailing each new

Marine's name, rank, gender, Social Security number, and specific MOS training. I'd print out this roster, and once I'd gathered my new troops, I'd check it over before getting them settled in the barracks to ensure I wasn't missing anyone. No Marine should be dumped in Okinawa to figure things out unaided. That place was bewildering when you were sober.

I had just received a new gaggle of "data Marines," short for those of us who handled computers and networking. Like the Marine Corps itself, it was an exciting and terribly boring field at the same time. Email was new and vibrant at the start of the twenty-first century. Because it led the officer corps to send all sorts of unintended message traffic via abuse of the "Reply All" button, it could also be kind of fun. In between those amusing incidents, though, life got astoundingly dull watching a perfectly designed system run itself while you waited in vain for the servers to implode. So, preemptively managing potential misconduct before boredom set in, giving rise to all kinds of terrible ideas, was a top leadership priority.

As the cluster of twelve new joins gaggled together in the hallway outside our shop door, I looked down the roster to make sure I had everyone. I scanned the neat rows and columns on my paper and spotted the dreaded *F* for female marked out by one PFC's name. Sighing, I looked back up at the Marines. I saw every shape and size of identifiably male human being in the hallway but, except for me, no females. I frowned and looked back at the paper. *Yep, that's definitely an F.* I rescanned the hallway in case, in my haste, I'd misgendered someone. Finally, I gave up and just asked.

"Listen up! My roster says there's a female in your group. Does anyone know where she might be?"

They all looked confused, and one of them spoke up.

"There weren't any females that we saw, Corporal. Just us, and we all came together from comm school." PFC Desmond, who volunteered the information, had a distracting Boston accent but sounded sincere. I frowned again, glanced down at my paperwork, and then read out the name.

"It says PFC Fitzpatrick. Kelly Fitzpatrick. Is she here?"

There was a murmur and some snickering as one skinny Marine with very short, dark-brown hair spoke up in the middle of the group.

"I'm PFC Fitzpatrick, Corporal. I'm not female."

The Marines around him jabbed him in the arm and laughed.

Feeling a bit foolish at having been bested by a clerical error, I decided in that moment that equality meant equality.

"PFC Fitzpatrick, my roster says you're female."

Now the giggles and derision were more open. PFC Desmond made remarks under his breath to PFC Fitzpatrick, much to the amusement of the whole group.

PFC Fitzpatrick tried to reply without offending me.

"As you can see, Corporal, the roster is wrong."

He gave me a wry little smile. Staying stone-faced, I looked him dead in the eye.

"Fitzpatrick, if my roster says you're female, then I have to give you the don't-be-a-slut speech. I had it all planned out, and I'm not going to waste it."

Now the group was really getting into it, enjoying his discomfort as well as the quiet-part-loud of getting to hear a speech that normally wasn't for them. They were all ears. *Good.* After all, girls weren't committing all the sexual misconduct on their own.

"PFC Fitzpatrick, look to your left and to your right. You are not to sleep with these Marines. You are not to try to use your feminine wiles on them to charm them into doing your work for you. Do not date any of them. They are all a bunch of hornballs, and if you cause drama in my shop, I will remove you. Do you understand?"

The guys howled as PFC Fitzpatrick replied: "I understand, Corporal. I will restrain myself."

Inwardly, I smiled at his ability to ad lib. I appreciate a Marine who can take a joke, especially about his sexuality. During the era of "Don't Ask, Don't Tell"—then at its apogee—it could be a touchy subject, but PFC Fitzpatrick handled it with humor and grace.

Suddenly, he stepped through the fourth wall: "Corporal, were you really planning on saying that to the female?"

"Shut up, Fitzpatrick," I snapped. "PFC Desmond, take your group here over to the barracks across the street and check in with the company clerk. He'll get you all billeted. Report back here once you all have rooms assigned, and then I'll dismiss you for chow. Any questions? Good. Be back by noon."

I turned, scribbled on my sheet, and went back in my office. Thanks, company clerk. Love it when you fuck up my paperwork.

Our little comm shop was extraordinary. Not because we handled messages, worked all the hours the gods sent, or had the most consistently air-conditioned room on-base. We were exceptional because of the very rare alignment of leadership. Not only was I, the platoon sergeant, female, but the staff sergeant above me was also female. And the gunnery sergeant above her. And the master gunnery sergeant who ran our crypto vault. And the officer in charge. All females.

I hadn't seen this many women in a Marine Corps chain of command since I left 4th Battalion at Parris Island. Since we made up less than 10 percent of the Marine Corps, the probability of this happening organically was very, very low. When I was finally promoted to sergeant, and I inherited a female corporal from another unit, who served as my backup, the stars had aligned about as well as I could imagine. That's when I really found out how female Marines would treat each other if we were insulated a bit from external pressures. To my delight, we seemed to get along and function just fine. We managed all the humdrum affairs like physical training (GySgt Schnepp[17] could run anyone's ass off), leave (which had many extra layers because of the long commute from Japan to the US), and professional skills for the platoon very smoothly. Even better, I got to see some of my seniors in action.

Part of the training we were required to secure for our platoon was in martial arts. Martial arts belts were becoming exceedingly important for Marines to attain so that they would be eligible for promotion. Spots in a martial arts certification class were therefore coveted. When a new class was announced, responsible members of the chain of command had to get names submitted as soon as humanly possible. Every Marine we put forward to attend training had to meet all the requirements exactly or be summarily dropped from consideration. There was also a small catch.

The Marine Corps operates on a sort of economy of favors. A smart Marine tries to befriend everyone he or she can in the company offices, where administrative decisions are made. That way, when a new class is about to open up, maybe you'll hear about it a couple hours prior to submissions and get your people to the front of the line. You would be expected to return the favor at some future point, provided the deed falls within your reasonable powers and is not illicit. However, as I am sure you can imagine, this system occasionally gets abused.

The company gunnery sergeant empowered to select Marines to attend the latest martial arts certification course for gray-belt level had decided that no one below the rank of corporal should be allowed to attend. That

---

17   Only sort of her real name

wasn't in the rule book, and there were many lance corporals who fully qualified for the training according to the actual published stipulations. But the company gunnery sergeant shot down every single submission we sent up that contained lance corporals or PFCs. Frustrated with this blockage, I took my issues to SSgt Dexter. Dexter was tall, spoke slowly, always had a sly smile that could mean *anything*, and we knew each other from our previous duty station at MCRD San Diego. When Dexter listened to my complaint, she nodded slowly and replied, "Okay, we'll handle it."

How? I couldn't think of a way around the company guns. He outranked us not only by, well, rank but also by billet. The system in the Marines is billet first, rank second. If I'm a staff sergeant and Dexter is a staff sergeant (not the case at this time; just for the sake of argument), but Dexter is tasked with fulfilling the duties of the company gunnery sergeant—i.e., billeted as such—then she trumps me on every call. I can't overwhelm her authority without getting someone more senior to her to invoke *their* authority. But SSgt Dexter sounded like she had a plan.

That Friday was the battalion run. We all formed up in this huge, three-hundred-plus-person formation and went for a four-mile run, singing running cadences and otherwise building *esprit de corps*. SSgt Dexter was an excellent runner, so she led our part of the formation, and I ran in back with Gunny Schnepp to keep everyone together. This run was only a challenge because of the accordion effect, where the groups slowed way down and then suddenly had to sprint as the runners ahead of them finally had room to run.

The battalion commander, Colonel Paisano, was leading the way. When we reached the end point on the big grass field in front the battalion offices, we all came to a stop and then stood at attention, waiting for permission to "fall out," or leave the formation. Colonel Paisano climbed onto a big, red, wooden table in the middle of the field, and the battalion segreant major gave us the command to fall out and gather around so the colonel could speak to us. Sweaty, stinking, and thirsty, we all clustered up to the table. Okinawa's humidity made even standing feel like it required gills to breathe.

Colonel Paisano stood with his hands on his hips, beaming at his battalion, evidently pleased with our performance. Being near a happy battalion commander is like being near a soothing warm light. If he was happy, we were all probably going to be okay and get liberty for the coming weekend. That was always good news. Colonel Paisano told us about the plans for the second half of the year's physical fitness test, congratulated us on a steep decline of disciplinary incidents, and encouraged everyone to get moving on their martial arts belt certifications.

SSgt Dexter chose that moment to strike.

She raised her hand, letting Colonel Paisano know that she had a question. I can't stress how huge this is. In the Marine Corps, asking the battalion commander something that you haven't previously asked every single person in the chain of command between you and him, which is a significant number of people, is akin to a deep betrayal. The battalion commander was about to be asked something that none of his underlings knew about, and that would send ripples of reckoning almost immediately. If the question or comment caused even very slight embarrassment, the reckoning would be much worse. Speaking up as a mere staff sergeant to the battalion commander in front of the entire battalion was *huge*.

Knowing all that but blissfully aware that it was everyone else's problem, Colonel Paisano pointed to her.

"Yes, Marine! What is your question?" he boomed cheerfully.

SSgt Dexter lowered her hand and gave him a pleasant smile. Every head in the vicinity turned to stare at her.

"Sir, may I ask why lance corporals are not permitted to attend gray-belt training?"

I gasped, and I was not alone. *Holy shit.* The question was a shout from the mountaintops that the company gunnery sergeant was blocking our nominees. I couldn't see him, but I knew that the company guns had probably gone rigid with shock. Now came the moment of truth. Would Colonel Paisano back him up on this policy or shoot him down in front of everyone? Every frustrated NCO, who, like me, had been submitting names that got denied over and over, waited with bated breath for the colonel's answer.

Colonel Paisano frowned. He scanned the crowds and spotted company guns. "I don't know. Why are we not permitting lance corporals to go through gray belt, Gunnery Sergeant?"

Every eye fell on the company guns, who looked like he was living a nightmare. He stood there, owl eyed, blinking for a moment while he tried to come up with some defense.

"Um, sir, we're, um, prioritizing NCOs, um . . . but lance corporals, uh—"

Colonel Paisano cut him off with the wave of a hand. He turned back to SSgt Dexter and said, "Submit your Marines, whatever their rank. We'll get them all through. Isn't that right, Gunny?"

Company Guns gulped. "Yes, sir."

"Very good. Any other questions?"

No one made a sound. After that little show, no one had any questions except maybe when they could get those names submitted following dismissal. Colonel Paisano nodded at the battalion sergeant major, who called everyone to attention as the battalion commander hopped down and departed the field. When the commander was sufficiently distant, the battalion sergeant major shouted, "DISMISSED!" and we all filtered away.

When I caught sight of SSgt Dexter in the departing masses, I saw the battalion sergeant major had beaten me there. He was smiling at her, and I read his lips as he said, "Good work" before disappearing in the throngs. I ran up to her. She still had her mysterious little smile as she wiped her face of sweat.

"Holy hell. Good work, Staff Sergeant!" I was utterly floored. Talk about the direct approach. Dexter just kept grinning and walked away.

We got nine Marines into gray-belt training before the weekend.

16.

GATE TWO: AUBREY BEFRIENDS A HONCHO

Besides working with lots of female Marines, I also participated in the extremely popular sport of getting drunk on Gate Two street with the other ladies. On weekend nights, since hardly anyone was allowed to own and operate a vehicle, we'd all meet up at the barracks and then begin the long migration down the hill to where the Okinawan taxis waited in neat, orderly lines.

The term for the taxis was "honcho," and I have no idea where that came from. I just knew that every driver was "honcho," and I'd learned the important Japanese phrases to communicate with them, despite the fact they all spoke drunk English quite well. "Hubba hubba, honcho!" and "San-Nana-Yon, honcho!" were, for instance, necessary because the first one said you were in a hurry (curfews will do that to you) and the second was the building number for our barracks on-base where we needed to be dropped off.

Learning Japanese is a very common pastime for Oki Marines. The guys who learn it with the most enthusiasm are the ones looking to participate in the civilian dating scene. Marines might eat crayons by the handful, but when there's a chance of having sex, they become acutely intelligent in breaking down language and culture barriers. Some of my platoon-mates were so fluent that I reevaluated my opinion of them, as I had never achieved that level of skill at anything before. Perhaps it was because the Japanese men on the island expressed nearly zero interest in dating American military girls. Go figure.

I still tried to learn the language anyway. I lived out in town and wanted to be hospitable and well regarded by my neighbors, be able to pay my bills, and do some shopping without having to hope they understood me. I took some classes on-base and developed a few close friendships with the women my male friends dated. One thing I learned about the Japanese was that they can be very blunt. On one shopping trip with my friend Megumi, I asked for help figuring out what Japanese clothing sizes might work for me, to which she laughed and said, "No, Tracy, you are too big for Japanese clothes." *Ouch.*

As we reached the taxis one evening, Cpl Haffield approached the first one with its roof light on, and we all piled in. Haffield had mastered Japanese after three years on the island, so he plopped in the passenger seat while the rest of us filled in the back, and he conversed with the driver. Within fifteen minutes, we'd made it to the party district right outside Kadena Air Force Base's Gate Two. The whole street was lit up with neon signs, bright streetlights, and revelers wearing flashy clothes of all descriptions. The honcho dropped us off in front of one particular club and drove off. Music of every sort blared from different bar and club doorways, and cigarette smoke hung in a low fog inside and out. A few night-market stalls lined the sidewalks and sold chicken yakitori on a stick to those with the drunk munchies.

A very strange man with long, shaggy hair sat cross-legged on one corner, playing a guitar with only two strings that were wildly out of tune. For one hundred yen, he'd play you any song you wanted, provided that you didn't mind he had no clue how to play it. The military people loved him and would throw coins and cheer his rendition of "Free Bird," "Sweet Home Alabama," and "Stairway to Heaven," which were all exactly the same song in his hands. He filled the interlude between songs by making Gene Simmons faces and yelling. It was great.

That evening, when 0100 was closing in, my friend Aubrey and I staggered out of the final bar and began searching for a honcho. It felt like we searched forever, but one waited only a few meters away. We waved and he gestured to the passenger doors, indicating he was free.

"Oh my Goooood, that last song was so good!" Aubrey giggled as we climbed in.

I flopped onto the back seat, nearly hitting her with my flailing limbs. She leaned back and put her head against the window, singing not-so-quietly to the whole car. The honcho got in the driver's seat with the stoic expression of a man who earns his living by driving drunk foreigners home for hours every single night. He was unflappable.

I wasn't talking because I kept giggling at my own private thoughts, all of which swam in a nice, expensive alcohol marinade. Aubrey sang, I made weird hyena noises that passed as laughter, and the honcho made clear he didn't see or hear any of it.

"HEY, hey, hey. I wanna be his friend!" Aubrey announced.

"Whose friendsss?" I mumbled

"His! The taxi driver! Hey, honcho, let's be friends!" She sounded that special kind of earnest that only the very intoxicated can pull off. But the taxi driver was unresponsive. Aubrey frowned. "Maybe he doesn't understand me."

"I highly doubt that," I snickered.

"How do I say, 'Let's be friends' in Japanese? Tell me! I want to tell him we're friends!"

I grinned and closed my eyes to think.

"Okay, it goes like this: *Sumimasen* . . ."

Aubrey leaned toward the driver's seat and repeated after me: "*SUMIMASEN!*"—confusing volume of speech for proficiency.

Sngh, sngh. I smothered my snorts of laughter. ". . . *watashi wa* . . ."

"*WATASHI WA!* Be serious, Salz!"

". . . *bakka gaijin desu.*"

"*BAKKA GAIJIN DESU!*"

I couldn't control it any longer, and when the honcho started laughing, I joined in. Aubrey was completely delighted.

"Oh my God, HE LIKES ME! WE'RE FRIENDS!"

She fell back in the seat and laughed, too.

"Good job!" I burbled, slowly sliding down the seat in an arc from vertical to horizontal. "Probably never had a female Marine friend before."

She'd said to our driver, "Excuse me, I am a stupid foreigner." And that kept me amused all the way back to base.

17.

WALKER GETS HIGH AND PLOTS A MURDER

A s a day of the week, Monday was one I dreaded more than the average person. Monday morning was when the Marines came back from a weekend of carousing around Okinawa, and I got to find out exactly how many calls I was about to receive from First Sergeant to discuss exactly what the actual fuck I thought I was doing with my platoon. Never mind that I hadn't gone out partying with them; even when I was sleeping, I was responsible for their behavior. No wonder no one else had wanted the platoon sergeant job.

As the clock struck 0830, I took my normal seat in the back of the meeting room and looked up at my gaggle of shift workers. As a local control center, we were a twenty-four-hour shop, so normally no more than ten Marines were on deck at any one time. Today's pack included Pricer, Roberts, Smith, Rogers, Jaime, Gonzalez . . .

I frowned and looked back at the schedule in my notebook. There it was on the page. PFC Walker, first shift, 0900 to 1700. I looked back up. PFC Walker was missing.

"Cpl Stroyer, do you have any idea where Walker is?"

Marines trickled in late to work from time to time, but usually the policy was that if you weren't fifteen minutes early to formation, you were late. So long as PFC Walker showed up by 0845, I'd be willing to let it slide. After all, it wasn't like a hangover had never slowed me down.

Cpl Stroyer laughed, and a couple of the other Marines snickered.

"I have no idea, Sergeant. Haven't seen him today."

Their amusement aroused my suspicion. Marines acting shady should not be ignored by any leader who hopes to hold on to her position. I calculated my possible success at wheedling the truth out of them and then decided, *Fuck it. I'm a sergeant. Let's do this like a Marine sergeant.*

"Okay, I'll draw up your counseling for failure to maintain accountability after we finish this. Thank you."

Cpl Stroyer stiffened and dropped the coy grin. One thing I had learned in Marine leadership by now was that pain transference was far more effective than head-on conflict. I made my problem into their problem, and whaddya know? Solutions popped up like mushrooms after rain.

"Uh, uh, could I send a runner to the barracks, Sergeant? Maybe see if he just took a bit longer at the chow hall?"

It was my turn to smile. "Why, certainly. What a good idea."

Cpl Stroyer gestured to LCpl Lambert and nodded toward the exit. LCpl Lambert took off to search for Walker with the light-hearted attitude of someone who knew that no matter what he did or did not find, it wasn't going to be him in hot water.

We plunged through the morning brief and then wrapped up. I dismissed the late watch to their racks and everyone else to their workspaces. I asked Cpl Stroyer to stand by until the other Marines had departed.

The door closed. I set my notebook down.

"Stroyer, tell me what happened. You know something. Let's hear it from you before I get to hear it from company office."

Another unofficial policy, to go along with the fifteen-minutes-early one, was the policy of handling trouble at the lowest level. If something went sideways, a good NCO tried to get out in front of it before his or her higher-ups learned about it. If I could get ahold of the details before my bosses did, there was a chance I could mitigate the damage. Besides, young Marines sometimes hid really dumb secrets that didn't have the consequences they feared, and it gave me the opportunity to build trust. I rearranged my face into a reassuring expression. Cpl Stroyer sighed and sagged his shoulders.

"We went out to Gate Two street this weekend, and PFC Walker went with us. Most of us were just drinking beer, but I think a couple of the guys got some mushrooms."

In 2002, Japanese pubs sold *Psilocybe* under the counter and alcohol above. The average-size bag for sale contained about twenty-two mushroom caps and cost about ¥5,000. Only a few bars on the island sold these to military service members because they knew we weren't allowed to have it and they didn't want the trouble that the US military could cause for their establishment. Our average economic contribution to Okinawa's marketplace was roughly $700 million annually. That buys a lot of clout at town hall.

"Walker bought his own bag, and then we all went to hang out on the beach. When we left that night, he wasn't with us."

Okay. Okay. I was floored. That was not the confession I was expecting. I thought maybe he met a lady or just spent all night puking his guts out, or something else that was pretty common. But leaving a Marine sitting on the beach at night in a foreign country, smacked out of his skull on powerful hallucinogens, was an entirely different basket of bullshit. I opted to just get angry because I wasn't ready to deal with being horrified.

"What?! Holy fuckballs, he might've drowned! Or been picked up by the Japanese police! Or assaulted someone! What the HELL, Stroyer!?"

Cpl Stroyer took a step back toward the door.

"FIND HIM. NOW!"

I began frantically rehearsing in my mind how I was going to explain this to Master Sergeant. Was there a way I could maybe hide the part about the mushrooms? What if the Marine was in the hospital? If the Japanese police had him, we were screwed. Getting in trouble with the civilian authorities was a surefire way to bring all hell down on yourself and your command. *Fuuuu—*

The door cracked open, smacking into Cpl Stroyer's back. It was LCpl Lambert. We both turned to look at Lambert, and our expressions must've been something else because he stared back with confusion.

"PFC Walker is here, Sergeant."

I exhaled and leaned on the table. *Okay. All right. False alarm. Everything's fine. We're fine. I'll talk to the young man about not taking mushrooms, and then we'll sort it out at my level. It's all going to be okay—*

There was a shout from the watch floor, and Lambert, Stroyer, and I all pushed through the double doors leading to the main floor. There, sprawled on the ground, was PFC Walker.

He was a slender, smallish Marine, but he was putting up a fight against two others who had taken him to the ground. A foot or two away from his outstretched arm, which was pinned to the floor by another Marine, was a set of brass knuckles. Stroyer picked them up, and the others slowly let Walker up from the floor. He cursed at everyone.

"Get the fuck off me, man!"

At this point, it should probably be added that our workplace was a sensitive compartmented information facility (SCIF). This means that controlled information is received, processed, and stored there. Therefore, we had very clear rules about not bringing certain items into our workspace. No cell phones, no electronics, and most definitely NO weapons. The brass knuckles qualified as a weapon. Its presence constituted a clear violation of the SCIF rules and carried the possible repercussion of loss of the violator's security clearance, which meant the immediate loss of his job in the SCIF. Marines who lost their security clearance were pushed out to the far less hospitable realms of 7th Communications Battalion on Camp Hansen, or worse. Camp Hansen was stripped of all the luxuries that Camp Foster afforded Marines and was frequently under lockdown for some alcohol-related criminal mishap or another. A tour spent in 7th Comm Bn was a long, grueling tour indeed, which is why I had jumped at the chance to be reassigned to Camp Foster.

We took the brass knuckles away.

"Walker, what the fuck are you doing?!" Cpl Stroyer asked.

"Nothing, Corporal," Walker mumbled, rubbing his wrist.

Nothing indeed. The kind of nothing that had irrevocable consequences.

Because of the seriousness of Walker's violations up to this point, Cpl Stroyer told him to take a walk and calm the hell down. This gave me a chance to think about what I had to do next while removing the immediate danger. His excuse was that he was very angry at being left on the beach and wanted to beat the Marine he thought was responsible. He didn't make clear *which* Marine he held responsible, just that he was really looking for a fight. Given the potency of consuming a whopping twenty-two mushrooms all in one go, it's very possible he still wasn't in his right mind. According to the other Marines, he'd never had exposure to drugs like that before, which increased the likelihood that the whole experience had been a serious kick in his mental balls. That was no excuse for bringing a weapon into the shop, though.

But oh no, Walker wasn't done yet. Instead of going back to his room and thinking about the consequences of his actions, he used that cooldown time to walk to the PX.

Cpl Stroyer handed me the brass knuckles.

"What do we do now, Sergeant?"

I had no idea. As much as I hated to admit it, this was rapidly passing any point where I could fix it. I mulled it over, figuring I had a good thirty minutes at least to come up with something, anything, that might prevent this from going even more badly. I had no idea where the Marine had gone to calm down, but going anywhere on Camp Foster by foot took a while.

I went back to my office to think, but I didn't get the opportunity. Within fifteen minutes, Walker had returned. Only this time, he had a knife.

Before I even laid eyes on him, the Marines in the shop had gotten it off him. GySgt Schnepp saw the whole thing go down. By the time I knew what was happening, Walker was being escorted out and handed over to the military police, who had been summoned from their headquarters down the road. I tried to ask questions, but GySgt Schnepp adamantly refused to disclose any more details, only that I was down one Marine now and should probably go work on the watch schedule to cover his shifts.

Well.

Shit.

18.

PFC CARSON LOOKS FOR HIS LADY BITS

I never imagined that one day I'd find a Marine who would treat me with respect *because* I was female. I did think about how cool it would be if I were admired for my femininity, unlike the more realistic state of affairs, in which I was being admired *in spite* of my gender.

"Wow, Salzgeber! You're actually pretty good at such and such, for a girl!" or "You aren't like the other girls [barf] because most of them suck at their job." Yes, yes, I've overcome my disability and become medium-level good at computers. Wonderful! Life goals achieved.

In my platoon in Okinawa, there was an especially unusual man. PFC Carson was big. He was over six feet tall, over two hundred pounds, Black, and bespectacled. These traits were not the source of his uniqueness, however.

Marines are not the people you hang out with if you are looking for stories of happy families. Enlisted Marines, in fact, pride themselves on how screwed up their childhoods were. The smoke-pit game was to talk about who had it the hardest growing up, and it rivaled most Jewish grandmothers' abilities for describing intense suffering. Extra points were awarded to those with severe substance abuse and abandonment in their lineage.

In the poverty Olympics, the winners were usually all public assistance children from broken homes. It got so ridiculous, and was so consistent throughout the Corps, that later when I gave my DLI (Defense Language Institute) platoon the command to fall out of formation, instead of shouting some motivated phrase like "Oo-rah" or "Iwo Jima" I ordered them to all shout, "GOVERNMENT CHEESE!!!" That's just how it was.

In this case, PFC Carson had four moms, as he told the story. His birth mom and dad had divorced, and his mom had married (not legally, which was not at the time allowed in the United States, but unofficially married nonetheless) another woman, while his father had a sex change, became a woman, and married another woman (Carson's words, not mine).

Thus, PFC Carson had a very different outlook on women than other male Marines. He looked up to females, in his own special way. It was a bit odd, if for no other reason than I wasn't accustomed to anyone looking at me like I was something magical. I can't say it was upsetting.

But it turned out PFC Carson could not restrain his own desires to be female. Previously, I had to pull him aside and discuss his looking up things on the government internet that were probably not okay. PFC Carson was constantly researching prosthetic female body parts, which gave the rest of us some serious serial-killer vibes. Breast implants, padded undergarments—all of it fell into a gray area that was probably best handled by a simple, verbal "Stop that" request. If Marines weren't allowed to purchase "marital aids" at work, ordering him to stop reviewing silicon breasts wouldn't cross any boundaries.

I figured that was the end of the issue.

But one day, as I was fiddling with problematic log entries on the watch computer, PFC Bryant approached me in obvious discomfort. He was an average-size Marine with no distinctive characteristics, but I will never forget him on account of the following conversation:

"Um, Sergeant? Um . . ."

"Yeah, Bryant, what's up?" I mumbled as I tried to wrestle Microsoft Word into making the kind of formatting required by the command for watch log entries while the godsdamned paper-clip cartoon character suggested all sorts of other formatting that I didn't want.

"Sergeant, I'm having a problem with my roommate in the barracks, PFC Carson, and I was hoping, um, you might speak with him?" Bryant fidgeted, twiddling a pencil with nervous energy.

"What, does he stink or something? You know I can't change room assignments."

Backspace, backspace, tab, what the hell? Why is my paragraph now three inches indented? What the fu—

"He's wearing women's underwear!" PFC Bryant blurted out. "I hate it; it makes me really uncomfortable. He wears nighties to clean the room on field day!" It was almost a wail. PFC Bryant was genuinely distressed.

His big, honest face was contorted into an expression of confusion. I stopped my keyboard fight and looked up.

"What?"

PFC Bryant blushed. "It's pink. And frilly. And he wears a wig, too. Please, I can't take it. Can you do something?"

I sat for a minute with my thought process paused.

"He . . . um? Have you told him that you're uncomfortable?"

I was barely twenty-two years old, and these types of situations had never been my problem before. "Don't Ask, Don't Tell" was still being enforced, although now with everyone frozen on active duty thanks to the events of September 11, 2001, there was even less desire to kick people out[18] for being outside societal norms than before. I didn't want to see anyone get processed out, much less be the cause of such an action. But there was also no way to move Marines around in a packed barracks unless someone volunteered to switch. PFC Carson was not so popular with the rest of the platoon that willing participants would be easy to find.

"Yes! I've told him, I've asked him, I've begged him, but he just does it anyway! He watches these really weird animes and tries to cook for us, and it's so uncomfortable. Please talk to him! Please get him to stop!"

PFC Bryant was sincerely fed up. He came from a conservative upbringing somewhere in Louisiana or some such and probably had grown up with "views" on gay and transgender people. I was from Florida, mostly, so the thriving community there was a bit more colorful and diverse. But I could also understand that it was one thing to accept people in public and entirely another to be forced to live in a situation that seemed impossible for both sides. Something had to be done. If I left them to sort it out, things might escalate in who knew what direction. That wasn't good for anybody.

I sighed and turned back to the computer. "Yeah, yeah, I'll talk to him when he comes on shift. Maybe we can move your shifts around. Or at least get him to scale it back a bit."

I returned to my word processor fight. After a few more frustrating minutes, I finally got the bloody paragraph into the right place, saved the document, and rolled back from the desk. Now I could go find Carson and put an end to this. If I could tame Microsoft Word, I could do anything.

PFC Carson had arrived with the 1400 shift and was taking inventory.

---

18   "Stop Loss, Stop Move" was brutal.

Every shift was required to confirm every piece of gear being turned over from the previous watch via a long checklist. If the oncoming Marine signed for a cryptographic tape or device, they became legally responsible for the item until the next Marine verified and received it, so inventory was taken a bit more seriously than other turnover procedures. No one wanted to go to the brig because of lackadaisical stock-taking. I walked over to where Carson was verifying the serial number on a tape and leaned against the shelf.

"Hey, Carson. How's things?"

"Good, Sergeant. How are you today?" PFC Carson was soft-spoken, as many large men are. He didn't need a booming voice to get noticed. PFC Carson sort of bent the scenery around him just by standing there. He adjusted his glasses and initialed next to the serial number, placing the gear back in the safe and pushing the drawer shut. He looked up and smiled.

"I'm fine. Listen, I've got to ask, are you having issues with your roommate, PFC Bryant? Only, he seemed a bit distressed earlier today. Something about women's clothes?" I was trying approach things obliquely. No need to cause embarrassment if the accusations were just an attempt to get a new roommate. That wasn't uncommon in a full barracks.

PFC Carson sniffed disdainfully. "He doesn't like when I get comfortable after work. There's nothing wrong with wearing those! There's no order against it!"

I was totally at sea here. I knew how to tell a young Marine to stop being dirty or gross or leaving spit bottles all over the place. I knew how to enforce things like making sure he washed his dirty drawers (yes, that was my responsibility from time to time). But technically Carson was right. There were no written rules about that kind of conduct. For many long years, the Marines themselves enforced the necessary cultural rule without anything so bothersome as paperwork. But times had changed, and hazing was strictly frowned upon. Unofficial corrections had gotten way out of hand too often in the recent past, and now everything needed to be handled with a keener eye on how it looked to others.

As a female Marine, I was definitely not going to advocate for a return to the old days of sorting things out in a broom closet. PFC Carson stood a better chance at handling *that*, anyway. He might act and sound as soft as warm marshmallows, but his hand was the size of my face, and he could probably put me through the thin drywall without much effort.

"Carson, I totally agree, but maybe you could try to be a bit more considerate. You know, Bryant comes from a different place. Could you restrict your comfort time to when he's out of the room? Maybe I can switch your shifts around so you aren't sharing as much time together."

The barracks rooms were small, with two sets of bunk beds and small pieces of furniture in between. Marines who wanted privacy had to either rely on the head (bathroom) or else try to catch a time when the other Marines in their room were out. Our barracks had two Marines to a room, which was actually a luxury level of occupancy for Okinawa. Other barracks sometimes went as high as three, and in those instances, far smaller differences resulted in all-out combat from time to time. As a twenty-four-hour shop, our scheduling could be crafted to give the Marines the nearest approximation to their own rooms that I could achieve through clever manipulation.

PFC Carson, however, just sighed and said, "I wish I could have children."

I was thrown by the non sequitur. It was known by now in the shop that I was pregnant, and while it didn't really show yet, he was looking at my midsection. I frowned but tried to take things in stride. "Don't worry, Carson. You'll meet a girl one day."

I patted him on the shoulder with a faint smile.

"No. No, I mean, I wish *I* could have children. *You* can have babies! You can feed them and everything!"

Okay . . . Now, this was some awkward shit. I wasn't all that comfortable with my own physiology, and I definitely had no idea how to relate that to someone who, well, didn't have girl parts. *What the hell do I say to that?* I mean, I'd never thought about it much. Women had babies, ducks liked water, Marines hit stuff. These things weren't even up for debate.

"Uh, well. I can't help you there. I don't even know where technology has gotten to on that front." Groping for a transition, I took a deep breath, let it out, then continued: "Look, Carson, fix the situation with your roommate, okay? This has got to give, all right?"

It was a terrible way to close the conversation because I hadn't provided any solution other than "Fix it, goddamn it." But I was beyond my bounds and fresh out of paradigms at this point, so I had my hands full trying to extract myself back to what I knew as normal as fast as possible.

PFC Carson just nodded and said, "Aye, Sergeant." Then he stood and grabbed his clipboard, leaving the room to finish watch changeover. I tried to collect my thoughts. *Nope, no clue what to do with that.* I walked back out to supervise turnover.

Later that week, after the normal working hours of 0800 to 1630 had expired, I walked over to the barracks (which was directly across the street from our offices) to check on my Marines. Even though I didn't live there, I still came by at times to see how everyone was doing. This is expected of NCOs and leadership to maintain visibility of their troops' living conditions and morale.

I entered the four-story building and made my way to third deck, where my platoon lived together as a unit in rows of rooms. The usual background noise filled the hallway. The sound of music, movies, video games, laughing, shouting, and the occasional door slamming as Marines departed to the chow hall or, more likely, the PX to get some fast food all combined into the soundtrack of communal living at its most Marine Corps-y. I didn't bother anyone who had their door shut, and anyway, I'd really come for one reason.

Room 316 was indistinguishable from every other door except for the small nameplate under the number that read, *PFC Bryant/ PFC Carson.* I heard the squeaky sounds of anime inside and marveled at the rapid-fire nature of the Japanese language. I knocked and waited as I heard the bustling sounds of someone coming to the door. Within moments, PFC Carson answered, holding a broom in one hand and still in his cammies.

"Good evening, Sergeant!" Carson boomed cheerfully.

"Uh . . ." I couldn't help staring. "Hi . . . Carson. Um. How's it going? Everything okay?" *Stop looking at his hair. Stop looking at his hair.* I maintained my bearing as best I could.

"Great, Sergeant! Just cleaning up a bit. Need anything?"

I paused. *How do I say this? Carson, did you know you're wearing a . . . No, probably not polite. I mean, he has to know, right? It's on his head.*

"That's, uh, a nice wig, Carson. Where'd you get it?"

PFC Carson patted his faux tresses and smiled. His normally shaved head was currently adorned with lovely brown locks that stopped right at his jawline and no-nonsense bangs cut straight across the center of his forehead. He looked like he'd taken his inspiration from a Queen music video. "I brought it with me when I transferred here. Do you like it?"

"I'm not sure I could pull it off quite like you do, Carson." I didn't know what else to say. "Just seeing how you were getting on. I'll let you get back to cleaning. Is Bryant here?"

"No, Sergeant. He went to the movies."

"Okay, well, just try to be considerate of him. Cool?"

"Yep!"

"All right, have a good night. See you tomorrow."

Carson shut the door, and I left the building to go home. After all, I had my own sweeping to do.

19.

PUNCH ME IN THE FACE

'T was the season for the Marine Corps Birthday Ball again. This year, I was going in a dress instead of my stuffy dress blues, which made the whole ball event much more enjoyable from where I sat. Okinawa was inhospitable to every kind of clothing except bare skin, even in November. The idea that I could go out to the Marine Corps Birthday Ball in a chic black dress instead of the thick, woolen, dress-blue uniform was so amazing that I went a little overboard getting ready for it. I did my everything, bought high heels—I was dolled up to the nines.

My unit had a pretty fancy affair by Marine Corps standards. It was held on Futenma, the Marine Corps Air Base, in a huge ballroom. The commanding general of Marine Corps Base Camp Butler would be there, so everyone went all out.

My platoon showed up, and we went through all the normal ceremony and pomp of the occasion. There was the pageantry of the historic uniform parade, where Marines modeled every uniform the Corps had worn since its inception in 1775. The reading of the birthday message by General John A. Lejeune went by, the cutting of the cake, the first piece given to the youngest Marine present and the oldest, and the singing of the "Marine Corps Hymn." Everyone sounded off loudly during the first and third verses while making a spirited drunken effort at the second verse we never remembered correctly. By the time we were allowed to seat ourselves for food, we were all in a positively motivated mood.

My shop was seated at four tables situated close together on the right-hand side of the room, a short stroll from the open bar that served Marines all night until we ran out of money or they ran out of bottles, whichever came first. As much as we might bitch about paying $80 per person to attend a mandatory event we never seemed to stop fundraising for, no one seemed to have a problem buying drinks.

When alcohol flows at Marine shindigs, one can rightly suspect that misconduct will soon follow. But we policed ourselves that night, as we did many others. The first line of protection against career-ending shenanigans was each other. I was sober because for the first time in my career, I was attending with *my* troops. I was their platoon sergeant, and not being a drunken ass felt like a good example to set. But that didn't mean I wasn't out to have a good time.

At ten or eleven that evening, I floated around the ball, snapping pictures with my platoon-mates, socializing with my seniors, and generally just being outgoing, which was not my normal personality. I walked up to a gaggle of Marines who hadn't yet decided to hit the dance floor.

"Hey, Carpenter! Pricer! What's up, guys!" I crowed. I felt pretty good, even if my cheeks were flushed from makeup and not alcohol. The guys turned and raised their glasses, cheering my arrival.

"Sergeant! What's going on! Happy birthday!" LCpl Roberts called to me.

We called him Bob-Bob because his parents had chosen to name him Robert Roberts and, well, that was about as creative with nicknames as we got. I gave him a brief smile and glanced around, noticing the NCOs were missing.

"Where's Cpl Hogan and Cpl Parker? I haven't seen them in hours!" I asked.

Those two were particularly macho, and I wanted to verify they hadn't come to any harm. I knew Parker from MOS school in Twentynine Palms a few years back. He had joined the Marines young, just seventeen when he enlisted. Parker could come up with bad ideas at an alarming rate. He was a bit of a jock and thought most things came down to physical contests of some type or another. As I mentioned previously, the Marine Corps was cracking down on hazing. There had been some bad headlines back in the States about young people getting seriously hurt by overeager Marines ritually beating them into inclusion in a platoon or unit. So any perceived violence between Marines, especially where those in leadership roles were concerned, had gone from a minor nuisance to a severe discipline issue to be handled at the highest levels. Parker occasionally worried me if I took my eyes off him for too long. He was a great Marine, but new ideas sometimes needed to be pushed hard to get through his skull—by a crowbar, for example.

Bob-Bob burped and tried to focus his short-term memory. "I think they went outside to smoke. Might find 'em there."

I nodded and stopped by my table to nab my sister-in-law, Heidi. Heidi had moved to Okinawa to take care of our daughter, and she lived with us. But things were tight at my unit, and we were all the same age, so there was no point in not involving her in everything Marine-related, as pretty much all my life there was. The Marines in my unit had become so accustomed to her presence with me that she was treated like one of us. She came out and ran the PFT with me at 0500 in the morning and, to my chagrin, beat my score by twenty-five points, outran my gunnery sergeant, told me to go fuck myself, and went back home to bed. She came to our martial arts matches as her older brother, Jens, taught the classes, and she even grappled with the Marines in my shop. She partied with us, fought with us, and befriended everyone. She was a fantastic buddy to take to things like this.

"Heidi, come on. I gotta find Parker and Hogan. They've disappeared."

Heidi just nodded, threw back the rest of her drink, and hiked up the hem of her dress so we could walk faster. We headed through the lobby of the event hall, pausing to make pleasant conversation with the company gunnery sergeant, and then went out into the surprisingly refreshing air outside. I sniffed and detected cigarette smoke, following it to the curb a couple dozen feet from the doorway. There was a cluster of male Marines, all in dress blues, smoking and laughing. I strolled up with Heidi, doing our best impression of regular young ladies seeing what all the fuss was—totally not a sergeant trying to find out what her minions were up to.

As we got to the edge of the group, I spotted between shoulders that Cpl Hogan and Cpl Parker were standing in the middle of the gaggle. I politely shoulder tapped, asking for a smoke and a lighter as a way of easing myself into the throng.

Cpl Parker was tall, slender, and pale blond, whereas Cpl Hogan was big, gangly, and had jet-black hair. The two faced each other as though squaring off for a fight. I wiggled my way to the front and shouted, "Hey, Parker, what the hell are you two doing?" I laughed because there was no way these two were actually going to throw down. They were friends, and the atmosphere was far too relaxed. Cpl Parker ignored me, and Cpl Hogan was laughing, staggering back a bit but not turning away.

Heidi peered at them. "I think they're gonna fight. HEY, ARE YOU ABOUT TO FIGHT?"

Subtlety was not Heidi's style, and what could I say? She didn't have to answer to anyone in the chain of command whatsoever. The worst anyone could do to her was uninvite her.

Cpl Hogan covered his smile and shouted over to us, "He wants me to punch him the face! IN THE FACE!" He giggled. "This is nuts, man. Why do you want me to hit you?"

Cpl Parker took deep breaths, amping himself up. "Come on, man. We're Marines! We can take a punch! I want you to punch me! Then I'll punch you, and it'll be great! We're men!"

I was confused. I thought being a man was about more than their stance on hitting people. I mean, my mom had a mean right hand, and I was pretty sure she wasn't a man, technically. What I did know was that if the officers swanning back and forth from the event hall to the parking lot saw two male NCOs hitting each other, things could get . . . misinterpreted. You know. With consequences.

These were *my* NCOs. I couldn't let them do that. But you also can't tell a couple of drunk-ass Marines not to do silly punching games. So, woman powers, ACTIVATE!

"Hey, wait! WAAAIT! Let *me* punch you!" I shouted.

It was an insane proposal, but I couldn't think of anything else.

Everyone turned to stare. I blushed. "Well, if I punch you, right, no one will think it's the beginning of a brawl! You won't get in any trouble because you aren't going to get in a fistfight with a girl. No one would think that's what's happening. If I hit you, then everyone gets to go home with no NJP,[19] and I get to hit some people. It'll be fun."

I wasn't sure my logic would pass the sniff test, but hey, they were drunk. Cpl Parker looked at Cpl Hogan, shrugged, and they both turned to me.

"Yeah, okay. But don't be a wuss about it, Sergeant. Make this shit good, or else we're going back to the original plan."

I smiled. I might be in a dress and heels, but Heidi and I both liked to box at the gym in the evenings and on weekends. The first time I ever threw a punch, I was horribly embarrassed by how weak it was and how I rolled my wrist and yelped. After that awful beginning, I'd sneak into the heavy-bag room at the gym when the guys weren't using it and—with gloves because I'd also learned how fast skin comes off bare knuckles— whale on the bag until I thought I might puke. I'd *practiced* for this occasion, even though I never knew it was coming.

I walked up and assumed the stance, which caused some snickering because of my dress and heels. Cpl Parker turned his head so I'd have a clear shot at the side of his jaw, and he waited. I hauled back and threw my weight behind it, using my shoulder to push a bit of extra force. I didn't want to seem weak to my corporal.

BAM.

To my private delight, Cpl Parker jerked and half spun. His eyes went totally blank for a moment, and then he shook it off. Cpl Hogan looked excited, and everyone cheered. *Whew!* I hadn't blown it. My hand hurt, but I was pleased with myself. *Well done, Salz!*

"Goddamn, good punch, Sergeant!"

"Thank you, Parker," I preened.

I never thought a guy would compliment me on my face strikes. My

---

19   Nonjudicial punishment. It's basically where the commander scolds you and potentially demotes you but doesn't throw you in the brig.

ego swelled.

"My turn!"

Cpl Hogan had to lean down; even in high heels, I wasn't up to his six-foot-one frame. He braced himself. I was so giddy from my first punch that on the second one, I may or may not have gotten sloppy. A bit sloppy. Or I suck at aiming.

The punch missed Cpl Hogan's jaw, and about half of the impact hit his ear. He jerked back, everyone gasped and outright laughed, I shook my hand because *ooow*, and Cpl Hogan rubbed the side of his face. Cpl Parker cackled, slapped him on the shoulder, and dragged him back into the event hall to buy him another beer.

I turned to Heidi as everyone faded away, finally smoking my bummed cigarette. "That hurt, oh my God."

Heidi shrugged. "You panicked. Shouldn't have done that. But hey, no one called the cops, so crisis averted, right?" She looked bored again, so I finished the cigarette, and we went back inside to find a fresh beverage and more fun things to get into.

As Bob-Bob told me later, Cpl Hogan came banging on his barracks room door around 0300. When Roberts answered it, Cpl Hogan asked him, highly inebriated by this point, "Dude, why'd you punch me in the ear?"

20.

MEANWHILE, ON CAMP SCHWAB, COLONEL BRISTOL RISES

I was assigned to Camp Foster for most of my stretch on Okinawa. It was one of the most civilized Marine bases on Oki, having all the luxuries, such as a huge department store of a PX, several different eateries, an enlisted club, and a movie theater. There were families everywhere who lived in base housing, and Marines from Camp Courtney and Camp Hansen regularly came to Camp Foster for their liberty time. Compared to that, the island's other Marine bases were practically monasteries.

Camp Schwab was one such godforsaken base, located on the north side of the island near the city of Nago. It was so out of the way that when the Okinawans wanted to hold their annual protests over the bases being on their island, they only sent one little bald monk to sit outside Camp Schwab. He'd sit quietly near the front gate, slowly banging a drum, and once in a while, if he was feeling truly festive, he'd hang a giant banner on the fence that read, *SAVE DUGONG FROM US BASE!* The Marines liked him, often waved to him, and once hung their own banner next to his that had a picture of a giant manatee (dugong) attacking the barracks. The text read, *SAVE US BASE FROM DUGONG!* It was some beautiful synergy.

Schwab was primarily inhabited by the all-male 3rd Force Reconnaissance Battalion. The location was surrounded by pig farms, which stank to high heavens, and habu-infested jungles, but it did have one jewel everyone admired: Oura Wan Beach. With crystal-blue waters as far as the eye could see, beautiful sandy beaches that looked straight out of a tourism-ministry advert, and concrete pavilions with grills for making whatever type of grilled food a person desired, it was gorgeous.

My spouse at the time was a Marine in 3rd Recon, so I was invited to a battalion beach bash at Oura Wan on a very pleasant afternoon in September. There was a cookout, music, and as much swimming as any person could want. Colonel Bristol, the battalion commander, famous throughout the Corps for being a badass with a nearly insane level of belief that he was a reincarnated Spartan, was in attendance. The battalion sergeant major was there as well, providing his services as enlisted liaison.

I brought my infant daughter, Taely, and mingled with the other ladies. I wasn't there as a Marine, just as a wife, and it was really cool to masquerade as a civilian for a while. Wives are often referred to by the pejorative term "dependent" and regarded with a medium level of contempt by most active-duty service members. I traded my rank for the title of "wife" for the day, even though it was a sacrifice in status. Compared to a Recon Marine, I wasn't very highly regarded in any case, so it wasn't a huge sacrifice.

Just before the cookout was about to climax in a chow line for hot dogs and burgers, Colonel Bristol called for all the spouses to gather in a "school circle" around him and the sergeant major. It was off to the side and away from the carousing men, who were finishing off the first six-pack of the day. As the women gathered around him, I noticed Colonel Bristol's body language becoming increasingly awkward and uncomfortable. He knew exactly how to speak to Recon Marines and instill a warrior spirit with every word. When faced with a bunch of worried-looking young women, however, he was far outside of his comfort zone.

Oh boy.

He rubbed his hands together, kicking sand with his feet and looking very much like a man who was about to explain to his own wife that he'd spent all their money on a new tattoo. Sergeant Major looked on with apprehension just behind Colonel Bristol's right shoulder. The ladies waited quietly, especially the women whose first languages weren't English. Hell, even for those who spoke English, Marine speak was still its own beast. "Daggone," "Who-yah," "Roger," "Solid copy," etc., all required some mental translation as you went. Understanding was a task we had to undertake together. Because of this extra effort, I was really floored by the message we received.

Colonel Bristol steeled himself and began to speak.

"Good afternoon. Uh, thank you for coming. Sergeant Major and I feel these Marines, your Marines, deserve a good time like this. Uh . . . because we will have to send them—someday very soon, now that we're at war—into very dangerous places. They get dangerous missions, against brutal, vicious bastards that deserve the death we'll bring them. That does mean that these Marines could be asked to pay the ultimate price . . ."

I stood stock-still, a rictus of dismay creasing my features. *He's not . . . he's . . . where the fuck is he going with this?* I glanced to my right and left and saw wide-eyed horror on the faces of the other spouses. The Japanese women in particular looked confused, probably assuming something was being lost in translation. I half listened to the rest of his fumbling speech, my eyebrows climbing higher on my forehead as he started to wind down by talking about corpses.

". . . and sometimes we won't be able to bring their entire bodies home, although we don't leave a Marine behind, but we will at least have pieces, and, uh, it's important that those pieces get back to their families. We will always be fearless when we fight, and the bastards we're fighting deserve to be going home in pieces, too. Um . . ."

Colonel Bristol finally caved in to communication frustration and rushed to the point.

"Speak with Sergeant Major so we have a good address to get the bodies home. Thank you."

Exhausted by this entirely foreign experience, Colonel Bristol turned and stalked off, shouting for the Marines to get ready to distribute chow.

The sergeant major stood alone, surrounded by a semicircle of shell-shocked women—the irony was not lost on me—and now forced to do disaster recovery on the fly. One young girl next to me had started to cry, and I put an arm around her shoulders to comfort her while stifling my laughter. *What just happened? The only theater of combat is Afghanistan right now. We're in Japan! What the actual fuck?*

Sergeant Major cleared his throat and smiled brightly. Through smile-clenched teeth, he laughed nervously. "Haha, um, ladies, all the commanding officer means is we'd really appreciate it if you could stop by the tent at the front where you signed in on arrival and verify your contact information on the recall roster. It'll help us reach you if there's an emergency. Thank you again for coming, and we hope you're having a great time. Let's go eat!"

He led the way, joking and laughing with the wives closest to him, who were obviously more senior and had seen this type of shenanigan before. I followed the group in a state of mild alarm. If that was how bewildering being a dependent was, they could keep it. I'd stay active duty and get information from the main pipeline. Also, I'd know where my pieces would go in the event of disaster.

★ ★ ★

I came to regard Colonel Bristol as a masterful performance artist, however unintentional. Later that year, in November, I accompanied Jens to the 3rd Recon Marine Corps Birthday Ball at the Camp Schwab officers' club. By now, I knew most of the Marines in his shop, so I was warmly welcomed by them. The birthday ball is the highlight of the Marine Corps social calendar everywhere. I wore my dress blues, got my hair done, figured out how makeup worked, and away we went. I believed I would be in for an evening of hard drinking and all sorts of memorable incidents. Even so, I was totally unprepared for what the night had in store.

We were seated at our table in the banquet hall, which had been made resplendent by civilian employees with much better taste in decorations than the average grunt. The lights were low, the atmosphere was abuzz, and the Recon Marines were in their full glory. I might drag them a bit for some uncivilized behavior, but a Recon Marine in his highest dress blues is a thing to behold. They had every possible shiny object on their uniform: gold scuba bubbles, gold jump wings, stacks of ribbons, medals all over the place, service stripes for days, and physiques that would have inspired Michelangelo to sculpt something more glorious than *David*.

They were all queueing at the bar already—when no one has a car and the barracks is within crawling distance, who needs self-restraint?—and I inserted myself in the line at the back. After a few trips to and fro, I had scored a few drinks and was chatting merrily with everyone at our table. One Marine, Cpl Macon, was already pretty tipsy. I worried privately that the ceremonial part of the ball might be a struggle for someone who was seeing double, but hey, I wasn't his boss.

"Tracy! Traaaacy! How the hell are you!"

Macon hugged me briefly, breaking the no-touching protocol normally enforced when in uniform. I smiled. Being addressed by my first name always transported me a bit from the normal routine. No one anywhere called me Tracy while I was in uniform. Even at home, the joke was that we were Salz One and Salz Two. We sat and chatted, making small talk, although making small talk with a Recon Marine could go anywhere. After fifteen minutes or so, Macon blinked at me a couple times, and then, in a lower voice, he asked, "I've been wondering. What's it like being a parent?"

I'd had my first child only a few months ago, so I didn't have a volume of experience to draw on. I shrugged. "It's pretty good, Macon. Why do you ask?"

Macon hiccupped gently and replied, "There was this girl I did coke with a while back, and we were talking about having kids. Was just wondering if it was any good."

I snorted and covered my mouth, thinking he was obviously joking. When he looked confused about my laughter, I gasped. "Macon, yo, do you think a girl doing cocaine should be the mother of your kids? I mean . . ." I wasn't even going to broach the subject of *him* doing cocaine. Some things weren't my business, and I wanted it to stay that way.

Macon nodded. "Good point. That's a good point. Want a beer?"

With nothing else to say, I nodded mutely, and he swanned off across the ballroom.

When the time came in the evening's festivities, Colonel Bristol approached the podium to deliver his remarks to the battalion. Shaking off the previous weirdness, I gave this man my full attention. As an outsider, I knew that I must avoid even the shadow of disrespect toward the Recon Marines' esteemed leader, and Colonel Bristol was about as esteemed as a commanding officer could get without actual apotheosis.

At first it was the normal remarks about tradition, history, the sacred nature of Recon's mission in the Corps. But Colonel Bristol didn't much care for repressive formalities that would stifle a creative soul like his, and he soon deviated from the prepared speech. Clearing his throat, he reached into the recesses of his coat and pulled out a folded paper, smoothing it on the podium. He announced that he had written a poem to the "men of the forward shadow," his name for the Marines in 3rd Recon. In a clear and loud voice of pride, he proceeded to read his original poem to the ballroom of drunk Marines (and Navy corpsmen, who were as our brothers that night). I sat there stunned, yet again, by this unorthodox method of expression among Marines. But that was nothing.

Within minutes, he began to sing. In a vibrant baritone, Colonel Bristol serenaded the Marines with a song he had created out of pure love for them and for their mission. The Marines responded by standing at attention at their tables until the conclusion of the third and final verse, at which point the whole room exploded with barking noises and applause. I looked at my husband briefly with disbelief plain on my face, but he just grinned and continued applauding.

Holy crap. Love songs at the Recon Ball. What will they think of next, these macho men?

Colonel Bristol would continue to baffle and astonish the entire Corps as he went on to establish the Marine Corps Martial Arts School of Excellence, or MACE. In hindsight, I can see his fingerprints all over a program that called for hand-to-hand combat after being sprayed with OC spray several times in various places (such as the face) as a qualification for the black-belt instructor trainer rating. Makes perfect sense now. He might be a poet, but he was a warrior poet, which meant that he'd serenade you while beating someone's ass into the ground. Well, that works for me.

21.

ARE YOU SURE THIS IS E-OKAY?

As a platoon sergeant, I spent a lot of my time putting out fires that could land one of my troops in serious trouble with our command. This did not stop the junior Marines from carelessly starting fires, though. Every so often, one of them crossed the line, and I had no choice but to take company-required disciplinary actions.

Okinawa was infamous for being the place where military service members made near-fatal mistakes. Drunk driving, assault, and rape committed by military personnel made national headlines at one time or another back home.

One of my Marines, Cpl Rogers, was celebrating his twenty-first birthday. I knew he'd go out partying with a cluster of friends on Gate Two street, and it was almost certain the whole party would be blind drunk before sunrise. That's a perfect recipe for something to go horribly wrong. Therefore, I volunteered to be the designated driver for the evening and chauffer the lads from one bar to another. I did this for several reasons. For starters, I was one of the very few NCOs allowed to own and drive a car. That privilege was granted only to staff NCOs and officers; however, I had managed to wrest it from battalion's hands, and I cherished my driver's license. Next, chauffeuring them meant that I could prevent bad decisions from becoming catastrophic. If I failed in that regard, then I'd at least know what had happened firsthand.

That evening, Cpl Rogers was joined for his planned revelry by two platoon-mates. I picked all of them up from the barracks. I had also persuaded my civilian sister-in-law, Heidi, to come with us so I wouldn't get bored watching other people drink.

On the way to Gate Two, I asked Cpl Rogers which club we were going to crash first. After a little back-and-forth with the whole group, Cpl Rogers decided we should go to a club called Twentynine Palms. We had all come up through the Marine Corps communications school in Twentynine Palms, California, so I figured that must be why they wanted to go there.

Oh, I was so wrong.

We arrived at the club, and I noticed a small lit window next to the main entrance, similar to how some restaurants post their menus for customers to preview. Instead of a list of dishes and wine pairings, the display was covered in neat rows of polaroid pictures. Every single picture was of a scantily clad woman giving the photographer her best come-hither look. I couldn't read the kanji, and I was still a bit naïve about the world, so I didn't figure out what was up until we were inside.

Young Filipina women were lounging all over place, wearing nothing (or very close to nothing) but high heels and makeup. I was gobsmacked. Sex workers were uncharted territory for me, and I didn't know how to behave. Rogers and his friends peeled off to go pay attention to the naked women, while Heidi, it seemed, had her own ideas. She found the couch where the girls were clustered, resting after their last "dates," and she beelined over to them, ready to make new and unusual friends. Heidi didn't judge; she just loved people.

That left me by myself. I decided I'd just go sit at the bar and hang out while people watching. After all, if I was supposed to be keeping a sober eye out for trouble, that was the best place to do it. I looked for the bartender in the hope of getting a soda while I waited. Moments later, a waitress approached me. I could tell she was a waitress because she was wearing normal clothes instead of strings with tassels. She bore a drink tray carrying a single can of Budweiser. She set the can of beer on the bar in front of me and smiled. I assumed this was one of the usual drink-buying schemes created by establishments in Okinawa that took advantage of American guys' willingness to buy drinks for cute "buy-me-drinky" girls at exorbitant prices.

Either way, I definitely hadn't ordered a beer, and I politely objected. "Oh, no thank you. I can't drink any because I'm the designated driver tonight. But I appreciate it."

She laughed at me and pointed at the beer. "He order for you. He order for you. Is okay."

I was sure we must be misunderstanding each other. Who the hell would be buying me drinks in a brothel? Maybe it was the language barrier or some esoteric brothel etiquette I didn't know about. Or did Cpl Rogers or his companions order it for me out of courtesy? Buying drinks for the DD is exactly the sort of shit Marines do without thinking. The waitress gestured to the end of the bar and repeated one more time, "He buy for you."

I swiveled my seat and peered through the dark and smoky room, trying to identify my sudden benefactor. I saw the outline of a man, and that outline felt familiar. He looked like a very stocky Black man.

Oh no. Oh hell no.

There sat MGySgt Roberts, the battalion's equal opportunity advocate. Equal opportunity advocates are tasked to handle accusations of sexual harassment, assault, or discrimination within the battalion, along with racial discrimination and any other EO-violating behaviors. I had dealt with him once before. Running into anyone from battalion HQ while I was in a whorehouse was mortifying, even if I was only a bystander. Running into a master gunny who knew me personally was worse. *Fuck.*

Three of the establishment's moneymakers were hanging on and around him. He smiled at me and gave a little wave. "Salzgeber! Good to see you! How's your evening going?"

"Oh my God, what the hell are *you* doing here?" I exclaimed. That was the only thought in my head, apart from trying to figure out how to react without crossing the line of disrespect.

His smile turned mischievous. "Me? Field research, of course. You could learn a lot about sexual harassment in the workplace from these lovely ladies."

One of the prostitutes giggled at that remark.

"What the heck are *you* doing here?" he continued. "I didn't know girls were your thing."

I was soaked in embarrassment. I felt like he had just busted me doing something wrong, but I couldn't figure out what, and that last remark of his made me even more uncomfortable. I gave a nervous laugh and nodded. "Fair point, Master Guns. Well, this is awkward."

He slapped the barstool next to his. "Come on down here! I'll buy you another drink."

I scooched down to the proffered seat, raising my current can of beer.

"I actually can't accept another drink, Master Guns. I'm the designated driver tonight. But thank you anyhow." I didn't like beer much anyway. But I was brought up to be polite, and refusing food or beverage is rude, so I settled for taking very tiny sips as we gossiped.

"So, how's things? Work treating you well?"

"Yes, Master Guns. One of my guys turned twenty-one, so I thought I'd be my brother's keeper for the night. Um. How's your work? Everything quiet?" *God, my conversation skills suck.*

"Yeah, it's great! We've got a tournament coming up. Battalion football team is taking on MCAS Futenma's team. Going to beat their air-wing asses."

Master Guns took a pull of his beer. For reasons I never fully grasped, throughout the Marine Corps air-wingers had the reputation of getting an easy ride. I sympathized with that. The joke was that the only exercise air-wingers ever did was "twelve-ounce curls" because they carried their twelve-ounce beer to their lips and then set it back on the bar. Har, har. That's clever!

I continued to flail in my sputtering conversation with Master Guns, hoping he'd never ever bring this up when we got back to work. My leadership was a touch more conservative than his and probably wouldn't find the humor in this. Technically, prostitution and the patronizing of sex workers were both illegal activities if anyone cared enough to prosecute it.

Cpl Rogers finally reappeared roughly thirty minutes after we arrived, wobbling down the stairs that led to the girls', uh, workspaces. He got to the last step and fell over onto one of several couches in the main room. He was laughing so hard that his eyes were tearing up. I did not ask why. The working girl who followed behind him gave him a deeply disgusted look. (It turned out later he had sneezed while going down on her, which was considered pretty gross.) She strolled off to the couches where the ladies took their breaks while Cpl Rogers gasped for air between fits of hilarity. I went over to see if he was going to make it.

"Rogers, you okay? Can we move on to the next spot now? It is getting a bit boring."

Rogers kept on chortling, flopping over like a discarded rag doll on a stripper couch. I gave up and went to find Heidi.

Heidi was having a moment of her own. Surrounded by the ladies of negotiable affection, Heidi was giving what looked like a motivational speech. The girls were laughing and speaking to Heidi in broken English. I gestured to her, indicating that we wanted to leave. This club's atmosphere was over, for me, and we were hopefully going to a spot that was not a brothel.

Heidi stood to go, and all the working girls called out, "Bye, Heidi! Byyyyyyye!" That made me smile. I flashed Master Guns one more sheepish glance, and we all left. The next club was a normal bar with a live band, and I decided the whole previous club was going in the vault. We're just not going to think about that anymore.

22.

THAT CUT DEEP

I was on barracks duty one night. Doesn't matter where or when. It was nothing special. The basic idea of duty is that two Marines are assigned to stand a twenty-four-hour watch over the entrances to the barracks and take turns walking through them to catch any unsafe or illegal behavior. We were to report anything unusual. If it got wild enough, we had to alert the chain of command, no exceptions, but it was mostly boring and uneventful. Chasing a naked drunk back into his room, chasing the naked girl out of his room, telling people to turn their crappy music down, blah, blah, blah. Any Marine on duty should pray that it stays that way; what happens when it goes sideways is always bad.

I was seated at the duty desk facing the front doors, meticulously copying out the paragraph that had to head every single logbook entry in the ghastly-green, military-issue logbooks that were handed from watch to watch as a record of all that transpired during duty. First, I had to list my chain of command so that I knew who to contact and in what order should a problem arise. After that task was completed, I listed my name, the name of my assistant duty NCO (often a lance corporal or below), and then an inventory of everything we'd been given at the start of our shift. Two (2) duty logbooks, two (2) duty cell phones, one (1) set of barracks keys, two (2) duty belts, and so on.

It was getting late, but the nighttime hours rarely quieted down in the barracks until after midnight. Marines would probably be awake throughout my whole shift. While I was engaged in this activity, careful to make no typos or else risk having to tangle with the white-out, I heard the steps of a Marine approach behind me.

That in itself was no big deal. Marines came and went all night as their duties or their entertainments moved them in and out of the building. I ignored it and focused on *Why oh why is my penmanship so horrible?* Everything I wrote looked like it had been written while on a very shaky rollercoaster, probably because of the cheap pen that alternated between gushing and vanishing altogether throughout the strokes. Just as I was lining up the ruler to conclude the paragraph and separate it for the oncoming log entries, I heard a discreet cough.

"Sergeant?"

Without looking up I replied, "Yes, Marine?" I assumed by the tone and the title used that this person was a non-NCO. He sounded calm but slightly uncomfortable.

"Sergeant. Um. I cut myself in the shower."

"Grab a Band-Aid, then. Is the corpsman back from chow yet? Doc's in room 304, I think."

"Um . . ." His voice changed, *um* becoming less a verbal placeholder than something close to a moan.

I stopped. Something felt out of place.

Oh no.

I put the pen down slowly and turned in my seat, willing myself to look.

PFC Conner[20] stood behind me in nothing but running shorts and flip-flops. His chest was red with blood, and long, thin wounds had been carved into his flesh. His arms were bloody. There were gashes in his face.

I said nothing. Mute, I scanned his exposed torso and saw cuts everywhere, blood running down his legs and onto the hallway floor. My animal hindbrain grabbed for my vocal cords. If any time was a time to scream, this was it. But discipline grabbed harder.

PFC Conner was a skinny white kid with a shaved head who had always had the most positive, outgoing, *kind* attitude of anyone in our platoon, but he looked like someone had tried to murder him. As I forced myself to look at his face, I saw he was blissed out, drunk on the pain juices. I understood in that instant that *he* had attempted the murder.

I lifted myself from my seat ever so slowly. Keeping my voice as calm as I could, I shouted out to my assistant duty NCO to run for towels. *NOW.*

---

20   Not his real name

Despite my alarm, PFC Conner simply looked sad. He knew this couldn't end well, which was clearly no longer a frightening thought for him, just a sad one.

When I could manage it, I quietly asked, "Conner . . . what . . . the fuck, dude?"

I watched in horrified fascination as a small red rivulet reached a fingertip, pooled into a droplet, and fell. Part of my combat training caught up to me and said, *It's just dripping, not gushing. He didn't hit an artery.* It was very small comfort.

He sighed. "I'm feeling a little stressed out, Sergeant. Can I please go to medical?"

I nodded, everything now happening in a time warp of syrupy slow motion. *"I'm feeling a little stressed out."* Fucking understatement of the year right there.

"Are you . . . are you in pain?"

He nodded. "Yes, Sergeant. It hurts very badly. Especially this one where I caught my nipple." He gestured to a chest wound that was barely visible through the blood.

The assistant duty NCO arrived with the towels, handed them to me, turned his head, and threw up in the trash can. I began wrapping PFC Connor in the towels.

"Come on, man, you're upsetting people," I said softly to Connor. Then I turned to my queasy ADNCO. "Call 911; get an ambulance here right fucking now."

I did not raise my voice, and the Marine did as he was ordered.

While this was going on, I tried to get Conner out of the hallway. Marines gossip like fiends, and I didn't want his humiliation to go more viral than it already surely would. I guided him out to the front steps of the barracks where the ambulance would pick him up. He followed obediently, making no irrational threat or gesture, just oozing sadness and despair.

The night air was muggy. I asked if he would sit with me. He nodded slightly and sat.

"Sergeant? They're going to kick me out for this, aren't they?"

"Conner, man . . . why the fuck did you do that to yourself? I mean, I've heard of nicking yourself while shaving, but this is some next-level shit."

He laughed wearily. "I wanted to go home and see my little sister. I miss her. She's having a really bad time. But I can't get leave yet. I feel so helpless."

We talked a while longer. We talked about video games, the shop, how nice the evening air was. We talked about anything other than the fact that he was soaking government towels with his blood. Covered with them as he was, the Marines passing through the doors didn't comment. But their frowns were curious and disapproving. Who had leaked blood on the hall floor? That was bound to fuel the rumor mill.

Now, at last, I asked about the "incident."

"What did you . . . did you use?"

"A box cutter."

"FUCK, Conner, that's lethal!"

"I know," he responded, sounding already dead. The ambulance pulled up with sirens blaring, and that put an end to any semblance of the nothing-to-see-here I had managed to create.

The medics popped out, shooed me away from him, and began their triage. I stood, helpless now, watching Conner submit to every poke and question with a fatalist's acceptance of having thrown away his military career. Within five minutes, they had him on a gurney and then disappeared with PFC Conner as quickly as they had arrived.

I walked back into the barracks and looked at my chair. Blood. The floor around it. Blood. I stared at my ADNCO. He looked worse than I felt. I had to get it together—for myself and for him. Clearly, he wasn't going to do it on his own.

"Rodgers, get those assholes on restriction[21] down here with some swabs and buckets. Get this fuck-show cleaned up, all right? I'm going to call Sergeant Major and tell him what happened. Believe me, I've got the worse of the two jobs."

I picked up the duty cell phone and looked left and right down the fluorescent hallway, gleaming white tiles in all directions except for mine and an unsettling trail on the stairs.

"Follow the whole trail and use bleach, goddamn it," I ordered the restriction Marines as they arrived, their faces changing from annoyance to disbelief.

I turned and walked outside to the back parking lot of the barracks.

---

21 Marines "on restriction" have committed some violation of the rules and as a result are on a sort of house arrest. As the duty NCO, I had the power to employ them in doing tasks for the good of the unit when the occasion called, so long as I did not interfere with their chow, their sleep, or their work schedule.

On autopilot, I dialed Sergeant Major and relayed exactly what I had seen and what we had done about it. He acknowledged it, then said he'd call the commander and be at the barracks in ten.

"Roger that," I replied, and hung up.

I looked around for a minute. No one in sight. I sneaked behind the dumpster and wretched my guts out. I felt like I should be crying, like I should be feeling something more. But there was just a void where normal emotions should be.

What the fuck did I just see? How did I not see this coming? I stood like a lost child for a bit before I pulled it together, straightening my uniform and tugging my cover down low.

Conner was never seen again—not by me, not by anyone in the platoon. They say he was packed off to the hospital for a psych evaluation and then sent home to the United States.

23.

AMAZONS DO IT
DIFFERENT

A s I've mentioned elsewhere, in Okinawa I had a rare alignment in my chain of command, where nearly every single person up to company level was female. This included my officer in charge (OIC), 1stLt Coleman, the kind of inspirational character movies are made of. An orphan from South Korea, she had been adopted by loving American parents, and when she graduated from college, she really wanted to give back to the country to which she felt deep gratitude.

She joined the Marines, and while she was slight and small, weighing maybe 110 pounds if she kept her pack on, she was a powerhouse in her own right. We conducted shop PT once on Camp Schwab, where my friendship with 3rd Recon granted us access to the Red and Black Trail—a jungle running trail with hills so steep you needed ropes to get up them. But 1stLt Coleman ran that trail like she'd designed it, coming out at the end looking like she was just warmed up.

Unlike many female Marine officers I had dealt with, 1stLt Coleman was also very kindhearted. The female major above her was more like a woman-shaped battering ram going through a bad divorce, barely concealing her contempt for other females the same way many of the guys did, while 1stLt Coleman *cared*. She brought in cinnamon rolls for the platoon in the mornings. She cried when a PFC attempted suicide and we'd successfully saved her and got her to the hospital in time. She really, really wanted to do a great job, and she endeared herself to me. She wasn't a pushover, but she had one of the kindest and most sincere hearts I'd seen since joining.

Above all else, 1stLt Coleman never hesitated to ask the enlisted Marines beneath her for guidance. Struggling with an issue or a decision, she'd approach Gunny Schnepp and ask her for help. Or SSgt Dexter, or MGySgt Roberts—anyone who might give good advice. She had no reservations or pride issues with approaching us. I respected that.

As I said, though, not all female Marines treated each other very well. The hierarchy goes like this: Marine Corps Base (one- or two-star general), then subordinate commands like H&S Bn, 7th Comm Bn, III MEB, and so forth, all headed by colonels. There are a few structural layers in there because of course there are, but you get the idea. Because we were the local control center and, by some strange twist of fate, I was the only CAW[22] operator in Okinawa, when these subordinate commands went to the field or on exercises, they had to come to our shop to get the crypto needed for their communications to be secure. I was busy as hell, constantly either creating Fortezza cards from last-minute requests by units who had completely spaced the need to encrypt message traffic or running things as the LCC platoon sergeant.

My benevolent officer in charge had replaced another female officer, Capt Lim,[23] who had moved on to 7th Comm Bn, a subordinate command to our shop. Seventh Comm Bn was slated to go to the field one week, and as usual, they'd never filed requests with me to get crypto. Hours before they were supposed to depart, a harassed first lieutenant showed up at the service window, frantically pushing the button for service. I came to the window (customers are strictly forbidden from coming inside the center itself) and greeted him.

"Good afternoon, sir. What can I do for you?"

"Hi, good afternoon. Um, I'm from 7th Comm. From the data shop. We're, uh, we're supposed to be going to the field today, and we didn't get any Fortezza cards. Can I pick some up, please? I'll sign for them." There was a pleading note in his voice. Getting *anything* from anyone on short notice in the Marine Corps requires extensive prior networking, and this harried man was entirely unknown to my shop. I was already forty deep in my current request pile, but he looked so worried and miserable that I took pity on him.

---

22 A workstation that cut Fortezza cards, which were used on computer and phones lines to encrypt message traffic. CAW operators were rare and had to attend special training in the United States before being appointed directly by high-level commanders.

23 Not her real name

"Sir, the turnaround time for cards is usually two weeks. Do you have the paperwork? It's required by the authorities. I have to have the forms."

I saw him blanch at this. Today was definitely not going his way. He licked his lips.

"I uh, no . . . no, I don't have paperwork. Is there any way you can help me?"

I caved in. I couldn't send him back empty-handed. That would be like kicking a puppy. A devil puppy, true, but a puppy all the same.

"No worries, sir. I will go print out the forms, and I'll show you how to fill them out. Since it looks like you've been given a Message to Garcia[24] moment, I'll process your requests today. God willing, you can pick them up by 1800."

I dropped my other tasks and went to take care of this poor guy's request. After a few false starts, we got the forms signed, and I immediately took them back to the CAW and began making the cards. He returned at 1800, and after filling out the proper logbooks, I released the cards to him. His expression of gratitude when he finally had the crypto in hand was heartwarming. I felt good about myself and confident that I had a friend if I ever needed anything in the future. I picked up where I'd left off before his arrival and went back to work.

However, a week later, when 7th Comm Bn returned from their exercise, Capt Lim made a lot of bad noise up her chain of command to the CO about how the Fortezza cards hadn't worked and it was all the local control center's fault that her field systems couldn't encrypt. She sent emails shredding 1stLt Coleman for ineptitude (even though 1stLt Coleman had zero control over the CAW beyond telling me to do stuff) to every officer that would listen. Capt Lim strangely failed to mention the part about *her* ineptitude and failure to request the crypto well in advance, and that it was *her* lieutenant who had put the wrong details on the makeshift forms I'd tried to help him with, and how the fact that she had *any* cards at all was thanks only to my good graces.

My officer in charge was stung by these nasty remarks, especially since Capt Lim had made sure to humiliate her far and wide instead of

24 Getting a Message to Garcia means something like being given an impossible task with no other guidance beyond "Get it done" and doing your damnedest to figure it out and overcome all obstacles in the way. The origin of the phrase dates from the Spanish-American War and is the title of a 1899 Elbert Hubbard essay about carrying an urgent message from President McKinley to a Cuban insurgent leader.

one-on-one. Maybe she'd skipped the lesson about "public praise, private criticism" in leadership school. But since I knew that as a sergeant, I didn't feel very charitable toward the captain.

As I returned to the office from another part of the building, 1stLt Coleman poked her head out of her office. "Hey, Sergeant, do you have a moment?"

She had a strange expression on her face and had never called me into her office before.

"Sure, ma'am!" I stepped into the tiny office and took a seat in front of her desk. She sat behind it, sliding a printout of an email across the desk toward me. She folded her arms and leaned forward on the desk, resting her chin on her arms.

"What should I do about that?"

She looked very sad and confused. I was taken aback. Marine officers don't show their emotions freely, and they sure as hell don't show them to enlisted people at my level. It was unnerving to see her in distress. I scanned the email as instructed, hissing between my teeth when I read Capt Lim's extraordinarily unkind remarks.

It seemed 1stLt Coleman had taken initiative once she heard of Capt Lim's complaints and reached out to her to ask if they could arrange a meeting so they might discuss what went wrong. Capt Lim replied with venom that seemed almost personal. She excoriated 1stLt Coleman for having the audacity to speak to her betters and said that when she, Capt Lim, wanted a word with her, she'd fucking let her know, and until that far-off day arrived, 1stLt Coleman better learn her fucking place and never, ever talk to Capt Lim again. She would be given a chance to speak once she was summoned before the colonel CO of 7th Comm Bn. Capt Lim went one step further, telling 1stLt Coleman that this kind of fuckup would *never* have happened on Capt Lim's watch, so she was certain that 1stLt Coleman was a pile of shit unworthy of the Marine uniform.

Yikes.

I was seething with barely controlled fury. I had hooked that motherfucker up, and here his boss thought she was going to step on 1stLt Coleman like a dead bug who deserved no better. Clenching my teeth, I set the email on the desk and looked at 1stLt Coleman. I decided now was no time for tact. Disrespect toward an officer was an easy thing to do unintentionally, so if I was going to do it intentionally, I wanted it to be just right.

"Well, ma'am, I'm only a sergeant. The way *enlisted* Marines would handle it would be to go punch that bitch in the face."

She managed a tiny, sad smile but was obviously still morose. I was firm in my conviction that this could not be allowed to go unanswered. If 1stLt Coleman was ever going to be respected and avoid the pervasive bullying that infested the officer corps (if Capt Lim's behavior was any indicator), she could not let this pass. Capt Lim would have to be reminded of *her* place.

Which, through a glorious technicality, was subordinate to us.

Well, why not? We could do it. I had an idea how to do this and do it right. I cleared my throat. "But you're an officer. So, we should do this the officer way. Answer her email. Say something like 'Thank you for your feedback; I will take that into consideration in the future.' Wait, no. Don't do that. She'll use it as a jump point to get even further in your ass. Don't say anything. Let her think you're defeated. I think I know how we can get this situation straight, prevent future incidents, and recover your dignity."

Looking unhopeful, 1stLt Coleman nodded and sighed, staring at the printout. I asked to be dismissed, she granted it, and I beelined back to my office.

She might be an officer and my OIC, but 1stLt Coleman was on my team. In a way, she was *my* Marine, and my Marine was being bullied. No fucking way was I going to pass up a chance to set this right. You don't ever hurt my people, *Captain.*

As Marine Corps Base G-6, we were headed by a lieutenant colonel whose billet was "assistant chief of staff." As I mentioned before concerning the difference between rank and billet, that meant that he had a higher billet than even the full colonels beneath him and therefore was able to craft policy and guidance that applied to them, backed by the full authority of the commanding general. In other words, he could make rules that they had to follow. Let's see how much Capt Lim's colonel liked suddenly finding policies and processes that restrict last-minute crypto requests thanks to her venting spleen via email on a junior. Crushing your enemies with paperwork was such an officer move that I felt elevated just thinking about this.

First, I'd have to get LtCol Gordon[25] on board with writing a policy. He didn't come to our office except when he needed to view controlled-

---

25   Not his real name

message traffic. Plus, the barriers between his rank and billet and mine meant that any attempt to approach him directly about this would be considered highly inappropriate. We needed to ingratiate ourselves with him before asking for any sort of favor. Commanders are sensitive to these things, and base level is a protocol palace on par with the Sun King's court.

I had heard through the rumor mill that LtCol Gordon was approaching retirement. He was scheduled to conclude his time in the Corps in a few months and move back to the United States. I had noticed that when Marines start to reach the end of their careers, especially from exalted positions like LtCol Gordon's, they begin to consider their legacy and their achievements. They want to impart to other Marines the lessons and wisdom they have gained before they leave for good. So I struck upon the idea of asking him to give a speech about leadership to my platoon. Not just come to my shop and speak; he was too important and needed to be seen. I set up breakfast reservations at a restaurant off-base called the Rose Garden, looked up the proper protocols for issuing him an invitation, and then went forth.

I sent two Marines from our platoon in full dress blues to his office. They arrived and reported in formally to his assistant, who cleared them to report to him directly. When he received them, they had a fancy printed invitation we created and which they delivered into his hands, officially requesting that he be the guest speaker at our leadership breakfast and honor us with his guidance. 1stLt Coleman knew what I was up to and that I was taking every precaution to make sure my ambitious plans could not somehow reflect poorly on her. I mean, this was the guy who wrote the fitness reports that determined her future promotion prospects. *Don't screw this up, Salz.*

LtCol Gordon graciously accepted, and the event was planned for that Friday. I rushed to the plaque shop on-base to have a small, tasteful gift made with an inscription thanking LtCol Gordon once he had finished speaking. Wrangling my Marines into civilian attire, I got the whole shop to the restaurant and made sure that LtCol Gordon's breakfast would be on my check. The whole event went off better than I could have hoped. He was in a great mood and spoke eloquently to the troops, who enjoyed food not from the chow hall. 1stLt Coleman looked to be actually enjoying herself. It was all perfect.

Once we returned to the shop and started our workday in earnest, I went to 1stLt Coleman's office and knocked on the door.

"Come."

"Ma'am, do you have a moment? I have something I need your feedback on, please."

"Sure, have a seat. What can I do for you, Sergeant?"

Now it was my turn to hand her papers across the desk. "Ma'am, I realized that 7th Comm Bn has abused our lack of formal written policy about submissions for Fortezza cards. I took the liberty of drafting a policy letter we can submit to LtCol Gordon for approval, which would protect us in the future from those incidents."

She gave me a confused look but took the letter anyway. I'd taken pains to look up proper naval formatting and then let fly with draconian suggestions for preventing any future requests for hookups. Realization dawned on 1stLt Coleman as she went through the paragraphs.

"Well, Sergeant, I think some of this language might need to be toned down." She gave me a wry grin. "But I think the idea overall is excellent. I'll go over this with GySgt Schnepp this afternoon."

I thanked her and left her office. I sent the electronic copy along, and inside a week, the new policy was signed by the assistant chief of staff for G-6 to MCB Camp Butler. When the message was published, I took a small, evil delight in making sure that Capt Lim was cc'd on the traffic, along with her colonel. Not only would her attempts to slander my OIC now fall on deaf ears, but the complaints were also already neutered by this new policy. If she wanted to pass fault around like an angry monkey flinging feces, her range had just been severely limited. Complaining about inadequate support while being in flagrant violation of every existing process only invites ridicule and criticism. If Capt Lim wanted to tell everyone *we* screwed up, she'd open the floor to a long, fruitful discussion of her own myriad fuckups. Personally, I was there for that.

And that's how *we* handle things. Back to you . . . *ma'am.*

PART FOUR:

TAMPA, FLORIDA

24.

USSOCOM GETS THE GIRL: NO PRESSURE

When I first checked in at USSOCOM (United States Special Operations Command) in April 2004, I was nine months pregnant with my second daughter and therefore wasn't getting up to any amusing trouble. I had to wear maternity cammies (the best cammies in the whole world, not even lying), which were light, cool, and gave me the basic color and shape of a robust pine tree. As I waddled around USSOCOM, working my way through the list of people and places I needed to notify of my arrival, I felt really out of place. Everyone there was svelte, trim, and ready to fight for four months in mountainous terrain with only a ham sandwich and a canteen of water. I looked better adapted for couch-like terrain. I had a few hard months of working out and weight loss ahead of me after my daughter was born.

The last stop on any check-in process is the commanding officer of the unit. Since there were a grand total of thirteen other Marines in the entire four-star command, it was a very short trip to the top of the Marine food chain. The officer acting as our collective commander was Col Hand,[26] and his office was a bit of a walk across the campus in the afternoon heat of a Florida summer. Upon arriving at his air-conditioned domain on the second floor, I took a moment to collect myself and wipe the sweat off my face. I didn't want to look gross at our first meeting. His aide-de-camp greeted me with a skeptical smile and then informed Col Hand I had arrived. After about five minutes, I was summoned into his office by a booming "COME IN."

---

26 Actual name, not a masturbation joke

Col Hand and his office both looked like something straight out of a movie set. It was all wood-paneled walls, carpeting, and bookshelves filled with the collected works of every battle commander I'd ever heard of. Col Hand was tall and had a chiseled face, broad, square shoulders, piercing eyes, and salt-and-pepper hair. Decked out in cammies, he stood with his arms crossed and frowned when he saw my impressive bulk pass through the door. I knew right away that I was not what he'd been expecting and definitely not what he'd hoped for. After giving me a once-over, he sighed his undisguised disappointment but went ahead with his prepared remarks after I completed my formulaic speech reporting in.

"Sergeant, listen to me. I've been asking Manpower to send me a female for months. They wouldn't send anyone because they thought this was a combatant command, which it technically is. Now you're here. I had no idea you were pregnant. I hope you have a healthy baby, but I also want you to know that you are not going to be a fat body. If you intend to participate in anything representing the Marines while you are here, you had better be within standards or else. We are going through a sensitive period where President Bush has ordered the Marine Corps to join SOCOM, and let me be abundantly clear: if you do *anything to fuck this up, I will END YOU.*"

Ooo-kay.

I had not expected tea and cakes, but being made to feel responsible for the entire future of the Marine Corps in the special operations community was a touch beyond my comprehension. Keeping my features as still as I could, I replied with a loud and clear "Aye, sir!"

He nodded and dismissed me after initialing my worksheet to prove I had presented myself as required. I left with a crystal-clear picture of what expectations were for my role. I was only there to join the data/computer shop, so I didn't see any way I could be a visible disappointment, but Col Hand knew that Marines made their own arrangements to be embarrassing.

A month later, I had my baby, a daughter named Ava. As soon as the doctors said I could go back to working out, I hit the track, the gym, and the salad bar (in that order) several times a day. I drank water like a fish. Everything I could think of to avoid pissing off Col Hand with my existence, I undertook it.

As I slowly got back into fighting shape, I gathered an unusual workout partner. LtCol Turing, from the US Army, was in charge of the comm shop and asked if we could work out together. He was pretty damn cool, and he figured that as a Marine, I'd probably work out with intensity.

The thing is, now that I was under pressure to impress an Army lieutenant colonel, I *did* work out much harder.

USSOCOM during this period attracted some very high-level visitors. President George W. Bush visited. The commandant of the Marine Corps visited. When LtCol Turing and I went to the gym during lunch, some visiting dignitary was frequently being given wide berth by the other fitness seekers. On one particular day, LtCol Turing and I were doing sit-ups. Since I had a C-section, sit-ups fucking sucked. But I had pushed through this before, and I was rapidly closing in on reaching one hundred in two minutes, much to my delight. LtCol Turing found no such joy in abdominal pain, and as I held his feet and counted out each rep, he muttered under his breath.

"Fucking crazy-ass Marines. Crazy . . . (huff) . . . Marines and their . . . (grunt) . . . stupid fucking sit-ups. Argh." LtCol Turing was a very tall man, so getting through each rep required closing a much greater distance than I had to go through. I laughed at his grumbling and kept counting. Then I looked at the pull-up bar directly behind where we were working out.

There, on the pull-up bar, in an exercise world of his own, was Commandant of the Marine Corps General Michael W. Hagee. The man was normally surrounded by a bevy of junior officers who did everything they could for him, like pay for his meals, take his cover (hat), and laugh at his jokes on cue. Seeing him by himself, in the green PT uniform, and working out quietly in the gym was like seeing the queen of England stroll unattended into a tea shop. I had to check twice to make sure I wasn't losing my mind.

"Fucking . . . uh, seventy-eight . . . Marines, I hate all of you bastards."

LtCol Turing lay back to take a breather. With my eyes and a nod of my head, I tried to communicate urgently that someone important was nearby. When he didn't seem to catch my expression, I looked down at him and whispered, "Col Turing! Shhh, don't say that. That's the commandant of the Marine Corps behind you!"

LtCol Turing gave me an irritated expression as he got his breath back. "What the fuck is a commandant?!" he barked.

I let go of his legs and covered my face. But luck was with us, and Gen Hagee hadn't deigned to notice us. Gen Hagee dropped from the pull-up bar, wiped his face with a towel, and left. Afterward, I explained things to LtCol Turing, and we both had an even better ab workout, laughing at how that might have played out. I was pretty sure Col Hand might've ended not only me but a couple generations of my family if that had gone wrong.

A bit later, I attended a retirement ceremony (it was mandatory, of course; can't have someone retire with a paltry group in attendance) where I witnessed something that shocked my Marine Corps soul. There, as the color guard entered the room to present the American flag flanked by the flags of each branch of the military and the unit, was the Marine Corps flag. Being carried by a soldier. Not a Marine. *A SOLDIER.*

Oh HELL no. This was not to be borne. That was a certain kind of sacrilege.

After the ceremony, I beelined to the color guard offices to ask what was up with that. I didn't think of myself as a "motivator" or a hardcore, lifelong Marine, but there were *standards*, for Chesty Puller's sake.

Once I was there, a very kind Air Force staff sergeant explained that no Marines had volunteered. Most Marines in the unit were officers, and the three other enlisted were all crushed with responsibilities that precluded the frequent trips and performances the color guard required. SSgt Holmes gave me a persuasive smile and asked if I'd like to volunteer.

I'll admit it: I balked. I had a new baby at home and a toddler on top of that. Would I have any time to devote to this? Then SSgt Holmes dropped his biggest selling point to me.

"You know, Sergeant, if you volunteer, we'll buy you a complete brand-new set of dress blues and pay for the tailoring as well." He leered at me, knowing that $300 to $400 in new uniforms was something few enlisted could sneeze at.

I thrust my hand across the counter toward him, ready to shake on it.

"Staff Sergeant, it would be my tremendous honor!"

There were some bureaucratic hoops to jump through, and I was required to present my weigh-in and PFT results before I could be approved. Once the uniforms had been issued and fitted, I also had to present myself for inspection to make sure I didn't look fat in the uniform. To a normal person, this may sound oppressive or antiquated, but the Marine Corps cherishes its reputation, and letting someone stand for all of us while looking less than fit in uniform invites ridicule from outsiders. That cannot be allowed.

After I was confirmed and approved, I came to practice drill with the other team members. I teased them without mercy about their less precise drill movements; drill is something Marines have intense pride in being good at. One sailor in particular somehow made the move "right shoulder arms" into an eleven or twelve-count maneuver (it's supposed to be four). Regardless of my razzing, they were very helpful in teaching me their performance routine and were glad to have a Marine on the team. I volunteered for every single performance because, in my heart, I felt that it should be a Marine carrying the Marine Corps colors, and to let that slide in the name of my own comfort was a terrible lapse in duty.

It wasn't all altruistic pride, though. We traveled to some cool places and performed for really great people. On one occasion, we performed for the opening of the New York Yankees' spring training. Since I know less about baseball than I know about quantum chemistry, the whole experience was surreal. At first, we had civilian employees of the Yankees management team sticking with us as we walked through the building to our staging area—not to make sure we didn't get lost, but to stop any of us from suddenly going into a fan frenzy at the sight of the players. I walked right past Wade Boggs, and he offered to sign a hat for me. I accepted, even though I had no idea who he was, just in case someone else in the unit back at SOCOM was a huge fan.

It took less than an hour before the employees realized that while we were in uniform, screaming and fainting were not likely to occur of our own volition. In fact, when we were prepping to march, I was looking up in the sky to see if I could spot where the F-16 flyover was going to come from and nearly tripped on Derek Jeter doing stretches. That was something else Col Hand probably would have strangled me for.

Apart from the color guard, I volunteered for every single thing I could fit into the schedule. Toys for Tots coordinator for the unit? Done. A major dinner event at the Ritz Carlton that requested a military team in full dress uniform to attend? Ah, the sacrifices I must make for my art. Volunteer work for a yacht race in which every captain was a disabled vet? I had no idea what that entailed, but sure, let's do this. Every event usually fed us good, free meals, and even threw in drinks on occasion.

Free drinks? Marine catnip.

Something I learned about myself in the Corps was the duality of my personality. Sober me was always trying to find clever answers to the problems I faced and was very conscious of how I presented myself to my peers and other Marines. Drunk me, on the other hand, was a bit more like F*CK THE PO-LICE and did whatever I thought would be funny in the moment, consequences be damned.

In 2006, the color guard was requested by the Special Forces Association, Cowboy Chapter LXXI in Cody, Wyoming. We arrived to perform the opening ceremony for a black-tie fundraiser for the Special Operations Warrior Foundation; there was an open bar that would serve free drinks until they ran out of alcohol, and there were rumors of dinner coming as well. As I waited on the side of the event space, making sure everything was ready to roll when the ceremonies began, I spotted someone headed straight for me out of the corner of my eye. I stared as an older gentlemen wearing a cowboy hat swooped in with glee.

"OH, FINALLY! A Marine I can hug!"

Before I had time to blink, he seized my shoulders and subjected me to the kind of heartfelt squeeze I usually associated with my grandparents. I froze up for a moment. Protocol dictates no physical forms of affection are allowed in uniform, but this guy didn't seem threatening, and it wasn't like anyone could reasonably blame me for this. Nonetheless, I opened my mouth to say something, only to catch a stern nudge from the right. It was one of the attending Marine officers.

"Don't. Say. A. Word," he quietly instructed.

Welp. Guess I'm getting a hug.

My embracer beamed at me. "It's so good to see a woman Marine! Thank you for your service!"

I smiled with surprise plain on my face, and he seemed content with that. He turned and departed, chatting with other guests as he went. After he left, the officer enlightened me.

"That man fought at the Battle of Tarawa. He's a legend."

With that fact out of the way, the officer also wandered off, and I absorbed what had just happened. "Terrible Tarawa" was one of the most famous Marine battles of the Pacific campaign in World War II. The Japanese said that a million men assaulting the island for a million years would never be able to take it. The Marine Corps took it in three days.

If a Marine from Tarawa wanted to hug me, then by the gods, I felt honored to the core. Or the Corps. Whatever. He was one of the living ancestors. With awe fresh in my mind, I got back to my duties. This night was starting out great.

After concluding my color guard duties (and acquitting ourselves very well, in my opinion), I changed out of my uniform into civilian attire and went to get a rum and coke. We were expected to mingle with the crowd and chat up donors as they participated in a silent auction. This event had brought out the Navy SEALS (we called them "frogs" and "pretty boys"), the Rangers, and the Pararescue-men (Air Force PJs, as they were otherwise known).

Because I have always suffered from moderate social anxiety, I drank a little faster than was probably a good idea. After I made a couple trips to the free bar for refills, the bartender got tired of me and started making my drinks in full-size glasses instead of cocktail cups. That should have been a warning sign if I'd had any interest in such things. But it suited me fine, and I spent the time in between new drinks at my table, laughing and playing jokes on my color guard team members. They were also partaking in the alcohol, but far more reasonably, whereas Marines were originally founded in revolutionary Philadelphia's Tun Tavern and were paid in rations of rum way back in 1775; I felt I should keep up traditions.

Then they said there'd be no dinner. Now I found myself something like ten drinks deep on an empty stomach. Welp, there was no going back. Dialing back a rum drunk isn't easily done, even with food. With no food, the brakes came off.

The announcer got up to address the assembled donors and thank them for their support of the organization. Then he proceeded to thank the sailors, soldiers, and airmen in attendance. But he left out the Marines. I couldn't let that pass, not in my state. So, I stood and shouted, in the middle of a black-tie affair, "WHAT ABOUT THE MARINES!?!"

There was a smattering of laughter from the audience.

The announcer paused and then wryly commented into the mic, "I see the Marines are here tonight as well."

This prompted more laughter and the signature barking from all other Marines present—the few who were clandestine in their tuxedos (those who had left active duty and were now present in their retired splendor) along with a few officers who didn't seem upset by my callout.

I shouted back, "Oo-rah!" and then collapsed into my seat with everyone at my table giggling in fits and starts. We'd been acknowledged. The night could go on.

A couple of us got into a wrestling match outside the venue after things had wound down. It started because I tackled one of my Air Force color guard teammates while yelling, "Come on, Fred! Let's WRASTLE!" (His name was Frank.)

He laughed while trying to ignore my attempts at a headlock.

"Why, Salz?"

I jumped on his back as if he were giving me a piggyback ride.

"Because! For the Corps!"

"I'm Air Force!" he protested as we fell into the grass.

To my mind, the donors would appreciate a good tale to tell after a fundraiser, and all the special operators present were being completely professional. So boring. No one came out to stop or scold us, so I figured it was a win. Frank/Fred let me claim victory, and we all laughed and headed back inside, dusting off grass and dirt.

After the event was over, the collection of service members from all branches of the military went downtown together and played pool, danced, drank more, and committed other shenanigans. At one point, a Navy SEAL was doing push-ups, and donors were throwing money for each one he did. I have no idea what number he was on, but I invited myself in and sat on his back, yelling, "Come on! You got this! Do it for Dick Marcinko!"[27]

The crowd laughed and threw more money as the SEAL finished six or seven more push-ups before he collapsed on the floor and I finally got off him.

When a bar fight broke out in one of the two bars that existed in downtown Cody, I jumped out of the way and physically blocked a gunnery sergeant in his service alphas from getting any beer spilled on him. After the combatants had been sorted out by the bouncers, Gunny tapped me on the shoulder while I had my back pressed against him, and I turned around.

He gestured to a tricolor ribbon on his chest and asked, "Do you know what this is?"

I shook my head no.

"It's a Combat Action Ribbon. Did you need to protect me?"

I was stunned by his indignant question.

"Yes, Gunnery Sergeant, I did! What kind of sergeant would I be if I let your uniform get soiled by beer when I'm in civvies and able to stop it? I protected the uniform. It's just that *you* happened to be wearing it."

It was his turn to look gobsmacked. That was the truth, though. As

---

27   Per Wikipedia: "A retired US Navy SEAL commander and Vietnam War veteran, he was the first commanding officer of SEAL Team Six."

a member of the color guard, I was keenly aware of dry-cleaning costs. Who wanted that bill just because two local drunks decided to try to beat some sense into each other?

Later that night, the bar was graced with a Wild Bill Cody impersonator, whom I coerced into doing the twist with me á la *Pulp Fiction.*

The next day my head felt like I'd slammed it in a door, and I groaned in my hotel bed, refusing even to attempt making it to breakfast. We weren't scheduled to fly home on the C-130 until 3 or 4 p.m., so I drank water and told myself that I hadn't really tried to show everyone my slick moves to the song "Pour Some Sugar on Me" by Def Leppard. I filed it all in the vault, under the heading of "Things Col Hand Must Never Find Out About."

Sorry, sir.

25.

SENSEI PENCE AND THE WAY OF THE EXECUTIVE

t USSOCOM, there were a *lot* of officers. The Marines numbered fewer than twenty, and of that number, just four or five were enlisted. All of us were ranked sergeant or higher, so our little coterie was pretty tight.

One of us was Sgt Pence. There is a saying I don't quite remember that Marines are either Doberman pinschers or Rottweilers because something-something Devil Dogs, but some of us are skinny and mean and some of us are big and mean. While I'm tempted to stretch that metaphor to include other types of dogs that are black with orange eyebrows, the point is that Sgt Pence was more in the Doberman category. He was so skinny that he would probably be rejected as a POW for fear that his appearance would bring accusations of torture and deprivation. He was tall, too, which made his slender frame even more painful to look at. What made Pence a real Marine was that, despite his delicate stature, he was powered by bubbling anger and hatred. Not unsavory hatred toward a particular group, just the kind of rage-filled madness that could drive a person's face through a stack of bricks. Pence was never happy.

Sgt Pence ran the equipment warehouse for Comm. Whenever we needed a new desktop computer for an arriving colonel (there were so many colonels they traveled the SOCOM campus in flocks), or a new printer, or any other IT gadget that every single officer simply had to have once the chief of staff had it, we went to Pence and asked nicely. He'd shred the paperwork (we always sent electronic copies as well, so this was strictly symbolic), curse the entire officer corps as a whole, storm off to a far corner of the massive storage facility, and return with the requested item while barely concealing his resentment at the imposition of doing his job.

Therefore, I was very, very surprised when I heard that Sgt Pence was running an "executive gray belt" course. The "executive" part of that title indicated that all the students would be officers. Just as our enlisted clique was all sergeant and up, the officers were all majors or higher. This course was being held specifically for the USSOCOM chief of staff, BGen Franklin, and his staff. Sgt Pence was qualified as a green-belt instructor, so he was authorized to certify others to the level of gray belt. Besides him, I was the only other green belt in the command, and Sgt Pence asked if I would come to the course and be his *uki*.[28]

Specifically, he said, "Salz, you fucking shitbag, come let me kick your ass so these officers can see how it's done."

By Pence standards, that was a flowery request, and I simply couldn't refuse such a kind offer. Jens had gone all the way to black belt–instructor trainer, so I'd already been thrashed regularly when we practiced for his tests. No matter how crazy he was, Pence couldn't hold a candle to a Recon Marine who needed every move to be *just right*.

The course was conducted in a grassy field next to the warehouse. On the first day, I walked up to the gathering of Marines and looked to see what we were getting into. When Marines train in martial arts, the uniform is "boots and utes": T-shirts, cammie trousers, boots, and sometimes flak jackets. No blouses, no rank insignia. Therefore, I needed to look carefully at their asses to see who each person was. From the name tapes on the right butt cheek of each Marine's trousers, I could extrapolate ranks.

BGen Franklin was obvious. A general officer is like the sun around which his junior staff orbits. You could pick him out by measuring the field of obsequious gravity he exuded. BGen Franklin was short, maybe five foot eight, while his officers were all pushing five-eleven and six foot. I counted five lieutenant colonels and two majors. By MACE rules, that meant there should be two of us to run the course, even if only one had the authority to certify. I felt pride at that. I qualified to help out!

Sgt Pence's first demonstration to the executive students was the leg sweep. It's hard to describe, but basically you seize the other person's shoulders, pushing them slightly off balance, and then complete the move

---

28   Passive partner in a martial arts demonstration

by using your right leg to hook and pull their right leg out from under them, knocking them to the ground. I stood, squaring myself physically against Sgt Pence's stance. Pence performed the move slowly, letting me fall gently into the grass while providing detailed instructions as he went. His tone was far more respectful to these Marines, which told me he wasn't really as insane as he acted and was in fact capable of calculating his own survival odds and adjusting accordingly.

I must have let my amusement show, because when Pence went to perform the move full speed, he did it so quickly that I lost my footing and landed like a sack of flour right on his boot. It knocked the wind out of me for a split second, and I rolled over, struggling to my feet to hide the fuckup. Technically, hitting his boot was my mistake. Pence smugly turned to the students and directed them to pair off and "do it better than what Salz just did." Then he turned back, walked closer to me, and asked softly, "You okay?"

"Yeah, I'm fine. That sucked."

"Stop falling like an idiot, then."

The next few moves were less difficult, and when the end of our time came, the officers dispersed, and we all went back to work. That night, when I got home and went to take a shower, Jens caught sight of my back and burst out laughing. Right in the middle of my spine was a giant black-and-purple bruise, with eyelets and laces clearly marked out. I told him to shut up and went to take my grumpy, aching shower in peace.

Over the next two days, we did groundwork, which meant pairing off to practice grappling on the ground. Gray belt involved at least three different moves that required one partner to lie flat on their back with knees apart while the other partner crouched between them and leaned forward, trying to choke the first person with both hands. Sgt Pence demonstrated this with me, which was really easy because I basically just tried to strangle him a bunch and failed to do so. (Damn.) But that day, one of the majors hadn't been able to make it for reasons. When Sgt Pence told everyone to pair off, one lieutenant colonel was left without a partner. He looked hopefully at Pence, but Pence had to decline. The rules regarding the course instruction demanded that the instructor be moving between students and making corrections. That couldn't happen if Pence was grappling.

Which left me.

Before now, I would have considered making a lieutenant colonel look at me in mute terror awesome and empowering. Instead, I felt embarrassed and decided to try to set him at his ease by demonstrating that we could both be professionals and get through this without anyone getting grabbed by accident in unintended ways. Unfortunately, I thought the best way to do that was by smiling a lot and then otherwise grappling with him as I would Pence. Pence was my friend, despite appearances to the contrary.

My unfortunate partner lay stone faced while I crawled on top of him to choke him. *Hey, I'm choking an officer! Dreams do come true.* His discomfort was palpable. The whole time I was partnered with him, he muttered under his breath and avoided eye contact with me. Smiling at him wasn't helping, but I was young and stupid, so I thought maybe if I smiled more, he'd feel better and realize this wasn't a big deal. After one or two tries at each move, he was definite about being done.

The other students were laughing and trying moves on each other over and over, but my partner's risk tolerance was simply not that high. He would storm beaches and charge hills, but rolling around in the grass with a young woman in front of his boss was too damn much. I drifted over to the shade trees to wait for the next part of the class.

When everyone gathered around the trees, Sgt Pence briefed them on what the next day's test would entail and how they should get ready. As he wound down, I realized that he was skipping part of the syllabus. It was my favorite part, so I wasn't about to let that stand.

"All right, gentlemen, any questions before we conclude?" Pence rubbed his hands together. I raised my hand, being a gentleman and all. He scowled. "What is it, Sergeant Salzgeber?"

"Sergeant Pence, what about the ground-fighting part? For gray belt, we're supposed to do two ground-fighting matches for qual."

"Well, not this time. These gentlemen have things to get back to." Sgt Pence tried again to conclude the class, but this time, he ran smack into an immovable object.

"Why are we skipping it if it's in the syllabus?" BGen Franklin asked. He was very hot on these martial arts belts, pushing all his Marines to get qual'd ASAP. He wasn't going to take a "gimme" belt. BGen Franklin wanted to earn it the right way, and if ground fighting was part of that, he wasn't going to skip it.

Sgt Pence squirmed under his gaze for a moment and then tried one more time.

"Sir, it probably isn't necessary for you to do it. It's more for the nonexecutive courses."

It was a flimsy defense, but the real reason behind his hesitation was that if one of these gentlemen hurt another under Sgt Pence's instruction, there could be ramifications. We didn't know what those were, but no one wants "ramifications" when it's coming from THE CHIEF OF STAFF. Of a four-star command. Hell no, not if you could avoid it.

"I think it *is* necessary, Sergeant. Get on with it."

Sgt Pence shot me a dirty look. I returned his expression with an innocent smile. Yeah, there would be payback for this. The universe decided not to keep me waiting.

"All right, Salz, you wanna go? You and I, as a, you know, *demonstration?*"

As one, the gathered officer corps looked at me. I gulped.

"Actually, BGen Franklin, sir, since you and I are about the same size, do you want me to be your fight partner?"

Now it was BGen Franklin's turn to look awkward. "NO, Sergeant, I don't. There's probably a PAO[29] Marine hiding in the bushes, waiting to snap a picture of me fighting a girl. If I win, I've beaten a girl. If I lose, I lost to a girl. Thanks, but no."

Well, that was blunt. Realizing this meant I was going to have to fight the fury ninja Pence, I sighed. *If you're going to lose, make a good show of it.*

"Hey, Pence, we're both sergeants, right?"

"Yeah, why?"

"Bring it, bitch."

The assembly ooohed and snickered. The challenge had been accepted. This might be good. Enlisted Marines sometimes act like assholes to each other in front of officers just to flaunt our coarseness. Don't ask why; I can't explain it. It's just a thing we do. We also drop decorum and fight dirty. Officers have to comport themselves in a careful manner at all times. I was just a fucking sergeant, though. It's pretty common to wear that rank at two different times in an enlisted career.

Sgt Pence smiled like a shark. He turned to the nearest student and explained the rules so that we'd have a referee. I mean, we had about ten miles worth of the chain of command watching, so procedure had to be followed carefully. Then he nodded at me, grinning evilly.

"Let's do this."

We sat flat on our asses, back-to-back, waiting for the word *go*.

---

29   Public Affairs Office—our journalists who publish news stories that go throughout the entire Marine Corps worldwide

Adrenaline dumped into my bloodstream. Pence and I might be the same size in terms of weight, but I didn't want to inflict damage on the world the way he clearly did. I was going to lose this fight; that was already known. The question was, how long could I make it last? Also, the audience was giving me a special dose of jitters. This might be the first time any of them had actually watched a female Marine fight. *I can't let down the squad.*

"GO!"

The word shot straight through my ears to my hindbrain, and I was scrambling before I was completely aware of what I'd heard. Sgt Pence went straight for my throat, knocking me backwards onto the grass. But I had learned to be really fucking quick when I fought. I wasn't any match for the males on upper-body strength, so my fighting style was more angry spider monkey than tiger style. I rolled, Pence missed me by less than an inch, and I scrabbled onto his back. *Get his neck, get his neck, get his neck!* I panted, trying to get my arm under his chin while he pressed as hard as he could with his fingers into a pressure point on my forearm that made me lose feeling. I gritted my teeth and wrapped my legs around his ribs, squeezing as hard as I could to deprive him of breathing space while I fought for control of his throat.

Pence fought back, tucking his chin and preventing access to his airway as he planned his next move. One of my boots slipped a bit as he writhed and went into his crotch. His head snapped back and smacked me square in the mouth. I felt the hot, sharp stinging start instantly, and then the taste of dirty pennies flooded my mouth. Blood flowed down my chin, getting in his hair, much to my private satisfaction.

"Stop! STOP! Someone's bleeding!" our referee yelled.

But we weren't ready to stop. You don't stop fighting for a busted lip. That's some weak shit. I hadn't quite got his neck yet. Just . . . a few seconds . . . more!

"STOP!" BGen Franklin issued the order unequivocally.

Defy a general in the presence of his staff at your own peril, but I would not. I started to let go. But like I said, Pence was fucking crazy. As I started to loosen up, Pence rolled over and, within fractions of a second, had me in an arm bar. I tapped frantically on the grass. *Fine, you win! Stop before we both go to the brig, you idiot!*

Sgt Pence stood, breathing heavy. I rolled over and got to my hands and knees, drooling blood into the grass and gasping for breath. I looked up at our spectators.

To a man, every one of the Marine officers was staring at me with horrified fascination. I tried to smile and realized my whole mouth and chin were bright red. I started to laugh because I probably looked like a crazy person. Also, I wanted them to know I was okay, so I got up, wiping my mouth and looking for my water bottle.

"It's all right, gentlemen. I see worse than this every month."

Their expressions worsened.

Sgt Pence took me to task. He shouted, "Fuck you, Salz, you went easy! You didn't give that everything you had. This is bullshit!" He stalked back and forth, glaring at me. I just kept wiping my mouth with a small towel I had originally brought for sweat, but inside I was flattered. Shouting at me might seem uncouth, but the subtext said, "That was a good fight. Don't think because you lost, you are less. I'll make sure they know that."

Then I realized I'd lost something else. *Oh no!* I groped my neck for the delicate chain of my necklace but felt only bare skin. *You moron! You didn't take your jewelry off before the match!* I grimaced. I loved that necklace, too. It was a little gold flower with rubies for petals and an emerald leaf. *Stupid, stupid, stupid!*

"Lose something, Sergeant?"

BGen Franklin was watching me closely, in case I was hurt and hiding it, and therefore he saw my frantic patting of my neck. I blushed, but when a general officer speaks to you, you answer him.

"Sir, it was just a necklace. I failed to take it off, and I lost it somewhere in the grass. I'll look for it once class is over. Thank you for asking."

He nodded, and then the officers paired off for their own fights. After seeing Pence and I go at each other, they seemed excited to have a turn. Maybe they would sort out some internecine office issues in the process or even some professional grudges.

BGen Franklin and I had something in common. None of the assembled officer corps wanted to fight us for fear of the institutional consequences. In his case, the matter of pride and privilege made any training accident a possible career suicide for the unfortunate officer who fought him. Directly challenging him was not to be attempted, either. They would have to wait and let him pick his unfortunate victim.

BGen Franklin decided on a prison strategy. He scanned his staff and chose the biggest hulking lieutenant colonel in the group and said, "You. We're fighting. Let's go."

LtCol Perlman did as he was bidden and got into our ring. The

Marines generally form the ring for the fight with their bodies so that there's a full 360 view in case of an injury. It made every Marine both spectator and referee. BGen Franklin sat back-to-back with him. The physical difference in size could not have been more pronounced. This was going to be some 4D chess if the lieutenant colonel wanted to walk away from this with any hope of getting his eagles one day.

When Pence yelled, "GO," BGen Franklin went at LtCol Perlman like the big man owed him money. Bleeding and forgotten, I watched in awe. LtCol Perlman had to go on the defensive almost immediately, and I could tell he was losing his cool. After a few seconds, he tried to grab BGen Franklin in a bear hug, getting only part of his torso. BGen Franklin dodged. They rolled over, and when LtCol Perlman was back to his knees, BGen Franklin was holding on like a bull rider trying to headlock a steer. His chin was pressed hard against LtCol Perlman's shoulder while they both tried to figure out what was next. Then he grunted.

"Sergeant . . . ugh, Sergeant!"

I realized he meant me, and I crawled closer.

"Sir?"

"Your . . . necklace . . . is right there!" He pointed with his eyes at a spot in the grass that looked like any other. I stared in disbelief. *Now? Really?*

LtCol Perlman decided at that moment to roll again and just crush his opponent by lying on him. It lacked grace and technical impressiveness, but there was no doubt it was effective. BGen Franklin could not be seen to lose, though, so he got free, got a choke hold on LtCol Perlman, and the wise man tapped out. It was just enough to show he hadn't handed his boss an unearned win while at the same time avoiding a pyrrhic victory. While his staff dutifully congratulated the BGen on his win, I dug through the grassy spot he'd indicated and grabbed my necklace, shining in the Florida sun. I backed away and gratefully washed it off.

"Did you get it, Sergeant?" BGen rasped. He looked very pleased with himself at his dual achievements.

"Yes, sir. Thank you, sir!" I bobbed my head in appreciation. I was so flattered he had cared about it all. I put it back on and tucked it inside my shirt. To this day, I always think of him when I wear it. What a way to go above and beyond.

The next day, everyone successfully passed their tests and went back to work, with brand-new gray belts—freshly minted ninjas. Sgt Pence returned to his tyrannical rule of the warehouse, and that was that.

26.

THAT'S A PADDLING

Sgt Brady decided he'd throw himself a going-away because there weren't enough Marines at SOCOM to plan it for him. He only knew me, GySgt Nolan, and Sgt Pence, so the party would include the other branches of service. Three Marines *can* party, but we really should have other people there to stop our more enthusiastic ideas.

By this time, SSgt Brady and I had worked together for about a year. I was a gawky new sergeant when we met, and he kept me sharp at our joint service command by doing things like sneaking up on me while I was at my desk and barking the greeting of the day in my ear as loud as he could, causing me to jump and hit the desk with my knees. When I was briefing GySgt Nolan on my progress with tasks and hardware deployments, SSgt Brady would suddenly put me in a choke hold and lift me, causing me to writhe like a trapped snake until he dropped me. When I was finally freed, I would scoop up my papers and keep briefing as though nothing had happened. Keeping my bearing and sticking to the mission was, I felt, the best way to respond. SSgt Brady would smile and walk out while GySgt Nolan looked momentarily taken aback.

The party was slated for August and being held on-base in Tampa, Florida. The ideal spot was the small enlisted club on the marina in MacDill AFB, where a few private boats were docked and a small indoor event space could hold a few dozen people. It was decorated in tacky, yellowish-gold wallpaper and curtains, with long folding tables and wooden furniture. Outside was covered in patio furniture that the Morale, Welfare, and

Recreation center had constructed from PVC pipe and dark-blue canvas.

When the evening came for the party, I showed up in jeans and T-shirt with a bottle of Malbec, ready to get down with my peers. Several other revelers were from the Air Force but worked in our shop, along with a couple Army guys. It was roughly six in the evening, and SSgt Brady had provided coolers of beer and a couple bottles of vodka and rum. I'd brought wine instead because I much preferred it, but to keep myself at the level of the event, I drank it straight from the bottle as I mingled with the other guests. My normal social anxiety melted with every sip, and when the time came to present SSgt Brady with his departing plaque, I was feeling pretty good.

To my horror, SSgt Brady had designed and bought his *own* going-away plaque. I was aghast. The plaque was supposed to be impressive in proportion with the unit's opinion of you. It was supposed to be a symbol of gratitude and honor. Buying one for *yourself* was like buying your own wedding gifts. Why would you do that?

Even more upsetting, he'd chosen for himself . . . a paddle.

The paddle is a symbol of having served in Recon. It is layered with rich meaning. The way the 550 cord is wrapped up the handle says different things about your time with them. The colors of the cord, the style of the braiding, all of it means something deeper, and it is almost always wrapped *by the team you served with.* It is done by hand, not manufactured, and the presentation of a paddle is done according to traditions that don't involve a mixed-service party and some self-promotion. This was absolutely mortifying. It was the equivalent of giving yourself a World's Best Boss award with a Microsoft logo on it. I don't care how good a job you did as a data nerd at USSOCOM; you don't fucking rate a paddle.

But I couldn't bring myself to humiliate SSgt Brady at his own party (yet), so I drank more. Maybe I'd be able to overlook the violation if I got good and drunk.

After SSgt Brady had finished congratulating himself, the party split up, and most of us went out to sit by the docks. Generic pop music played from the club's speakers to the outdoors, and everyone sprawled around in identical pipe-and-canvas chairs, enjoying the sunset. I engaged in banter with the other folks, but the part of me that felt a need to uphold the finest traditions of the United States Marine Corps was screaming that it was time to party like a Marine. *Give yourself a paddle, will you?*

By now, I was having trouble holding my head still while I looked at things. I squinted through my wine haze at SFC Gedding. He was lounging in his cammies in one of the deck chairs, laughing and joking about something. He was a big bald man that thought everything was funny, and I vaguely recalled that when I was sober, every time we shook hands, he'd scratch my palm with his ring finger. I had no idea what it meant, but at the moment all I could think was *The nerve! How dare he do a thing I don't understand? This cannot be let go.*

I stood and meandered toward his seat. Staff Sergeant[30] Varna called out to me. "Hey, Salz! How's that wine treating you?" He was grinning so wide I feared his head might split in half.

"It's great! You're great! This is all great!" I shouted back.

Everyone laughed. Varna's girlfriend laid her head on his shoulder, Sgt Nellis shifted in his seat, and someone else left to bring more beers. I must've appeared a bit suspicious because now that I'd stood up, everyone was watching me with big smiles. I took a big swig from the bottle and tried to think. *What should I do?* I was now standing right next to SFC Gedding, seated in that canvas chair, and I looked at him intently. He elbowed me in the leg.

"You good, Marine? Need to sit down?"

Yes, actually, not standing up sounded pretty attractive right then. Why had I come over here? *Oh my God. That's it. THAT'S IT.*

I should elbow drop this guy in the nuts.

My mind thought about this for fractions of a second and then went, *Yep, checks out.*

So, I (bottle still in hand) dropped all my body weight into my elbow and fell on SFC Gedding's lap, aiming ostensibly for his crotch.

A few things happened so quickly that I need to slow-motion replay this. First, wine bottles don't like sudden drops, so red wine went absolutely everywhere. Second, I misjudged where the male genitalia actually are anatomically and landed hard on his inner thigh instead, but still got a satisfying yelp out of SFC Gedding. Third, the canvas chair was not designed for over 140 pounds of weight plummeting onto another 180-plus pounds of weight already straining its meager construction. The chair broke and collapsed, with splinters flying in varying directions. Finally, SFC Gedding and I were sprawled on the deck, on top of chair pieces, covered in wine, with the rest of the crowd cracking up.

---

30   USAF not USMC

The shock of the moment sobered me for a minute or so, and I mumbled apologies while I rolled off of him, looking at the wreckage. SFC Gedding didn't move because he was gasping with laughter. "What the hell, Salz? Oh my God, hahahaha, you broke the *chair!*"

"Yeah, I don't know how that happened. I'm sorry. I, uh, fell."

I couldn't remember exactly why I had fallen, but I knew I'd done it on purpose, so I wasn't about to confess that. I stood back up and peered at my bottle. There was still a bit left, so I kept it. I helped SFC Gedding to his feet and then excused myself to the restroom. In my absence, SFC Gedding pushed the crushed chair remains to one side and dragged an identical chair over to his spot and resumed his previous lounging position.

By the time I returned, I had given up my wine bottle and decided maybe I should get some air. I was losing track of what I was thinking, but I felt fantastic and, besides, Jens would come pick me up later, so I didn't have to worry about driving. I could just cut loose, which I think is what led me to switch up to vodka and cranberry cocktails a bit later. How much later, I have no idea. Could've been minutes—felt like an hour.

I perched back on the dock and let my mind wander. Then I looked at my fellow partiers.

Hey, that's SFC Gedding! When did he get here? Isn't he the one who always scratches my palm? Fuck that guy. I need to . . . to . . .

Oh my GOD. I should elbow drop him in the nuts.

I paused, thinking for a moment. Hadn't I already been through this? Well, no, obviously I hadn't. The chair he was sitting in was intact, and in my daydream I'd broken it. I mean, clearly that was just fantasy; I didn't break chairs. *Anyway, even if I did, how much can a pipe-and-canvas chair cost? Ten dollars?*

I staggered to my feet and wandered closer to the conversation. I wasn't saying much, trying to look inconspicuous as I sidled up to SFC Gedding once more. He looked up and snickered as I weaved slowly left and right, blinking a bit.

"You want my chair?"

I looked at him owlishly. "Yes."

Then I dropped all my weight via my elbow into his lap. I missed his junk AGAIN, and the exact same thing happened as before. The chair crumbled, the drink went flying, everyone screamed and laughed, and I was on top of SFC Gedding, sprawled on the pavement, now with both of us trying to breathe through the giggles.

"Jesus Christ, Salz, what did I do to you! Hahahaha."

"I'm sorry, I did this already! I forgot!" I snorted.

But that was literally and figuratively the breaking point. SSgt Brady came charging outside from where he'd been admiring his ill-gotten plaque and grabbed me by the neck. I gurgled a bit as he dragged me physically back inside, letting the glass doors to the patio close slowly behind us. My friends outside made oohing noises and catcalled that I was now in trouble. I probably was. It's not like I hadn't earned it.

Inside, SSgt Brady put me in a headlock and leaned down next to my ear.

"You need to fucking stop, Salz."

"Yerg, Sertf Sergent." I couldn't quite breathe.

"You cut that shit out, you hear me? That's two fucking chairs!"

"Yerg, orkay."

"Now I'm going to let you go, and you're going to behave, all right?"

"Arye, Stref Ser—"

"Just shut up." SSgt Brady released his grip, and I almost hit the floor as the blood rushed back to my face. I shook my head a couple times. SSgt Brady gave me a look of disgust.

Where had my drink gone? *Oh well, probably not the time to get a refill.* I walked unsteadily back toward the glass doors, and everyone on the patio perked up when they saw me coming. The anticipation on their faces was clear.

I paused. *Tell me to behave, will he? Well, if it's a choice between him or them, I can't disappoint my dear public.*

I kicked open the glass doors, although not hard enough to damage them, and threw my arms in the air above my head, making the *V*-for-victory symbols with my fingers like I was Nixon fleeing from the South Lawn.

"I'm BACK, BITCHES!"

Everyone roared their approval, and I staggered back out to the party.

27.

THE CONTRACT

In 2004, a Marine Corps order was published containing a message about a very rare opportunity. When critical need arises for Marines in various job fields or when new fields are being opened, Marines have an opportunity to make a "lat move"—a lateral move from their current job into a new one.

I was still stationed at USSOCOM on MacDill AFB, Tampa, Florida. Sitting at work, bored with my current assigned tasks, I used the break in my attention span to check my emails. I saw one from our administrative department announcing openings and clicked on it. They were usually for fields like counterintelligence, which was not open to women at the time, or openings for warrant officers and the like. This one, however, would change the course of my career.

The message called for any Marine, regardless of current MOS, who could pass the entrance exams for the Defense Language Institute and come to the school in Monterey, California, to learn Arabic. There was a critical shortage of Arabic linguists to meet the needs of the Marine Corps, and therefore they had opened the floor to all comers.

I gasped. That was the MOS I wanted when I first enlisted six years ago, and here it was. Now. I approached the message as a lepidopterist approaches a rare Palos Verdes blue butterfly. This was the most exquisite opportunity I could imagine. I worried I was missing some important part of the message that would disqualify me, like being female. After a close scan, I could not find a single thing that took me out of the running. I carefully printed out the email and folded it neatly in half. I was going to look into this.

I went the next day to our admin shop and asked to speak to the career retention specialist (a.k.a. the career planner), the person who handled reenlistments. I knew for certain that a chance like this would require me to sign a few more years of my life away, but I didn't care. That was a minor tradeoff for the chance to attend the best foreign-language school in the United States. It was the Juilliard of terp work. You could not buy your way into it; your only option was to be good enough to be accepted, and to hang in with the accelerated pace of study. When the career planner, SSgt Kaplan, called me into his office, I was nervous and even shivering—just a bit. I had not wanted anything from the Marine Corps in a while, but this felt like my first enlistment all over again. Clutching the printout and licking my lips, I tried to explain myself.

"Hi, Staff Sergeant! Um, I'm coming up on the end of my current enlistment and, um, I thought I should come talk to you about my options."

I cringed at how shaky I sounded. Where was all my normal bravado now?

SSgt Kaplan smiled warmly. "Sure, no problem! Take a seat and tell me what your current MOS is. Let's see what we have available. Are you looking to stay in your field or lat move?"

"Actually, um . . . I wanted to ask you about this."

I pushed the paper across the desk to him with the lines that I was specifically referencing highlighted in bright yellow. That is always the best policy when asking people to look at any naval message traffic. At first glance, those messages always look like someone has broken the caps lock key and then slammed their face on a keyboard. It can be tricky to find the part where actual human communication is recognizable. SSgt Kaplan reviewed the message. He frowned and turned to his own computer, logging into the system and finding the message in its official electronic form. He scanned it, looking for the part that provided directions for him specifically on how to handle applications for the program. Then he nodded and looked back at me.

"Yep, that just opened up. Is that something you are interested in? It's not a lat move but an additional MOS. You'll stay a data Marine, but you'll add on Arabic interpreter."

I confirmed I wanted to apply, and he ran through my records to verify I met all my basic schools and training requirements. Once that part was done, he scheduled the DLAB, a test to see how well I learned foreign languages. A score of 100 was required to be admitted to the school.

I came back to his office a month later when it was ready to be proctored. I thought it would be like any other academic-style exam I'd taken, but no one there had ever administered it or knew what it was. When I showed up, contractors were doing some remodeling on the walls, and I was seated a few tables away from the workmen. The proctor gave me a tape player, headphones, and a paper booklet with instructions on the questions and time limits in the test. I signed a sheet of paper acknowledging I had been told the rules, and then the corporal looked at her watch and said, "Begin."

She went to a desk to keep an eye on me while she filed some paperwork. In between drilling, I listened to the gobbledygook that passed for a pretend language on the tape and tried to puzzle the meaning out as I went. Two hours later when I finally closed the booklet, I was tired but still excited. That had been fun! I got up and let the corporal know I was done and handed her the test materials. She had me sign a paper saying I'd submitted the whole thing and nothing but the things, so help me thing, and I left. Now there was nothing to do but wait for the scores and see what happened next.

After another month, SSgt Kaplan called me up and said I scored a 112 or thereabouts. He had run the scores up to command, and after consultation with Manpower in Quantico, Virginia, the school seat could be confirmed for November 2006. I would have to process my reenlistment before they secured the seat. Moreover, I qualified for a very tidy sum in reenlistment bonus money once I completed and graduated DLI. I was overjoyed.

More paperwork and months later, the reenlistment was completed in October 2006 with the only minor issue being the officer failing to show up to swear me in. That was corrected by a handy Marine colonel who had graced my ceremony and agreed to stand in for the lieutenant colonel who had disappeared. I'll say this for working at USSOCOM: there were plenty of officers around willing to help out a sergeant in need. With the documents and ceremony done and dusted, there was naught to do but pack my things and plan to be in California on or about 6 November.

At least, that's what I thought.

Two weeks later, I got called over to the office. The monitor, a

Marine at Manpower named GySgt Dunkirk who controlled duty-station assignments for Marines in a particular MOS, had decided I was going to report to Camp Lejeune, North Carolina, instead. Stunned, I pointed out that the reenlistment contract very clearly stated that I was slated for DLI and asked the monitor to correct the orders. He replied nope, sorry, but my MOS was at a low enough staffing point that the DLI thing would have to be cancelled.

I was distraught. I took a walk, smoked some cigarettes, and asked myself some very hard questions about how much I really wanted this for my life. Most of all, I was furious. Did he think he was just going to yadda-yadda my contract and reassign me for his own requirements?

The Marine Corps always told me that we were supposed to be fearless in the face of any opposition. Honor, courage, commitment. I had given my word, and they had given their word, all written down on the contract. They promised me the school, the language training. I didn't know anything at all about Arabic and had no real urge for that language in particular, but I saw a lifetime opportunity disappearing into the tall grass if I didn't make some moves and fast. What could be more courageous than facing up to a senior-ranking Marine with more power, connections, and clout than some no-name sergeant to seize *my* career, to take *my* proverbial hill? *To hell with that; I will not be moved.*

I went back to the admin office and politely informed the admin chief that I understood my orders and therefore would like my reenlistment contract to be shredded. I would get out of the Marines instead.

The admin chief looked at me like I was out of my mind.

"You . . . are going to renege on enlistment?"

In ordinary circumstances, that is not possible. Once the contract has been submitted and approved by Manpower, that's it. The Marine Corps owns your ass. However, in my case, there was a tiny hiccup. If Manpower was not able to complete the terms of the contract, after approving it and filing it, then we had a legal issue to resolve. I imagine that the outcome they expected was that I'd bow my head, let them send me a new contract, and I'd sign it and go away, lamenting my lost DLI dreams. Instead, I chose not to reenlist at all if the contract was not going to be honored.

Gunnery Sergeant called me, bloody furious. He shouted at me that I was going to lose all MOS credibility and never see promotion. Since I had already learned I was slated to pick up staff sergeant in a few months' time, I didn't feel that threat very keenly. I listened with the disciplined responses expected of a junior Marine, and when GySgt Dunkirk wound down, I decided to make my case.

"Gunnery Sergeant, I made an agreement in good faith. I mean to keep my word if you will keep yours. Thank you."

I handed the phone back to the admin chief and then went to the waiting area to have the quietest meltdown of my life. I'm not going to pretend that wasn't incredibly stressful and mildly terrifying. Sticking to my guns was either going to be the best or worst decision I'd made so far. I tried to calm my fluttering nerves and stop wringing my hands. After a few minutes that seemed to go on forever, the admin chief came out. She smiled at me.

"You're orders for DLI have been released. Let's get your travel paperwork wrapped up."

I was nearly drunk and shaking with relief. He had relented, albeit probably because going to his boss and saying he needed to shred a reenlistment contract while the Marines were involved in two active war zones was not a very appealing option. I signed my documents, and a week later, with all my belongings packed into a tiny Toyota Prius, I drove to Monterey.

PART FIVE:

MONTEREY, CALIFORNIA

28.

THANK YOU FOR SMOKING

When I served, I smoked. Though no longer in vogue in civilian society, in the Marine Corps, smoking is about far more than just the habit of nicotine intake. Marines who would never otherwise talk to me like a person were more than happy to let me listen in on their gossip in the "smoke pit" that every shop in the Corps had. If I casually strolled out near the pit (you could easily find it by smell), lit a cigarette, and stood looking lost in my own head, the conversation would generally wash over me within no time. I'd get to hear about marital disputes, unrealistic alcohol consumption, dating, cars, guns, and incredibly weird political positions.

At first, I kept my mouth shut. Chiming in without being properly introduced is a quick way to get shunned. It's a weird society sort of thing. If I had a junior Marine with me and we were having a relaxed chat about some silly-ass inspection we'd been working on for weeks, then the rest of the herd around the smoke pit got a chance to evaluate me and decide how safe it was to talk while I was around. You know you are okay if someone approaches and asks to borrow a lighter or bum a smoke. If you comply, you are generally accepted on a temporary basis.

I don't advocate tobacco as a leadership tool, but if a leader wants to know what is really, really going on in the platoon, the smoke pit is where you need to be. The rules regarding it are unspoken and informal, but if you violate them, you are sure to know. Silence will greet you, and then the group physically pulls away, leaving you standing by yourself in an invisible circle barrier. Staff sergeant is about as high a rank as can safely integrate, and it still causes the different groups of Marines to separate by rank and affiliation.

So, when the commanding officer at DLI decided one day to stroll into the smoke pit, the Marines pulled away and looked straight at me. As a SNCO and the highest-ranking person there at that moment, I was expected to handle this intrusion into our sacred space. The major was "not our kind, dear." Therefore, it was up to me to usher him politely but firmly off our patch and back into his office, where he was far less likely to hear anything that might disturb him. I sighed, put out my cigarette, and saluted him. He returned the salute and scanned the crowd.

Major Mansfield most definitely did not smoke. He stood, hands on hips, squinting in defiance of the California sun, looking like a commander for all he was worth. I was slightly worried he was about to berate the troops for the state of the smoke pit. That was a very common point of conflict between our leadership, who hated all smokers and their consequential filth, and the troops who despised the supervision of every level of their lives. I suspected that might be his cause for invading. *Oh well, let's go deal with it.*

I approached, rendering the appropriate greeting of the day.

"Good afternoon, sir. Is there anything I can help you with?"

He nodded but said nothing. I waited obediently, not saying a word either in case he was about to speak. After a minute passed without verbal exchange, I decided to try again.

"Are the Marines being too messy? Or is it problems with cigarette butts being left everywhere, sir?"

Major Mansfield, still gazing around as if lost in thought, nodded again and then, finally, when I started to think that maybe I'd messed up and used Arabic when I meant to use English, said, "You know, Staff Sergeant, I tried to start a smoking cessation course at my last unit. We were in Iraq. Unfortunately, we couldn't hold the classes regularly thanks to being mortared. I was considering trying it again here."

So many responses fought for control of my mouth that I clenched my jaw to stop them from slipping out. How could I explain that a bunch of Marines already under massive academic stress, combined with the stress of being young and figuring out adulthood, would not be improved by the pressure to reduce a habit like smoking? Nicotine withdrawals would just heighten tension, and for some of these kids, who might only be eighteen or nineteen, this was a habit they'd learned at home.

I opted to say something I thought was funny. "Well, sir, it was probably hard to convince those Marines tobacco is a health risk when they were being mortared."

I grinned, thinking he would see the humor in it. He gave me a weird scowl, as if what I had said didn't make any sense at all. I rearranged my face and decided to pretend that I totally hadn't just said that.

After a few more moments, Major Mansfield nodded silently again and then saluted me. I returned his salute, and he walked back in the direction of his office. I stood for a moment, shrugged, and turned back to the Marines in the smoke pit. They came forward, eyeballing his retreating back warily.

"What did he want, Staff Sergeant?"

"Honestly, Hogan, I have no fucking idea."

29.

I SAVE AN AIRMAN'S ASS (I THINK), AND MY MARINES SAVE US ALL FROM MASTER GUNNY REX

Drinking underage has been happening for as long as there have been age limits on beverages. It's no secret that people serving in the military partake of alcohol, regardless of the legal drinking age. While underage drinking is formally frowned upon, actual punishments usually come down on the antics sub-twenty-one-year-old Marines get up to while drunk. The drinking itself is generally given a pass.

The first time I was caught intoxicated at the age of twenty, the gunnery sergeant on duty merely rolled his eyes and told me to take my ass back to bed. It scared me sober—at least until my next birthday—and I went straight to my room and stayed there. So, it was no surprise to me that the Marines in 5th Platoon who hadn't yet turned twenty-one still went out and drank on the weekends. They just drank in private places like hotel rooms instead of bars like the rest of us.

I had attended a few hotel parties myself as a young PFC, and the ones that got out of hand were both memorable and terrifying. One time, hookers showed up at 0600 on Sunday, which I had not known was even possible. (Welcome to Palm Springs, babe!) The Marines who had called for them were passed out drunk before the ladies arrived, so money well spent, I guess.

Another time, some idiot who had dropped acid wouldn't stop screaming in the bathtub, which meant none of the rest of the group got any sleep. The key to surviving these parties without actual military repercussions was to avoid detection by hotel staff. So long as we didn't bother other patrons or staff, we could usually pass our time as we liked.

Yet here I was, getting one of those midnight phone calls I grew to despise, on a Friday night in Monterey, California. I'd fallen asleep on my Arabic textbooks in my one-room apartment. I would have been out on the town myself, but the coming test was rumored to be a total bastard, where two wrong answers automatically set your grade at a C.

When my phone went off, I startled awake, going through the mental uncertainty of abruptly awakened persons everywhere. I grabbed my phone to shut it off, but something reminded me I was responsible for some people somewhere, so I answered it.

"Hello?"

"Hi, this is Monterey PD. Is Staff Sergeant Salzgeber there?" The caller had a pleasant male voice that still conveyed the police-ness underneath. I rubbed my face and sniffled, trying to get coherent thought operational. I looked down in dismay at the drool on my notes. *Damn it.*

"Yes, that's me. What can I do for you?"

"Hi. We received a noise complaint at the, um, hotel over on the Naval Postgraduate School campus. We've got three of your Marines here. They were drinking underage and playing guitar. We need you to come down and get them."

I sighed. "Did they hurt anyone? Themselves or others? Or just annoy the shit out of people?"

The police officer laughed. Monterey wasn't just home to the Presidio, where all branches trained in languages, but also the officers' school and the Monterey Institute of International Studies. In other words, students misbehaving was probably 70 percent of the police caseload.

"No one's been harmed. The hotel just wants them removed from the property. Can you come down?"

"Yes, Officer. I'll be on my way shortly. Thank you."

As I got myself cleaned up to leave, I made some phone calls and sent a few texts to my NCOs. The platoon sergeant and two corporals answered my messages and agreed to converge on NPS with me. I specified that no one was to take charge of the Marines until I arrived. My NCOs meant well, but two of them had transferred to DLI from grunt units.

Infantrymen have a whole different idea of how to deal with misconduct among the "boots" or newer Marines. I didn't want to add an insane hazing incident to the pile.

When I finally got on the campus, I saw the two cop cars and three very worried looking young men standing to one side as the cops scribbled notes on their paperwork. There were a couple backpacks and, yes, one guitar case, by their feet. I instantly recognized the Marines as mine. They had only been in my platoon for a couple months at this point, which by DLI standards was very new indeed.

I got out of my car and grabbed my military ID. As I walked across the parking lot, I saw Cpl Shaw, one of the NCOs I had called. He was pacing back and forth, clenching his fists, his pale face suffused with rage, giving his best death stare to the troops who'd caused the scene. Privately, I thought he might be overreacting, but it does not do to try to calm an NCO in front of his juniors. I introduced myself to the police, who seemed glad that I had finally gotten there. I handed them my ID card, and they explained that the guys had been playing music in their room and annoyed some lieutenants down the hall who were trying to study, like most of the sober adults in this town. They called the front desk, and when beer was found in the young Marines' room, the cops and I were summoned. Now, here we were.

The police officer handed me the Marines' ID cards and asked me to just take them back to the barracks.

"Sure, no problem, Officer. I can do that." I nodded to Sgt Charles, the platoon sergeant, and he got the young men moving toward the duty vehicle he commandeered for this purpose. As they scuttled off with their backpacks for the ride to base, the police officer turned back to me.

"Oh, by the way, could you take her, too? We can't get ahold of anyone in her chain of command." He handed me an extra ID card. "She was hanging out with them in their room, so we figured you might . . . ?"

"Who is 'she'?" I frowned. No one had mentioned a female Marine in the group. The cop gestured to a small, frightened girl who looked about nineteen. She had short-cropped, dark hair and features that looked all the worse for fear. She was hugging a small nondescript backpack to her chest, and when she saw me look at her, she flinched. I didn't recognize her from anywhere. She definitely was not in any of the Arabic platoons, and I knew all three of them pretty well. I looked more closely at the ID he'd handed me.

"Officer, she's Air Force. I'm Marines. I don't know where to take her or what their procedures are. You want me to take *her* with us?"

The Air Force barracks were just across the street from the Marine barracks on-base, but I'd never been inside them. I wasn't even sure what their duty rank structure looked like. They were all a bunch of blue stripes to me.

"Please, could you take her back to base? It'd really help us out." The cop looked tired, and I decided I could probably use some goodwill in the department in case of future incidents. He was clearly fed up and wanted to be done with this rather minor scene already.

I shrugged and pocketed her ID card with those of my Marines. "Okay, I'll take her." I turned to her and nodded in the direction of my car. "Come on, let's go."

The drive back to base took only ten minutes. When I pulled in, we both got out of the vehicle. I told her to wait by the car while I sorted out the problems I did know how to deal with.

The young Marines stood in a line at parade rest just outside the barracks. Their NCOs were snarling and ready to give them a serious ass-chewing that might take a while. Everyone was waiting for me to speak. If I told everyone to just go to bed, I'd look weak to the NCOs and possibly the Marines. If I yelled at them, well, my heart wasn't really in it. The officers at NPS could cope with some poor guitar playing, for fuck's sake. Otherwise, life was going to get much worse for them. Making up my mind, I took a deep breath and looked up at the sickly orange streetlamps.

"Guys, you fucked up. Tonight, you might be a little sleepless and uncomfortable. That's the price you pay. Your NCOs will deal with you. But judging from what the cops told me, it looks like there won't be anything on the blotter [the police report issued each morning to commanders, highlighting any interactions with civilian or military law enforcement]. I can't be bothered to do paperwork, either. So, tonight will suck, but it won't follow you for the rest of your careers. If this is acceptable, then I'll get out of the way and let your NCOs deal with you. But if you'd rather I do paperwork instead, speak now."

I waited, letting each man choose his fate. No one spoke. I nodded and turned to the NCOs.

"No hazing, do you hear me? You can have them clean, you can chew their ass, you can express your displeasure. But do not do anything that will make this situation worse, understood?"

Sgt Charles nodded, even as Cpl Shaw continued to pace like an angry tiger. I decided maybe a bit more was needed. "If this shit comes out as hazing, Charles, it's your ass."

He seemed to get it, even as his own features were locked in a scowl. I accepted this was probably as good a reply as I was going to get, handed the ID cards back to each Marine, and walked back to my car. The NCOs seized the moment and barked orders for everyone to get upstairs to their rooms right fucking now.

Now I had to figure out what the hell I was supposed to do with an airman. She was shaking even more visibly, now that she'd seen the NCOs turned loose on her friends. An angry infantryman in attack mode would get most people shaking—or worse—by design. I was very tired, unsure if I'd made the right call, and ready to get back home. I gestured to her.

"Come here."

She scurried up and waited, still silent. She hadn't said a single thing yet. I looked at her ID card one more time and then shrugged.

"Here. Have a good night." I gave her the card and got in my car. She looked astonished and disbelieving at her luck, but wisely nodded and sprinted into the Air Force barracks before I could change my mind. With luck, she and I would never see each other again. Unlike the Marine Corps, which merely disciplined troops or reassigned them, the Air Force at the time would eject her not only from the school but from active duty altogether for an underage-drinking offense. They did not play when it came to their linguists, not even a little bit. Whatever else had happened, I didn't want the destruction of a young woman's hopes and dreams on my conscience—not for youthful hijinks that harmed no one. For the next week or two, I wondered if she'd taken the near miss to heart, but I never tracked her down to find out.

Monday morning rolled around, and classes went how they normally went: one unbearable hour of struggle against a language I felt I'd never master after another. By the time 4:15 p.m. rolled around, I was mentally toast. I trudged back to the barracks, which was walking distance from Middle East III's schoolhouse. I'd been shut in a tiny, windowless room all day, surrounded by hyper young members of every branch of the military, all of whom seemed to find my amateur mistakes in Arabic incredibly amusing. I combined present and future tense by accident one time in speaking practice, and my classmates never let me live it down. As their class leader (yep, along with being a platoon commander, I was also the senior class leader—joy of joys), there was no end to the bruising my ego took if I goofed up or failed a test. I was cashed, done, finished, exhausted. I wanted a stiff drink that arrived in about nine glasses but knew exactly why I couldn't have it.

The barracks building was not just living space for the Marine students. The first floor served as the admin shop and company offices. The commanding officer, executive officer, and enlisted advisers all had their offices there as well. At the end of my day, my responsibility as a platoon commander meant I had to check in with the company gunnery sergeant and get any news that the platoon needed to know about. Such news often included things like urinalysis testing, scheduled events (such as PT tests), and any policy changes the commander saw fit to make. When I arrived on that day, however, GySgt Calvin hit me up almost immediately with a very unwelcome question.

"Hey, Salz, what's this I hear about a noise complaint from NPS? Your Marines having a party or something?" GySgt Calvin looked like he'd heard some delicious gossip and couldn't wait to find out if it was true. I dropped my pack and plopped down in the chair in front of his desk.

"Yeah, that's all it was. I picked them up, brought them back, and the NCOs had a chat with them about not doing shit like that." I stifled a yawn.

"Bring them to my office. I want to have a word with them." Gunny grinned at me. I knew what he was up to. He was digging to see if I was trying to keep something at my level when he would rather take it from me and deal with it at *his* level. *Ugh.* But I had to obey. He was well within his rights to demand any troop of mine appear and report to him.

"Roger that, Gunny."

I grabbed my bag and went out back where the Marines were forming up for unit PT. Today was scheduled to be a run. *This day is just not going to improve*, I thought. I got in front of my platoon and called out the three young men from Friday night. We gathered to the side while the platoon closed ranks to fill their missing spots. Lucky me, Sgt Charles was not here yet; otherwise, he'd have insisted on handling this, and I worried he'd fuck it up for all of us. Charles was a genius linguist (he fluently spoke Farsi, Dari, Urdu, and Arabic, which, considering he was born in Florida to a white-as-Wonder-Bread family, was impressive as shit) and he could run for days, but politics and subtlety were not his things.

I lowered my voice as the three huddled around me.

"Company Guns wants to speak to you guys about the incident Friday.

I think all he's heard is that there was a noise complaint. Don't go in there volunteering all sorts of details unless you really want the consequences. I'm not saying lie. Do NOT lie. But be mindful of what you say."

They nodded and followed me in an orderly line to the office. When we arrived, GySgt Calvin was already entertaining other guests, and his door was closed. The Marines lined up along the wall outside his office at parade rest and waited to be called in. I stood against the opposite wall, saying silent prayers to whatever gods had time for me that this was not about to go badly for us all.

As chance would have it, the next person to arrive on the scene was MGySgt Collins,[31] looking like a storm cloud with extra lightning. I calmed myself by noting that he *always* looked like that. He was a gnarled, crusty-looking old man who wore glasses and spontaneously shouted curse words for no apparent reason. He shouted things like, "NO FORNICATION IN MY GAWDDAMN BARRACKS, ROGER???" and everyone within hearing range was now not only deafened but also probably no longer in the mood for fornication or any other indulgence. He was ready to retire while simultaneously being completely unimaginable in any incarnation other than an old Marine. We were all wary of him.

And here he was, shoulders hunched, pushing through the hallway as if even air resistance pissed him off. My Marines and I pressed ourselves into our separate walls because accidentally brushing against Master Guns in the narrow passage was not to be thought of. He'd probably wig THE fuck out. Instead of continuing past us, though, he stopped. He glanced suspiciously at the three Marines in green PT gear waiting to see GySgt Calvin and then subjected me to a long stare. *Oh no. Please, no.*

"What the fuck are you idiots doing out here?" he barked at the troops. I opened my mouth to speak for them, but his withering glare stopped my reply in my throat. "I didn't fucking ask you there, Staff Sergeant. I know I fucking spoke to them, not you."

My teeth clicked, I shut my mouth so fast. *Fuck. He's going to interrogate them, and they're so new they'll decide now's the time to confess all their sins or something. Goddamn it. We're all screwed.*

PFC Wilson[32] moved from parade rest to attention. (Marines do not speak at parade rest, so they have to change positions to talk or answer.)

---

31   Not his real name; the real name escapes me. A master gunnery sergeant is like a sergeant major, but more technically proficient.

32   Also not his real name

Clearing his throat, he replied, "Master Guns, there was a noise complaint about us. GySgt Calvin ordered us to report to him."

The other two guys stayed still and silent. *Maybe if they don't move, Master Guns won't be able to see them*, I thought to myself.

Master Guns grunted and then faced me.

"See, Staff Sergeant? They didn't need your fucking help after all."

That was it. Master Guns was satisfied. He abruptly resumed his walk down the hall and went to his office, shutting the door. I breathed out and mouthed a silent thank-you to the universe in general.

Moments later, the only sound I heard in the hall was the susurration of Marines moving to the back of the building for the run and a muffled "FUCK" issuing from Master Guns' office, which was simply the sound of him operating within normal parameters.

GySgt Calvin finally opened his door, having changed into running gear, and nodded to the guys who had been waiting. "We'll talk after the run. Come on."

They followed him out and formed back up into 5th Platoon.

After the run, GySgt Calvin forgot about everything. It was never spoken of again.

30.

THE EXECUTIVE OFFICER LOSES HIS MIND: WHAT ARE BOOTS?

A t the Defense Language Institute, the Marine Detachment had a stealthily growing problem. It came in the form of the XO (executive officer), a man with a stocky build that suggested brawn was his main strength instead of brains. He had dark, buzz-cut hair and beady brown eyes, which burned with hatred for everyone he thought weaker than himself. He habitually abused his rank and privilege in the XO billet to the fullest. Every single Marine in the unit avoided him at all costs. He enjoyed punishing people for the least consequential offenses.

Bad as this was, Capt Curtz was becoming even more bizarre and aggressive, especially in his behavior toward the young, enlisted Marines. Personally, the title of "captain" stuck in my throat every time I had to address him as such. He had been a first lieutenant who flunked out of the French program but was kept around to fill the XO billet, which put him second in the chain of detachment command, behind the commanding officer (CO). For the sake of appearances, he was frocked to the rank of captain—given the captain's double bars without an advance beyond a first lieutenant's pay grade.

At first, he just came across as a taciturn guy who was quick to criticize every little thing. This rapidly devolved into more general abuse. When it came to PFCs and lance corporals, he seized on any opportunity to punish them, humiliate them, and exercise his control over them. He was not a Marine but a vicious schoolyard bully. He labored to make up excuses, usually an accusation that the Marine had lied to him in some form or fashion, and then proceeded to bring down the harshest consequences he could manage.

The first incident that really made me sit up and take notice was when the XO decided to go after one of my Marines, LCpl Goodman. On the day Goodman underwent knee surgery to correct an earlier injury in the Marine Corps, Capt Curtz ordered him to go straight back to class—basically from gurney to desk.

Now, this struck me as some next-level fuckery. Goodman absolutely had to have the operation. Without it, he could never leave DLI to go into an active unit. He was supposed to be recovering in his barracks room on convalescent leave, which is a nonnegotiable right granted to Marines who need to stay in their quarters and heal. By the book, no one in the unit could countermand the doctor's orders.

Capt Curtz didn't see it that way. Despite his initial approval for the surgery to go ahead, he now refused to understand any part of this situation or acknowledge his own culpability. He ordered GySgt Calvin to destroy the hospital-issued leave chits bearing approval signatures. He was—for reasons unknown and unfathomable—determined to destroy Goodman's career.

When the Marine showed up in the classroom, he was staggering with the new crutches, groggy, and almost completely out of it from the pain meds. The instructors, civilian and military, decided to override the XO and send LCpl Goodman back to his room.

Beyond pissed now that civilians and other Marines had thwarted his authority, Capt Curtz demanded that the Marine at least receive an official reprimand—a "page 11," as we called it—for having the surgery performed in the first place. The XO said Goodman had lied to him and disobeyed him by going forward with the surgery. This made no sense whatsoever because we had the existing, physical paperwork showing that the procedure had been approved a month earlier, signed in black ink by the entire chain of command, including Capt Curtz. The reprimand was still issued because the CO trusted that his XO wasn't being a total psychopath, and LCpl Goodman now had an illicit surgery on his record.

The Goodman affair was only one in a series of acts escalating day by day as Capt Curtz doubled his efforts in pursuing some personal vendetta—against whom, no one knew. He oscillated wildly, ranging from sick to straight-up sadistic. And he never, ever laughed unless it was at the sight of a young Marine's distress over the prospect of expulsion from the school.

He did things like take the Marines out on beach runs at 0430 and get all the troops neck-deep in the ocean while temperatures outside were only forty degrees Fahrenheit. He never brought along a corpsman, either, and left the emergency vehicle two miles back. When Marines started to fall out with signs of acute hypothermia, he simply made the rest of their squad carry them while he continued the run. By the time he felt he'd collected what was owed to him, three Marines were sent straight to the hospital, and the rest of us were so frozen that even uncurling our hands so we could remove our boots was nearly impossible.

One particular weeknight, Capt Curtz came to the barracks and stayed all night. His favorite thing was trying to catch someone doing something he could fry them for. On this occasion, I was on duty as the officer of the day (OOD), and my responsibilities included touring the barracks at least twice at random intervals and having the duty NCO report to me. I was otherwise allowed to leave the barracks so long as I answered my cell phone immediately if trouble appeared. The duty NCO (usually a sergeant or a corporal) had the exact same standing order that every duty NCO in the entire Marine Corps does—to notify the OOD immediately if something serious goes down.

But Capt Curtz much preferred trying to screw over the Marines on duty, like me, by making it look as if we had all failed in our reporting requirements. That night, one of our female lance corporals attempted suicide by swallowing a bunch of pills. Capt Curtz saw his chance and seized it.

It was not his chance to be decent or human by leaping to the aid of this young woman. No way. Instead, he ordered the duty NCO in the barracks not to inform the chain of command about it. That way, he could use it as a gotcha against the NCOs and SNCOs for not knowing. As luck would have it, though, the Lance Corporal Underground disregarded Curtz's instructions almost immediately. Thanks to the trust and rapport I'd established in the smoke pit, the duty NCO, Sgt Wannamaker, called my cell phone to give me the heads-up.

When I arrived at the barracks, I readied myself to hear the worst of the details. By that time the commanding officer, Maj Mansfield, had also arrived. Capt Curtz was in Maj Mansfield's office, complaining that none of the SNCOs had answered their phones or even come in for a tour, and he wanted permission to NJP us all. Just then, I pounded my fist against the hatch, as protocol demands, and reported in, standing center-squared on the CO's desk and looking straight ahead at the wall behind him.

Major Mansfield looked worried and tired, but Curtz was almost excited.

"Oh, well, guess who finally decided to show up there, Staff Sergeant. You were supposed to be touring the barracks, so how the hell did you not know about this?!"

I stayed at the position of attention and did not answer him at first because I might blurt out that he ordered that I not be told. The Lance Corporal Underground had given me the information, so I could not tell him that the duty NCO had defied his orders.

Capt Curtz found my silence irritating. "Tell me something, Staff Sergeant, did you even read the duty binder?[33] Don't even answer that because I know you didn't. And that's still no excuse because I read the entire duty binder out loud during the detachment formation last week! So, what's your fucking excuse?"

To say I was severely nonplussed is an understatement. I didn't even know where to begin so I could understand how he was making the leap from a suicide attempt to everything being my fault because something-something binder. He expected me to say something, so I tried.

"Sir, I wasn't here the day that you read that."

The whole detachment had been an unholy degree of pissed off over his little stunt. Reportedly, it was a complete shitshow that went on past the time the chow hall closed for the day. The tired, hungry Marines had stood outside in Monterey's chilly weather while Curtz, all bundled up in a bomber jacket, stood there on a table, reading every single page aloud (and there were nearly sixty pages) for nearly two and a half hours.

"Oh, is that fucking right, Staff Sergeant? You're a platoon commander. What's your excuse for missing formation?!" His voice oozed contempt for me, and he was berating me in front Maj Mansfield for the express purpose of destroying my reputation with the commander. But there was no way in hell I would let that little remark whizz by my head unanswered.

"I was in the hospital having a miscarriage, sir."

Curtz sneered and in a mocking voice replied, "Oh, don't give me that poor-me pity bullcrap—"

"I DIDN'T ASK FOR YOUR FUCKING PITY, SIR." *Now* I was pissed. "You asked why I wasn't there. That's why." I broke position to stare directly at his face, letting my own anger come to the surface for a split

---

33   A three-ring binder that contains all of the emergency phone numbers, threat condition warnings, procedures for specific events and emergencies, and so on

second. Throwing away my rank for the chance to kick him in his throat was becoming more and more appealing by the minute.

Curtz responded with disgust: "What are you, some kind of wordsmith or something? You damn well know what I'm talking about!"

He wasted no time getting in some good gloating over my obvious discomfort with discussing a personal loss in front of strangers. For my part, I thought, *Wordsmith? This fucker knows this is a language school, right? He's not that freaking dense.*

Fortunately, Maj Mansfield decided to step in. "We need to first figure out why the Marines are attempting suicide. Curtz, what's your take?"

Capt Curtz changed his manner and tone in an instant. Now he was talking to his boss, and being sycophantic was yet another of his talents. *Oh, yes please, Capt Curtz, give us all your hot take on this situation with your epic emotional intelligence and empathy.* I locked my jaws shut and went back to staring at the wall.

"Sir, it's my opinion that the boots[34] are not being properly supervised. They sit up there in their barracks night after—"

"What is wrong with their boots?" Maj Mansfield looked confused and irritated by this new information. Curtz also looked put off by the question.

"No, sir. The new Marines are who I'm referring to."

Maj Mansfield's scowl deepened. "What are the new Marines doing with their boots?" He sounded bewildered. I mentally rolled my eyes. Either Maj Mansfield was denser than concrete or he was a world-class troll. I opted for the latter. I didn't want to think it might be the former.

Capt Curtz decided on a new tack.

"Sir, the junior Marines are not being properly supervised. Not their boots."

Now I wanted to burst out laughing while simultaneously face-palming through my own head. If not for the fact that we were discussing someone trying to take their own life, I would have absolutely enjoyed telling anyone who would listen about this conversation.

Wow.

Shortly after that, Maj Mansfield dismissed me and stayed with the XO to chat. On my way out the door, I stopped in and thanked Sgt Wannamaker. If not for him, Curtz would have been able to spin this whole event however

---

34 Boots = the new Marines. Can be used for Marines straight out of basic as well as Marines joining the unit for the first time.

it pleased him. Then and there, I chose. *Someone has to stop this man.* He was actively hurting people for no reason. I began to plan.

31.

STRANGLING CHIP WITH MY BARE HANDS

L ife can be frustrating. Military life can be even more frustrating. For young Marines, the greatest source of frustration is found in the gap between what they thought being a Marine would be like and what being a Marine is. Recruiting command's messaging is all about warriors running boldly toward a fight, shouting commands while helicopters zoom over *and* an exciting soundtrack makes the whole thing look and sound like a rock music video.

Imagine their disappointment, then, when they find themselves studying the Arabic language for ten or more hours a day on a collegiate campus in Northern California. Far from a deeply masculine dream, this is the quiet, disciplined world of academia, and it goes on for over a year with very little time off. That's a lot of accumulated steam to let off, and weekends often loomed as an opportunity for drinking and running riot out in the small town that hosted us. The drinking part is pretty much necessary to the rioting part but is, for many Marines who are underage, off limits. Officially, anyway. So, time off becomes just another means of building tension.

The combination of classroom stress and discipline problems is a petri dish for the incubation of mental health issues, which regularly cropped up in the platoons. As the platoon commander for 5th Platoon, and the only female platoon commander in the det. (as, in detachment), I felt that I should probably do something about this situation before the poor kids got themselves into one career-ending mess or another. Most young people who enlist—and I speak from experience—aren't people who grew up amid a rich variety of healthy coping mechanisms.

In 2007, the Marine Corps was enjoying the continued renaissance of interest in hand-to-hand combat. The Marine Corps Martial Arts Center of Excellence (MACE) was opened, and clear-cut syllabi were issued, detailing what techniques should be mastered to achieve certification in different martial arts belts. As I've mentioned before, the most basic was the tan belt, for which most Marines were trained in boot camp, followed by gray, green, brown, and black. Because of my husband's instructor-trainer status, I had been arm barred, hip tossed, and wrestled with so much that it started to feel normal. Now it seemed to me that setting up some ground-fighting matches would be a great way for my Marines to blow off steam.

I scheduled several training sessions as activities for morning PT, much to the chagrin of my platoon sergeant, who loved nothing more than running for miles and miles. We booked a reservation in the gymnasium and dragged the blue floor pads out to the center of our space. One Marine, LCpl Goodman—the same Marine who had been the object of Capt Curtz's deranged wrath—was some crazy-skilled martial artist, like third-degree black belt in jujitsu or something. All I knew was that he'd kneel in the middle of the ring—all matches had to be done kneeling to avoid injury, according to the MACE rules—and take on six other Marines separately as a warm-up. The kid was insane.

After he had warmed up, he gave instruction informally to the rest of the troops. Having watched and/or been victims of his warm-up, they all listened with respect and interest. After an interval of practice and instruction, we would wrap up the lesson with ground fighting. Every Marine took a turn in the ring, facing an opponent nearest to his or her height and weight. The matches went two minutes, kneeling, and were supervised by an NCO to have eyes-on for any injuries.

As we wound down to the last few troops, I spied a thin blonde girl of about twenty. She looked despondent. Her name was LCpl Chip, and the other female with whom she would normally pair up was out sick that day. She would either have to go up against one of the bigger males, who had been saving up their hostility for this moment, or sit out. I didn't want to do either of these things to her, but being left out from a platoon activity was a worse option. It made being female feel even more "othering" than it already was.

When it was down to her, I dropped my blouse and got in the ring, clad in cammies, trousers, socks, and T-shirt. I took out the hairpins that kept my insanely long mane in regulations so that I just had a loose ponytail. I sat and looked over my shoulder.

"Come on, Chip. Let's do this."

The troops made whooping noises. She brightened up, albeit nervously.

"I'm fighting *you*, Staff Sergeant?"

"Yep, come on. I gotta get these people to chow at some time tonight."

She crawled into the ring and sat back-to-back with me. I looked up at Cpl Miner, who had been the acting referee because everyone was afraid to fight him. He looked like an all-American wonder boy from an '80s movie, and he was Mormon to boot, so he never swore (much) or drank (at all) and was insufferably cheerful, no matter what. I figured he'd be good at spotting whether anyone was about to accidentally kill each other—and would probably care if they did.

Cpl Miner nodded, put his hand on our shoulders, recited the rules, and then asked if we were ready. I nodded, feeling the pre-fight jitters start the adrenaline. Chip nodded.

"Fight!"

Cpl Miner jerked his hand off our shoulders, and we both spun around. At first, LCpl Chip was clearly hesitant to grab me. I was her platoon commander after all. I lunged at her to set the tone that it was all right, and she responded by grabbing my shoulders and sliding her legs toward me in a quick move to get around my waist. I pulled back and grabbed her throat with one hand, squeezing the carotid arteries in the hope of making her light-headed. Then I had the great idea to just squeeze her neck. The way I saw it, she would bring one of her arms down along the bend in my arm, where the elbow was, and then I would try to get her in an arm bar. It was the best strategy I could come up with.

Its only flaw was that Chip didn't do what I figured she'd do. Instead, she stayed gripping my shoulders, squeezing my midsection with her legs, and, well, staring at me. So, I had a good close-up view of her face as it got red and her eyes bulged. This made me wonder if maybe I was not squeezing as hard as I thought; clearly, it was not prompting her to take defensive action. For my part, I was unwilling to crush her throat. The larynx is notoriously fragile, and a crushed throat was not something I wanted to risk, if for no other reason than the very last thing I wanted was to have to report an injury to command.

But we were locked in a static situation because she continued to do nothing. She did not defend, and she did not tap. She just gave me a death stare.

Through clenched teeth, I mumbled, "Tap, Chip. Tap!"

Then I heard the gurgling. In her throat was this awful noise of fluid and strangulation.

That broke the deadlock. I gasped and immediately let go. She just rolled on her back, staring unblinkingly at the ceiling. My whole chest went cold, and I crouched over her, tapping her face frantically.

"Chip! Chip! Come on, baby, wake up. CHIP!"

I started shaking her and looked up at Cpl Miner. To my shock, he was simply standing there along with the whole platoon, staring down at the floor where Chip lay. He was smiling, and the other Marines were commenting among themselves to the effect of "Damn, these females play rough," which segued into "Holy shit" and "What happened?" and "Is she okay?"

I shouted at them to get help, but before I could do this a second time, I heard Chip gasp. That snapped my gaze back down to her bewildered face. She looked at me with puzzlement and asked, "Staff Sergeant? Why do you look like you're about to cry?"

I felt all the air rush out of me as I hugged her, clasping her to my chest, completely indifferent to the Marines watching us. I almost did cry.

"Chip, I thought I just fucking crushed your throat! I thought I killed you!"

She blinked. "When? Just now? I don't even remember what happened—"

Before I finished processing this, I leapt to my feet and charged at Cpl Miner, who was still standing among the other astonished Marines.

"What the actual FUCK, Miner! Why didn't you fucking SAY something???"

Cpl Miner looked taken aback, bewildered by my anger.

"Staff Sergeant, I thought you *knew* you knocked her out. You didn't *know*?"

I leaned down with my hands on my knees and breathed deeply. Then I straightened up, checked on Chip again once she was back on her feet, and let everyone have a good laugh. It was generally decided I won the match, and the murmurings left me with the impression that the incident was being regarded as ferocity worthy of Marines, regardless of gender. Chip and I had fought to the finish, as far as they were concerned.

Chip reassured me she was fine, and I quietly instructed her squad leader to check on her again this evening before lights-out. I dismissed the platoon, and everyone wandered out, headed to the barracks or the food court. Once I was by myself, the pieces of my uniform that I'd discarded before the fight scattered around me, I put my head on knees and rocked back and forth.

Jesus fucking Christ. I really thought I'd just killed another young woman with my bare hands. It was the most terrifying thing that ever happened to me, though it didn't seem to bother her in the least.

32.

EVEN WHEN EVERYTHING IS GREEN, YOU CAN STILL WEAR THE WRONG THING

L ike many others in the twenty-first century, Marines are always advertising their resumé. Because Marines don't wear unit patches like soldiers and airmen do, the uniform might look, well, *uniform*, so as to equalize all the troops. But there are little tells that to a properly educated and observant person speak volumes about the human being wearing the cammies.

Knowledge of these semantic signs marks you as an insider. It's not an easy knowledge to acquire. With nearly two enlistments down, I still had learning to do. No one, in fact, has ever articulated all the little rules that apply. Like everyone else, I stumbled into them and sometimes suffered the consequences of a hard impact.

One morning, at around 0500, I got up and started the morning rituals of cleaning up and leaving the house. Today, I was going to monitor a physical fitness test (PFT). For most Marines, this translates into wearing a green T-shirt, green shorts, white socks, and running shoes. A glow belt was added to diminish the number of Marines lost to cars, bikes, and other road hazards during the three-mile-run portion of the test. As a monitor, I wore tan boots, green cammie trousers, green T-shirt, and belt—in my case, green. I scrounged through my laundry until I located the correct items, and I got dressed. It was a chilly month in Monterey, so I sought a green sweatshirt to go with my ensemble.

The Marine Corps never went in for "comfort-based decisions," but there were allowances for wearing a sweatshirt for the sake of protecting your chest. The standard issue was plain olive green with a black Marine Corps logo on the chest, to right side. But different Marine units and shops designed and made their own olive-drab sweatshirts. Mine, from DLI, bore the unit logo in the right chest quadrant and a glorious eagle, globe, and anchor (EGA) on the back. The EGA was rendered in calligraphy rather than printed as a single image, the calligraphy comprised of all the different languages the Marines in the det. studied, such as Korean, Arabic, and Chinese. It was complex and quite beautiful.

I could not find that one at the moment, however, so I grabbed the first sweatshirt I saw before heading out the door. It was from 3rd Recon Battalion. Their motto, *Celer, Silens, Mortalis*—"Swift, Silent, Deadly"—was inscribed on a semi-triangular logo that contained paddles, skulls, and parachutes. I didn't think much about it beyond the fact that it was green, soft, and clean. About to stand outside for hours in the chill, I left with it.

I arrived at the Naval Postgraduate School, where we would start the test at 0630. The entire detachment was present, except for the officers, who preferred to test away from the critical eyes of the troops. We clustered around the pull-up bars where the first third of the test took place. I slipped on my Recon hoodie, got out of the car, grabbed my clipboard and stopwatch from the passenger seat, and walked up to take my place at the final bar.

Female Marines didn't do pull-ups. We did some awful alternative called the "flexed-arm hang." Basically, you get on the bar, are helped up until your chin is over the bar, and then, at the word *GO*, you are released and left to hang like a frightened possum until your arms are slowly pulled straight by gravity. As long as your elbows are bent, it counts. The moment they go straight, time stops, and the score is figured. Seventy seconds is a perfect score. The most I ever scored was sixty-nine.

The female Marines saw me and gravitated to where we would do our test, while the males used the rest of the bars for their pull-ups. I scribbled names and Social Security numbers on my roster so I could record each time as girl after girl did the hang. As I wrote, however, I became aware of strange looks thrown my way from the pull-up bars inhabited by 4th Platoon, our brothers in Arabic studies. I frowned but decided to ignore it. Fourth Platoon's platoon sergeant was Sgt Holland, a Marine from 2nd Recon in California, and I figured he was probably ogling my sweatshirt. *Whatever. I'm not shivering, and that's what's important, right?*

Moments before we were to start, Sgt Holland finally broke off from his troops and moseyed over to me. He was a man of medium height, muscled like the total gym rat he was, and, with his pale-blond hair and nearly colorless eyes, looked quite intimidating—like the kind of guy who might try to bite your eyeball out of your head during a fistfight.

We exchanged greetings, and I commented on Sgt Holland's very, very bright pink running shoes. He got a kick out of wearing them because any Marine who wanted to question his masculinity would find out that a Marine like him wears any-damn-color shoes he wants. At last, our small talk spent, Sgt Holland broke down and asked, "SSgt, where did you get that sweatshirt?"

He looked very concerned, as if I were wearing a blanket from a plague hospital.

"It's my husband's. I couldn't find anything else this morning. Why? It's not out of regulations, is it? Is there a dick on it or something?"

Sgt Holland coughed. He indicated with a nod that he'd like me to step away from the junior Marines for a moment. Once we were a few feet away, he explained what was going on—and put none too fine a point on it.

"Staff Sergeant, female Marines wearing Recon gear are women who were gangbanged by a recon team." He took a beat to let this sink in. "If it's a T-shirt, she slept with two members of the team, three if it's green shorts, and the entire team in one go if it's a sweatshirt. We don't give the gear to anyone outside the unit except in that case, and it's not so much an honor as it is a way of telling others she's a whore." He paused again before adding, "Your case is obviously different. You only slept with one Recon Marine." Another beat. "I hope."

In shock, I mumbled, "Yeah, well, I always did like a bargain."

Then he grinned.

Holy shit. I felt my face flush bright red. "Wow. Um. Holy shit. Yeah, that's not how I got this. I mean, it just ended up in my household goods when I moved here because movers can't tell one Marine's uniform gear from another's. I'd be very grateful if you could not tell the Marines here that little bit of information. I don't need more struggle."

Sgt Holland's smirk broadened into something worthy of the Cheshire cat. He was clearly enjoying my discomfort. But he graciously agreed that we would keep this particular piece of lore to ourselves. Fortunately for me, at this time, none of the other Marines at DLI came from Recon, so no one else was the wiser.

Once the physical fitness test was concluded, weigh-ins (where

Marines are checked to make sure they aren't becoming "fat bodies") and such recorded, we all dispersed to get ready for classes that day. I made a beeline for home, took off the sweatshirt, put it on a hanger, and never wore it outside the house again.

33.

WHO DRESSED YOU?

I t was a gorgeous Saturday morning in Monterey, and the platoon had formed up in the concrete loading bay just behind the barracks. Everyone, including me, was wearing desert cammies. The Marines joked and looked over each other's uniforms for flagrant violations of regs. My arrival signaled that things were about to get underway, so they started wrapping it up. I checked my watch just as the hour ticked over: 0700. Time to rock and roll.

I nodded to Sgt Charles, my platoon sergeant. He spat, and we headed for the gaggle of about forty Marines. Sgt Charles walked ahead of me to the front of the formation and came to attention. Everyone shifted into position, ready for the commands.

"PLATOON! AAA-TEEEN-TION!"

The Marines snapped smartly to the position of attention and waited. All movement stilled; all conversations died a sudden death. Sgt Charles continued.

"OPEN RANKS! MARCH!"[35]

The platoon opened up the formation so that there was walking room between each rank. The morning sunlight reflected off their uniforms, making the platoon not only smart but shiny too.

"DRESS RIIIGHT. DRESS!"[36]

---

35 All drill commands have two parts. The first word warns everyone what they are about to be ordered to do; the second word tells them when to do it.

36 This is a drill move involving a lot of elbow action to basically get everyone lined up properly.

"COVER!"[37]

Once the shuffling of feet came to a stop, it was my turn.

Walking briskly toward Sgt Charles, I arrived just after he completed an about-face, stopping six feet away from him. We faced each other, and he saluted.

"Good morning, Staff Sergeant. Fifth Platoon is formed up and ready for inspection."

I returned the salute. "Thank you."

Sgt Charles turned about-face once more and put the platoon at parade rest. As a pair, we then marched to the front of the platoon, stopping in front of the squad leader for first squad. Cpl Shaw snapped to attention and saluted. I saluted back, we exchanged greetings, and then I started the inspection.

"Is your squad all present and correct?" I inquired.

"Yes, Staff Sergeant."

"Have they eaten chow?" I knew it was early and the chow hall was barely open, but I wanted to see how far ahead Cpl Shaw had thought when it came to his troops' well-being.

"I brought them all granola bars," he responded smartly.

Privately, I was impressed. It was an interesting solution to the problem of early breakfast.

"Anyone in your squad going to surprise me when I step in front of them this morning?"

"Shouldn't be, Staff Sergeant."

I peered at his collar for any damage to his rank insignia and performed a close examination of his shave. "Cpl Shaw, most the Marines out here look like they tried to peel the skin off their faces. Your shave looks good and un-inflamed. What's your secret?"

Cpl Shaw winced, momentarily taken aback. Beauty routines were not a normal area of discussion during uniform inspections. Fighting back a smirk, he replied, "I use products, Staff Sergeant."

"Fantastic. Well done. Teach the rest of these yahoos, will you? I'm sure they're taking the term *leatherneck* far too seriously." I took one step back. "Corporal, I need you to lift your blouse so I can see your martial arts belt. If that makes you uncomfortable, Sgt Charles can inspect that."

There was a very soft snigger from someone within earshot. A female asking to look in the general area of a man's crotch should not be a cause

---

37   Now make sure you are directly behind the Marine in front of you.

for offense in their opinion, but then again, since I had the option of demanding a female inspector for my ribbons at chest height, I felt it was only fair to give the men the same option.

"Equal means equal, Corporal."

Again, with the hint of a smile, Cpl Shaw demurred. "It's fine, Staff Sergeant." Without moving his head or his gaze, Cpl Shaw lifted the bottom part of his blouse so that the belt was visible. It was exactly as I expected. His gray belt was clean, taut, and the black buckle un-scuffed.

"Very well, lower your blouse. Do you have your sergeant chevrons on you?"

One superstition that persists throughout the Corps is that a Marine should always have a pair of the next rank's chevrons pinned neatly somewhere on their person, such as under the chest-pocket flap. That way, if a situation suddenly arises where a field promotion is possible, they are ready and able to be promoted. I encouraged such optimism.

"Aye, Staff Sergeant."

"Very good. That will be all, Corporal Shaw."

With one final exchange of salutes, I turned on heel in sync with Sgt Charles and moved to the next Marine. Two Marines down the line, I stood in front of PFC Crowman. Crowman repeated the same inspection ritual. One aspect of performing inspections that I took very seriously was being standardized in my expectations and remarks. If I didn't go so far as X with one Marine, then, unless extenuating circumstances obtained, I would not deviate from that precedent.

"PFC Crowman, I need you to lift your blouse so I can see your martial arts belt. If that makes you uncomfortable, Sgt Charles can inspect that." It was the same mantra. This time, no one made a sound. Licking his lips, PFC Crowman hesitantly lifted the bottom edge of his blouse to reveal his belt.

It was . . .

What the fuck color is *that?* It looked nearly white but the sort of white you'd get if you washed something the color of seafoam green about a thousand times. *Maybe it's the sunlight?* I leaned to the left and then to the right, staring at the belt, willing it to be a color I recognized as within Marine Corps regulations. But nothing changed. Even worse, the belt buckle was some sort of brownish plastic, not black metal.

Finally, with my eyes still glued to the belt, I had to ask.

"Crowman, what color is your belt?"

This question should have been easy. Crowman should have been able to state clearly and unequivocally the color because it should have been the color he earned in the martial arts program. Tan, gray, green, whatever. No-brainer.

He pressed his lips together for a moment and then said, "Gray, Staff Ser— No, wait! Green! Maybe gray?"

He shifted his weight slightly but didn't break the thousand-yard stare to take a peek.

Oo-kay.

PFCs don't get green belts. That's usually reserved for corporals and above. So, where was the uncertainty here?

Exasperated, I barked, "Crowman, did you dress yourself this morning, or did the hookers?"

"What hookers?" PFC Crowman stammered.

Out of the corner of my eye, I saw Cpl Shaw close his eyes in embarrassment. I gave up.

"Marine, look down at your goddamn belt."

PFC Crowman broke position and looked. Then he returned to attention, still clutching the hem of his blouse.

"What. Color. Is. Your. Belt?" I asked slowly, increasing the volume at each word.

PFC Crowman caved. "I don't know, Staff Sergeant."

I lost it.

"IT'S A FUCKING *ARMY* BELT."

The pale colors of the Army battle dress uniform (BDU) were well known to us because the Presidio of Monterey was technically their base. Their uniform items were next to ours at the store.

PFC Crowman rallied.

"I bought it at the PX!"

I sighed. "Holy shit, fuckface. That's an auto-fail."

I turned my head to Cpl Shaw. "Fucking fix him after formation."

Cpl Shaw's cheeks were reddening. "Aye, Staff Sergeant."

PFC Crowman restored himself to the position of attention, saluted, and exhaled with relief as I moved on to the next Marine. Within fifteen minutes, I completed the inspection without further shenaniganry. Afterward, Sgt Charles called the whole formation to attention as I departed. I left them in his capable hands.

I mean, really? Who fucks up a *cammies inspection*?!

34.

MY AIR FORCE WISH

T here's an unrelenting stereotype about Marines loving Air Force girls. The United States Air Force is famous for recruiting the smart people, and the women who serve are desired for their beauty. Unlike Marine women, Air Force girls are culturally permitted to be female, and they really do it up. That's not to say there aren't any beautiful women in the Marines. There are. But female Marines aren't the first ones people bring up when talking about ladies in uniform. I hated this fact but couldn't articulate why. To blend into a macho culture like the Marines, sacrifices had to be made, and one of those was overtly feminine things.

At DLI, there were Air Force girls galore. The Air Force was far more lenient about females and LGBTQ+ people. One airman in the classroom next to mine swapped his uniform at the end of the day for a purse, scarf, blouse, and earrings. No one was pressing charges on *him*. I envied them. Being a Marine and being yourself was essentially incompatible, at least on most days.

When I picked up my Arabic class, I learned a few things that were quite humbling. My status as a Marine was still respected, and a lot of the young people in my class of twenty were very impressed by the uniform and our reputation for beastlike strength and hardheaded behavior, but all of that wouldn't save me when it came to learning Arabic. I might be an E-6, but if the E-2 sailor sitting next to me could translate written Arabic paragraphs faster or with a higher aptitude, my rank didn't mean squat. Having no idea what you're doing is a great equalizer. I figured out pretty quickly that standing on my past accomplishments was a route to embarrassment.

I was twenty-six, and I was intimidated by the other students. These eighteen- and nineteen-year-old kids absorbed our lessons with an alacrity I felt I could not match. I was still struggling with the alphabet while they joked around in class *in Arabic*. I didn't come this far to give up, though, so I heaped extra study time on myself and pushed through a growing feeling of hopelessness. What had I gotten myself into?

When I left MacDill AFB in Florida, I kind of left my marriage as well. Jens and I still cared about each other, but our ambitions were at cross purposes, and we both looked forward to separating. Because his progress through MECEP (Marine Enlisted Commissioning Program) would be hampered by single parenting, I moved our daughters to my parents' place across the state of Florida while I was at DLI. I couldn't bring them with me because the demands of the school were far too intense, and time off was strictly prohibited. Once you were a student at DLI, you had to stop being everything else or you would fail out.

I hadn't officially filed for divorce yet, but it was only a matter of time and paperwork. Nonetheless, I was bound by my technically married status to avoid romantic relationships. The Marine Corps isn't shy about taking someone down for adultery, and if I were thrown out, my reputation, hopes, and dreams wouldn't be the only things shattered. I'd have no way to funnel money to my family and provide for Taely and Ava. That was way too high stakes for me. If celibacy was required to keep my children fed, so be it.

My classmates and I settled in, and our vast differences in rank were forgotten once class was in session. When we started the course, we ditched our real names and took Arabic ones to use in the classroom. My name was now Fatima, although the instructors referred to me far more often as *Raqiba*—the equivalent of "Sergeant" but with the *a* at the end to indicate I was female. Because the Marines had taught me to think of myself as the same as the guys, I constantly referred to myself in the masculine forms of Arabic, much to my teachers' irritation. It killed me that I had to keep remembering I was female and alter my sentences accordingly. It presented the kind of dichotomy that's only interesting when you aren't living it.

In my class, there were two sailors, Muntusser and Fauwzi, two soldiers called Zoohair and Qassam, and two airmen, Bedr and Muna. These were the people with whom I was shut in a windowless room for eight hours every day through sixty-three weeks while being subjected to Arabic instruction whether I wanted it or not. I liked all of them on some level, but Muna was the one I had trouble with.

Muna means "wish" or "desire" in Arabic, and she was a twenty-something airman with the most stunning light-green eyes I'd ever seen. They were flecked with copper, and I'd catch myself staring at them anytime I could get her to look my way. She had a relaxed attitude about everything, born from already having a bachelor's degree and being familiar with academic environments. I found myself wishing I had her confidence. She had short dark hair with blonde streaks and, to my delight, seemed fascinated by the fact that I was a Marine.

When she complimented my appearance in the mornings, I blushed. I put in more effort during lessons in the hope that she'd notice me. If I could get her to smile at me, even if it was because I'd flubbed a line, it was worth it. I heard that she drank her coffee black, so when I was getting breakfast on my way to class, I'd grab an extra coffee for her—and then a couple of hot cocoas for the other kids so that it wouldn't look weird. She liked penguins, too, and every time I saw a penguin trinket when I was out in town, I wondered if she'd like it.

Realizing that my feelings were starting to approach a line, I exerted all the self-control I could muster to squash them.

This is not the time or the place. Get it together, Tracy—I mean, Raqiba. Aside from the fact that you're still married on paper, she's an E-4. Even if she were an E-6, she'd be off limits anyway because she is a she. (Don't Ask, Don't Tell was still a thing back then.) *Plus, you're something like coworkers. The whole idea of having a schoolgirl crush on her—dump it, for the sake of survival. You're here for classes. Fucking focus!*

I wasn't immune to masculine beauty either, and the Marines I served with sometimes had that in abundance, but I'd developed coping skills and defenses to keep it professional, and those skills came to my aid in class. Pretty quickly, I started to forget my silly crush and get on with things.

But Muna noticed my drop in interest, and *she* was disappointed. Muna decided that if I was not chasing her anymore, she would chase me instead.

I wandered into class one morning, stifling a yawn and with a killer study hangover. They had warned us when we arrived that the training could be brain-creakingly intense, and when I passed out on my notes the previous night, I'd dreamed that I was having a futile argument with a cat in Arabic and getting frustrated that it wouldn't answer me. The cat spoke English only and kept saying "meow" like a total bastard instead of عواء. *Neek nefsik, ya qita.* I hate you.

I dropped my pack at my seat and slouched into my chair. I'd skipped breakfast because I was running late and school policy was that once the classroom door was shut, students had to go to their commands and get a hall pass to get in. This morning, though, there was a hot cocoa waiting for me on my desk. I frowned at it and looked up to catch Muna glancing my way before averting her eyes to the whiteboard, her own coffee in hand.

O-kay. Um.

I said out loud, "*YaAllah, qaahoowa!*" (Oh my God, coffee!) even though it was cocoa, and slurped it with obvious relief. It was the most subtle way I could say thank you without calling her out. The corners of her mouth twitched. Message received.

The military wasn't the only culture struggling with same-sex relationships. Our Arabic instructors, though well adjusted to the United States, were hardly at home with the idea. There existed an unspoken agreement in which we students kept our love lives and trouser situations out of the classroom. In return, no one would throw real or proverbial stones at us. An uneasy peace that was holding—for now.

Between class sessions, we were permitted ten- or fifteen-minute breaks to step out, use the bathroom, smoke, whatever. I walked out to the *hamaam*, washing my face and hands so I could wake up a bit more. On my return to class, I saw Muna having a giggly conversation with another airman, whose name I couldn't remember. *Loren? Tory? Ugh, my brain is rotting soup right now.*

When I got to the door, they both looked at me, and Loren/Tory scowled. I held the door, and she swept past me, nose in the air, leaving in the manner of one who has been offended.

What did I do? I checked my watch. There were roughly five minutes remaining in our break. That might be enough. I let the door close and walked after her.

"Loren! Tory! Airman! Hey, wait up!"

I've never had issues projecting my voice. She turned on her heel and crossed her arms, waiting for me to catch up.

"My name is Zainab," she sniffed. "I thought Muna might've mentioned me." Zainab had bright-red hair and ice-blue eyes that communicated disapproval very effectively. I stopped a few feet away from her.

"Did I piss you off or something? I mean, I know I'm just a stupid Marine, but I do outrank you by a bit. Maybe give me the due respect instead of pushing past me, or something?"

I was feeling tired, short tempered, and privately worried I'd let standards slip too far by focusing on my studies instead of customs and courtesies at times. But Zainab was in the Air Force, and they gave their people more latitude than Marines got. She put her hands on her hips and looked directly at my eyes.

"What are your intentions with Muna?"

"Wha-what? What intentions?" I sputtered.

Zainab rolled her eyes. "I have to get to class, *Sergeant.* By your leave?"

I waved a hand, dismissing her, and returned to my own classroom. *What intentions?* Coffee and penguins weren't any betrothal etiquette I'd ever heard of; I wasn't even sure if Muna saw me like that. *Ugh, forget it.*

I washed my mind of the incident by trying to remember what the word for "utilization" was. *Is that measure twelve? Wait, if it's a noun form, then it's probably not measure twelve. Maybe?*

About a month later, Muna and I had figured out our dynamic. At least, I thought so. We teasingly called each other stupid names in Arabic during class, like *habibitee* (sweetie), *jameela* (beautiful), and *amira* (princess), snickering when our teachers shot us dirty looks. It was a game to act as gay as we could without revealing anything, and our teacher from Lebanon, *Usteth* Ghassan, would occasionally mock us by croaking, "*Ya amiraitee, ya habibitee*" in a falsetto but otherwise let it go. If the male Marines could slap each other in the nuts and do other humorous homoerotic things, I could damn well get away with making kissy faces at an airman for the fun of it. It was harmless, and we kept it to the classroom.

The loneliness of DLI was getting to me, though. I couldn't hang out with my platoon because I was their platoon commander. I couldn't make friends with the other SNCOs because spending any time at all, anywhere, with a male Marine would spark the gossip machine into full gear, and rumors could do the work of truth when it came to accusations of inappropriate conduct. Sitting in my tiny, one-room apartment, rewatching videos on YouTube, wasn't as fulfilling as human interactions. (Yeah, I said it. Fight me in a field!) I needed friends, or I was going to turn in on myself and go to the dark place. I didn't want to be in the dark place.

When Muna casually invited me to see a movie out in town one weekend, I accepted. *Elizabeth: The Golden Age* was playing in the small cinema down the hill from our campus, and it was a short walk and even shorter drive. I dressed in jeans and a T-shirt, putting on a bit of perfume and wrangling my absurdly long hair into a ponytail. It felt so good to be a person again! I was going to get out from under all my duties for a couple hours, and that in itself was exciting.

I hopped into my tiny Toyota Prius and drove the five minutes downhill, parallel parking on Alvarado Street and getting to the theater almost five minutes early. *Cool.* I could get the tickets before Muna showed up and treat her. I made a lot more than she did; plus, I had no student loans. This trip should be mine to cover.

I turned from the box office window and saw her crossing the street. I nearly dropped the tickets. Muna looked *amazing.*

Out of cammies, I could see she was curvy in very pleasing ways, and the skillful application of makeup highlighted her eyes so that I stopped breathing when she looked at me and smiled. She was wearing a loose white blouse, tight jeans, and sneakers, but she couldn't have been more beautiful if she had been attired in haute couture. I felt clumsy and dumb, but I liked it. *Wow.*

Then the thoughts started.

You need to leave. You can't be here. Look at her. You think you've been in trouble before? She's an entire catastrophe looking to happen. What will you do if someone sees you and reports it to the chain of command? You know Capt Curtz seizes on any chance to humiliate and drum out females. You're going to fuck up.

But I didn't leave. I felt rooted to the spot, and when Muna hugged me and I smelled her, I was done. The Marine Corps wasn't that cool anyway.

While Muna and I kept things platonic, when the Marine Corps Birthday Ball came around that year, I did something a little crazy. I got dressed in my highest dress blues, Muna got dressed up in a gown, jewelry, and heels, and together we went to the ball. When Marines came up to me to say hi or get some pictures, I introduced her as my date. They gave her big smiles, drinks, and other forms of welcome.

That was it. No one cared, not even a little bit. Part of me felt that it was anticlimactic. When you work yourself up to do something brave, it's humbling that no one else seems to have noticed much. Turns out, they didn't mind, so it didn't matter.

35.

CAPTAIN CURTZ BULKS UP HIS BAD-LEADERSHIP RESUME

Curtz kept his private, unselective revenge quest going for months after the attempted suicide. No matter how trivial the offense, Curtz was more than happy to bring about the worst possible outcome. Worse, Maj Mansfield was oblivious to what was happening. For instance, Curtz had one female Marine kicked out of DLI and stripped of her MOS because she had forged a dental hall pass so she could return to class right away and miss as little of the instruction as possible. He had refused to write the pass out for her when she asked him. Curtz also decided I needed some extra-special attention. He viewed nothing and no one as sacred, and therefore he disregarded what the consequences of his actions would be, both for himself and others.

He had me dragged out of my final exam, the Defense Language Proficiency Test (DLPT), which was the very last word in whether a student graduates from the school. Curtz straight up didn't give a shit. The cruelty was the point.

It was during the most difficult and critical part of the DLPT, the listening test, that he ordered me to report into his office so he could accuse me of lying to him about reading the duty binder. When I reported in, he castigated me as a liar, although he didn't say what lie I was supposed to have told or how it had negatively impacted him, the CO, or the unit. When he got tired of threatening me without eliciting the desired squirming response, he said he was going to give me a page 11 (letter of reprimand) and dismissed me.

Surprise, surprise, executive officers do not have the authority to do that. Only the commander does, and Curtz would have had to explain why he wanted to undertake that action to Maj Mansfield.

Curtz was checked here but hardly checkmated. He had another avenue of attack. The captain regularly hung out with the chief warrant officer in charge of the admin shop, and the two talked very loudly about each female Marine, from private all the way up, and whom he thought they might be sleeping with, how hot they were, and what they might be like in bed.

Meant to be overheard, the conversations disgusted the enlisted Marines who worked in the shop and could not help listening in. Rumor had gotten about that I had Curtz in my sights. So one of the sergeants in admin approached me clandestinely and reported the various remarks he and his team had been forced to listen to. Subsequently, another female staff sergeant found me and told me her own horror story of Curtz's behavior while she was on duty. I asked her to write down the whole event, sign, and date it. This would be the first of at least five signed, written statements I collected from different Marines who were fed up and thought I might stand a chance at changing things.

It all reached critical mass one day in 2008. Capt Curtz called two of my Marines from 5th Platoon, Cpl Shaw and LCpl Hayes, to his office in the barracks. Of course, he did this while they were both supposed to be in class. It wasn't *his* graduation and future on the line, after all. There he proceeded to berate them for some offense I don't recall.

Curtz did not seem to be getting enough satisfaction out of that, so he decided to improvise. He wanted the Marines to act out a little pantomime just for him. He lounged behind his desk and started his little show by making the lance corporal, who was female, role-play as the XO and have her demote the corporal. Not just turn and say, "You're demoted." No. He forced her to take her rank insignia off, take Cpl Shaw's off his collar, and then replace it with her own junior rank insignia. All this was to be done while Cpl Shaw stood at attention, enduring the humiliation.

Capt Curtz was clearly enjoying the show as the deeply uncomfortable Marines started to comply. But they just could not debase themselves like that, and LCpl Hayes finally refused to obey his orders any further. Enraged, Curtz shouted at Cpl Shaw, out of the blue, "It's your fucking fault your friends died in Iraq!"

This was so far outside the limits of what is acceptable that it almost could not be real. As an infantryman, Cpl Shaw had deployed to Iraq prior to his change in MOS and subsequent assignment to DLI. He had lost three Marines he was quite close with during a firefight with insurgents. And this slimy quasi-captain, who had never even been assigned to a real duty station, was torturing Cpl Shaw, relishing the anger and hurt he caused.

This time, however, Capt Curtz had indulged himself a little too much. He had called down the hall for the company gunnery sergeant to come to his office to watch it all with him, thus inviting a witness to his crime.

At length, Capt Curtz grew bored and told both Marines that they would be facing disciplinary action very soon. He didn't say what their misconduct had been, only that he was planning something worse for them in the future. Cpl Shaw and LCpl Hayes immediately sought me out. In shock and outrage, they reported in detail what happened.

I was enraged to the point of glowing in the dark. I decided then and there that Curtz needed to go down, hard, and it needed to happen right fucking now.

Demolishing a vicious prick like Capt Curtz would be a treat and a half. After a year or so working under him, I concluded that he was rotten and beyond redemption. He was a terrible cocktail of arrogance, malice, and cringing insecurity. Had he ever actually hit the fleet instead of hiding in an MOS school, I absolutely guarantee he would have gotten someone killed and done so without remorse.

On the other hand, I thank the gods of power plays that he was stupid and petty. Those were two traits that gave me, a lowly SNCO, a much-needed advantage.

The Uniform Code of Military Justice (UCMJ) prescribes specific punishments for enlisted servicemen who level accusations against officers, should those accusations fail to pan out. Once I had decided to take a swing at him, I needed to be certain I didn't miss. He would never, ever let that pass without exacting revenge. If I accused an officer of misconduct, the other officers—including Maj Mansfield, the CO—would most likely close ranks to protect one of their own. I had to make Curtz appear as a clear and present danger to the officers and enlisted alike. That way, he'd be without allies. Fortunately, I had thought of a plan.

There's a little-known and rarely used legal mechanism in Marine Corps processes for addressing issues far above your pay grade. It's called "Requesting MAST." Requesting MAST allows any Marine, regardless of rank, to take a problem or issue up to as high a level in the chain of command as they desire, even to the commandant of the Marine Corps. The rules state unequivocally that a request MAST has to be dealt with immediately, as an emergency. The entire chain of command between the Marine and the person or office they are requesting to speak to must take steps to handle or pass on the request within seventy-two hours. Any interference with the request is strictly forbidden and carries penalties ranging from demotion to incarceration. Finally, the request-MAST paperwork itself is filled out and put into a sealed envelope by the initiating Marine. No one is allowed to open it or read it without specific permission from the requestor.

For all these reasons, Marine officers, and most especially Marine commanders, react to the news of a request MAST with intense trepidation. If they fuck it up or break any of the rules, it is now *their* ass that is about to be court-martialed. There's also a very good chance that if the request goes above their level, it will give rise to some very pointed and serious questions as to why the hell they were not trusted to deal with the matter in the first place.

I decided to request MAST. After I had collected every single signed and dated statement from the other Marines Curtz had wronged, I filled out a request-MAST form, requesting to speak with Col Schneider, the commanding officer of all Marine Intel schools. Truthfully, I was ready to take this beyond our detachment if needed, but that was not the outcome I was actively going for. What I wanted was to give Maj Mansfield a clear wake-up call that his XO was dangerously close to damaging the major's own career—permanently.

I dropped the request off the very day Maj Mansfield returned from leave. I didn't trust Curtz *not* to break rules about interference. The captain, after all, had no scruples or ethics whatsoever. When I got to the part of the MAST form that asked me to describe my complaint in detail, the only thing I wrote was *For Colonel Schneider's Eyes Only*. I also did not include copies of the written statements along with the form. I could envision Capt Curtz opening the envelope despite it being addressed to someone else, shredding the supporting paperwork I'd gathered, and then trying to press charges against me for false statements.

Nope, the form was going to be sent up all by itself and with as much ambiguity as I could get away with.

As expected, Maj Mansfield seemed very worried and anxious when I was summoned to his office later that afternoon. When I entered, he was seated behind his desk, the palms of his hands flat on either side of the official envelope while he stared at it like it was unexploded ordnance.

He invited me in, asked me to take a seat, and then took a deep breath. Part of the courtesies surrounding these requests states that leadership is allowed to politely ask the requesting Marine if they would be willing to give their leadership a chance to resolve whatever the issue is in lieu of MAST. Maj Mansfield also had the S-1 admin chief, CWO3 Polk, sitting in. It was my right to ask him to leave, but I wanted at least one witness for this. I knew Polk was sweating the possibility of his own name being in my complaint, thanks to those loud conversations he and Curtz had. *All right, sir, let's see how close to Curtz you really want to be after this.*

Still fixated on the envelope and its dangerous secrets, Maj Mansfield came right out and asked me, "Staff Sergeant, I understand that you've requested MAST to Col Schneider. Before I send it up, is there any way you'd be willing to let me have a chance to resolve it? Is this something you'd be satisfied with, attempting to address this at my level instead?"

Here it comes. Let's get this started.

"Sir, I would be delighted if you can resolve this at your level. I'd only requested to speak with Col Schneider because you were out on leave [even if a Marine is away on leave, once MAST has been requested, it must reach the Marine and be dealt with ASAP], and I did not think this could wait. Now that you're back, I am confident we can sort this out."

Maj Mansfield exhaled and let his posture relax.

"Thank you, Staff Sergeant. Do I have your permission to read the complaint?"

"Yes, sir. The form in the envelope does not have any information, though. I brought that with me separately."

I held up a manila folder with all the documents in my hand, slid it across his desk, and watched him open the envelope first. Then he turned his attention to the folder.

"Is this the specifics of the issue right here?" He opened the folder and scanned the top page. As he started reading, I backfilled him with an overview of the entire situation, making sure to touch on every event for which I had evidence. I failed to mention CWO3 Polk's name. No point in giving Curtz an ally. Partners in crime always seem to burn alone. At the conclusion, I stated what my desired outcome[38] was.

I wanted Maj Mansfield to rein in the XO because he was "bad for good

---

38   Requesting MAST requires the requestor to have a clearly stated objective that they want to achieve and would consider a satisfactory resolution.

order and discipline within the unit." I was very careful not to ask for the XO to be reprimanded or to suffer any other specific disciplinary action. I needed this to sound like a very sincere and honest concern, not a personal grudge against an officer for being a hard-ass. All I wanted, I told the major, was for the CO to look into Capt Curtz's increasingly bizarre behavior.

After we exchanged a few more questions and answers, Maj Mansfield and I reached an agreement that he would immediately look into the issues I brought up. If his inquiries did not bring about the desired outcome, then Maj Mansfield would at least be able to say to Col Schneider that he had given it his best effort before sending it up further.

Maj Mansfield asked to keep the statements, and I agreed, having already made photocopies just in case. I expressed my belief that Capt Curtz would be all over those papers the minute the CO's back was turned. Maj Mansfield put them in a safe, which Curtz opened only days later because he knew the combo. He waited until Maj Mansfield left his office to attend a graduation ceremony and stole the papers, read everything, and then put them back. The only reason I know he did this is because that same afternoon, he called to his office each Marine who had made a statement about his behavior. None were afraid to answer him, especially not LCpl Hayes and Cpl Shaw. Curtz had grossly violated the rules of MAST by seizing the evidence, and if he tried anything that even looked or sounded like retaliation, he was toast.

On my final day in the command, I was about to depart from the offices when a clerk stopped me.

"Staff Sergeant, Capt Curtz wants you to come to his office."

Well. Shit. Obediently, I took my service-record book and went to stand outside the XO's office, waiting for whatever chaos he was about to unleash. Whatever else, he was still my XO, and I owed him the obedience. I had hoped to get a jump on afternoon traffic, but this was probably going to take a minute.

As I stood clutching my folders, CWO3 Polk walked by. He stopped and glanced up at the sign over the door. Then he looked back at me. "Why are you out here, Staff Sergeant?"

"Sir, Capt Curtz ordered me to come to his office." I stared at the end of the hall.

CWO3 Polk frowned and saw my record book in my arms. He held out his hand for it, and I gave it to him unquestioningly. He opened it, flipped through the pages, and then closed it. He looked me dead in the eyes as he handed it over and said one word: "Leave."

"Aye, sir." I fled the building and never saw any of them again.

I later ran into the company gunnery sergeant, GySgt Calvin, in Iraq on Al-Asad. He informed me that after I had left the command, Maj Mansfield "got deep in the weeds" investigating Capt Curtz. Maj Mansfield interviewed everyone the statements even mentioned in passing, including GySgt Calvin himself and MGySgt Collins (a.k.a. MSgt T. Rex). That pleased me immensely because before I dropped the MAST paperwork, MGySgt had suggested that I should try to understand that the captain was going through a divorce and maybe I should hold my fire. Another member of the chain of command suggested that since I was departing a mere week after the allegations were made, I shouldn't pursue this because I would not be present to stop Curtz from tormenting the Marines who had trusted me with their statements. Both arguments only supported my hypothesis that many people knew what Curtz was doing and decided to look the other way. That convinced me even more that I had done the right thing.

GySgt Calvin shook his head and sighed. "I don't know what you did to him, Salz, but he's no longer in the Marine Corps. He was gone within months of your departure."

Fuck him.

PART SIX:

CAMP LEJEUNE, NORTH CAROLINA

36.

HAVING A FIELD DAY WITH THE GUN BUNNIES

Near the end of 2008, I was attached to 2/10 artillery battalion as an Arabic linguist. I was fresh out of DLI and excited to use the skills I had just learned. While there was no pressing need for artillery guns in Al-Anbar at that time, there was civil affairs work to be done; the Marine Corps had been given the mission to help rebuild Iraqi communities damaged in the war, and the commander of 2/10 volunteered his troops because deployment as a commanding officer was the pathway toward higher promotions.[39] We were given a one-week course in what being Civil Affairs Marines meant and how to do it.

It was a good deal of accounting work, like knowing how to manage a couple million dollars in reconstruction budgets to fix issues and help open shops to rebuild the economy that communities in Iraq relied upon to stay peaceful. I chose this mission out of several offered to me because I liked the idea of using my newfound Arabic powers for good, like a white-girl superhero.

There were also work-ups to do. This meant lots of field exercises to remember our basic Marine skills, such as shooting, surviving Humvee rollovers, and field hygiene. We might be headed out to blow large sums of money (and Marines are *really* good at that), but we wouldn't be doing it in luxury. We went to Fort Bragg for a weeklong field exercise. It was, like

---

39 Ideally, if a commander could lead Marines in both Afghanistan and Iraq, he would have a shot at stars on his collar one day. This led to some chicanery that I'm still angry about.

so many other things in the Corps, boring. Out in the backwoods, it was humid, dirty, grimy, and smelled like a forest's butthole. The addition of dirty, sweaty Marines did not improve the bouquet. But Marines embrace the suck, so I wasn't going to complain. I packed my things and brought a few extras for the sake of comfort. One of these was my hookah.

A hookah, for those who don't know about them, is a tall water pipe common all over the Middle East and used for smoking tobacco. It's like a bong[40] but with extra steps. Instead of setting fire to the tobacco, the crushed leaves are smeared into a flavored paste and then piled into a ceramic dish. The paste might be passion fruit, strawberry, or other flavors, and it makes the mixture smell sweet as candy. Once pressed into the ceramic dish, it is covered with tin foil. Next, small lit charcoals are placed on the foil, and the mixture is cooked. The smokers take a deep breath on the smoking tube, and flavored smoke is pulled through the pipe, through the water in the base, and into the smoker's lungs, where it feels much less harsh than cigarettes and tastes better. It was vaping before there was vaping.

I had been tasked with teaching the Marines some useful Arabic phrases and things like numbers, so I figured the hookah would bring out curious gun bunnies, whom I could instruct while they explored this new device. Hookahs were a communal pipe, unlike personal things like cigarettes, and Marines do love community. Winning!

You wouldn't think that a new device for ingesting nicotine would cause comment. But oh did it. Marine Corps culture does not like change or things that are different.

When we got back to our bivouac site at the end of the day, I set up the hookah outside my tent and lit a couple candles. Marines wandered by out of curiosity and then stayed and hung out, smoking hookah and gossiping into the night. It was a Middle Eastern way of moving the smoke pit to my front door. Crusty, old-fashioned Marines quietly and not so quietly bitched about how much attention and use the hookah was getting, and at one point, someone asked the CO if they could ban me from using it. It was far too similar to *paraphernalia*, you know, for *drugs*, which are *bad*.

In a subtle but strong and unexpected display of support, LtCol Brightman agreed to ban my hookah—but only if the complainers were willing to ban all tobacco consumption for the rest of the op. A bridge far too far, my hookah was left alone.

---

40   With marijuana legalization happening all over the US, I presume we all know what this is.

Another fine thing, in my opinion, was that as the Arabic instructor, I had rare license to actually talk to all the Marines without fear of rank differences disrupting the dynamic. In turn, I kept the conversation mostly to the professional topic at hand.

We were all sitting, passing the pipe from person to person, while I taught them how to count to twenty in Arabic. Of course, the first words people of any military branch want to learn in a foreign language are the dirty ones; Marines want to gain access to phrases like "go fuck yourself" before figuring out how to say boring things like "car" and "food." As much as I resisted, when their attention started to flag, I'd give up some ground and pull out a book called *The Dirty Side of Arabic*, laying out a few profanities to reenergize my class.

So, I was reasonably confused with their sudden delight in counting to twenty. I didn't get it at first, and was like, "Wow, Salz! You're a really good teacher! Look at how happy they are. They seem to get more giddy as we get up into the teens. This is great!"

"*A'ashera, 'hiddash, itna'asher, thelat'asher,*" I counted, with the Marines repeating after me. They snickered and elbowed each other. Here it comes! Blissfully unaware, I continued.

"*Arba'tasher, khamstashera . . .*" I paused because the class had all pronounced the word for "fifteen" and then burst out with the kind of glee Marines usually reserve for foul bodily functions.

"What the hell is so damn funny?" No one seemed ready to speak up. Corporal Yi passed off the pipe and clued me in.

"Staff Sergeant, it sounds like you're saying *cum 'stache.*"

Now that someone finally said it, the guys let their mirth go, looking at me to see if this made me uncomfortable. I rolled my eyes at the juvenile joke but otherwise made us keep going.

Whatever. I've suffered worse embarrassments.

We got to twenty, and the hookah charcoals died down shortly after. I took the pipe back and started to clean it and prep it for storage. My students dispersed, and that was that.

Later that evening, I was hanging around near the field kitchen, chatting with a young female corporal from the Public Affairs Office who had been sent out to write a story on our preparations for the coming deployment. She was a graduate of an Ivy League university who had, "for personal reasons," nonetheless decided to enlist instead of becoming an officer. Because everyone was deeply uncomfortable with a journalist (and a *female*) being in their midst, I was assigned to escort her around the camp and keep her from seeing anything too distressing beyond the number of dicks drawn on the walls of the port-o-shitters. I kept the conversation pleasant but minded what I said, in case she decided to publish anything that would come back and bite me in the ass.

Evening chow was about to be served, and Marines were lining up for food. The Marine Corps has a strict tradition that the lowest-ranking Marines eat first and staff NCOs and officers serve the troops before eating any food themselves. Thus, I was hanging out near the back of the line with Cpl Young, watching to make sure no one got left out.

Everyone in the camp knew who I was by now, and every single Marine who had attended my classes walked by me, merrily waving and shouting Arabic stuff at me. LtCol Brightman came up next to Cpl Young and me and listened for a moment, not knowing any Arabic himself. The most common remarks from the troops were along the lines of, "Hey, Staff Sergeant! Hey! *Khamstash*! Hahahahaha!"

The Marines continued to shout to me as they got in line. I stood stoic, letting one corner of my mouth turn up but no more. I was not about to acknowledge some porn shit while being flanked by a reporter and the CO. Nope. After a few minutes of this, LtCol Brightman turned to me and nodded approvingly.

"Well done, Staff Sergeant! They seem to be picking up Arabic pretty well!" I kept my eyes forward and mumbled, "Thank you, sir" as he walked off in a confident manner toward the command post.

Cpl Young turned to me and said, "Yeah, this is great!"

She scribbled in her notebook and then went after LtCol Brightman to get a few quotes for her story. I exhaled as she departed. *Thanks, guys. Glad the number fifteen amuses you.*

★ ★ ★

The next day, I saw Cpl Yi sneaking off with a large, tan-colored water can she'd "liberated" from the back of a Humvee, dragging it in the direction of the tree line. Wondering what she was up to, I followed along, not bothering to keep any distance between us. She saw me following and waved me urgently over.

"What's up, Yi?"

She set the heavy can down and shot furtive glances around the woods in case any pesky eavesdroppers were around. "I feel disgusting, Staff

Sergeant. We haven't showered in days. I'm going to do something about it."

She reached in her cargo pockets and produced the contraband stashed there. It was a full-size bottle of shampoo and a full-size bottle of conditioner. She gave me a shifty look.

"You in?"

This was exactly the kind of drug deal I was hoping for.

"Uh, hells yes I'm in. Do you have towels?" Yi and I both had long hair that went almost all the way down our backs. Washing it without towels was not to be thought of. She nodded and handed me the bottles, then picked up the can, leading me deeper into the privacy of the trees, away from the camp. We arrived at our makeshift salon.

I was truly impressed. Yi had found a camp stool we could sit on, dug a little hole to catch the water, and a couple of towels were stacked on the seat. This was field luxury at its finest. We propped our weapons within arm's reach and in our direct line of sight. Then, because this was her spa day, Yi went first.

She took all the pins, bands, and the rolled-up sock out of her black hair and shook it out. In my backpack, I always carried a hairbrush and a few other items because I never knew when I might have a wardrobe malfunction like losing a bobby pin, and the males had no tolerance for hair that was out of regulations. Instead of sitting on the camp stool, Yi propped her elbows on it and shook her hair out. I grabbed the water can and poured the lukewarm water over her hair into the little pit. Within ten or fifteen minutes, we both had clean, washed hair. In the afterglow of our ablutions, we dried our hair and then restyled it. It was only hair, but I felt like I'd just luxuriated in a hot bath instead of having tepid, barely potable water dumped on me. This is how the other half lives.

As we went about hiding the traces of our act, a male Marine came crashing through the bushes. *Shit. Shit, shit. He's probably looking for somewhere to pee, and he's going to catch us.* We both jumped up and nonchalantly tried to block as much of our contraband as we could with our bodies.

Sgt Compton cleared the bushes and looked up in surprise. He stood for a moment, taking in the scene while we both shifted uncomfortably. He glanced at the water can.

Shit. He knows.

"Is that you? That smell?"

Smell? SHIT. In our haste to get clean, we'd completely forgotten that clean hair smells strongly of, you know, shampoo. The smell was normally just part of the pleasure, but in the field, that scent wafted. He gave us an accusing stare, and finally we crumpled. I decided to take the hit since Cpl Yi was junior.

"Yeah, that's us. Sorry." I waited for him to admonish me. I outranked him, but he was within rights to at least give me a reproachful remark or two. That was better than if he went back to camp and told other people. We were wasting water, an unforgivable sin, especially when it wasn't us who had to go fill the damn water cans at the source. We were giving away our unit's position with the pleasing scent of lavender and verbena as well—another no-no.

Sgt Compton came a bit closer and lowered his voice.

"Um, uh . . . could you wash mine?" He removed his cover and looked hopefully at the water can. Cpl Yi recovered from her astonishment first and flashed a bright smile.

"Sergeant, it would be our pleasure."

On the last day of the field op, we were given a reveille time of 0500 to begin breaking down camp and packing up for movement back to Camp Lejeune. Leaving the field was a cause for celebration, although the process itself was frustrating, slow, and dull, much like everything else. I went to bed in my cammies, although I changed into my last clean green T-shirt and shorts, which I wore underneath my uniform while we were out there. No socks, though. When a Marine gets the opportunity to let their feet air out, it is vital that they take it. Poor foot hygiene is anathema to Marines. Play fast and loose with wearing clean socks and keeping dry feet, and you pay the price.

I was pulled out of a dreamless sleep by the sounds of Marines rising early to get a jump on the camp breakdown. It wasn't anywhere near 0500 yet, so I burrowed deeper in my sleeping bag, hoping to snatch a few shreds of good rest from the maw of the coming day. But artillery Marines are not Recon Marines. Recon is all about stealth and being undetected. Gun bunnies, on the other hand, don't see the point. When you're firing a triple-seven big gun, noise is not your primary concern. A gun crew doesn't whisper to each other. Every statement needs to be said at the top of your lungs in a rapid-fire code to ensure the right round, the right windage, and right timing is executed in a hot combat environment.

In other words, these guys were LOUD.

Outside my tent, hyper young men were shouting to each other. The sounds of laughter echoed from far off in the camp but without any joke I could hear. I curled up tighter and pulled my field pillow over my head, but their voices carried right through the ineffective fibers, and within a few minutes, I was bloody furious. I'm already a total bitch when I first wake up in the morning, and that's when I wake up on my own time with coffee coming. Here and now, I was being sucker-punched with stupid and unnecessary noise, and I reached my boiling point fast.

Growling, I ripped open my tent flap and came storming out, snatching up the first Marine within reach. The young man looked shocked to see me appear like a pissed-off harpy but insisted on yelling, "I SEE RED!"[41] anyway. It was pitch black outside, but *I* was the one seeing red at that moment. I let go of him and proceeded to lose my mind, swearing, cursing, making bold statements about his questionable ancestry, and above all else ordering him to shut *the* fuck up. I couldn't see much of his face except for the bits illuminated by his flashlight, but I could tell he was staring wide eyed at the ground.

Good: contrition. I'll fucking take it.

When I ran out of creative fury, before I could get a second round going, the Marine breathed in a hoarse whisper, "Staff Sergeant . . . your toenails are painted!"

This derailed my tirade. *I'm freaking out at him, and he's worried about my* toenails? I mean, he was right. They were some shade of magenta at the moment, but I'd forgotten entirely about that because I'd painted them a week ago. But really? That's what he took away from my attempted ass-chewing? I threw my hands in the air and returned to my tent. They weren't listening anyway. Maybe they all had blown out their hearing by this point. I gave up.

I packed up my things that day, and after we returned to base and were set loose for the weekend, I swore never, ever to go back to the field with artillery. It's the Marine Corps, we're all mad here, but the gun bunnies are in their own lane. And they can keep it.

---

41 A phrase gun teams use to indicate that something is wrong and must be fixed before firing can commence

37.

IF YOU DON'T HAVE SOMETHING NICE TO SAY, SAY IT WHEN YOU'RE DRUNK

Marines often like to gut-check each other to see who can keep their cool when provoked. I can't count the number of times that Hispanic and Latino Marines were teased as having "snuck into the country," Black Marines ribbed about chicken, Middle Eastern Marines poked as "suicide bombers," and the number of kitchens and sandwiches I was directed to engage with by various men was off the charts. Such banter is offensive to outsiders, but inside the service, it's a kind of equality. No one is off limits or immune, not even white Marines. If you are short, tall, handsome, hideous, whatever, someone will skewer you for it. I once teased a Mormon Marine after he asked me for some of my M&Ms during a briefing.

"Would I get half your planet when I die if we married and divorced?"

He munched the candy for what seemed a genuinely thoughtful moment before tilting his hand side to side. "Could go either way. Depends on the size of the planet."

I don't know where I stood in his estimation as a result of my joke, but his reply elevated him several notches in mine.

Remarks stay within peer groups, though, and everyone knows where the line is just by being part of the group. Teasing should never cross into outright mockery and humiliation. The other side of this is that Marines gain respect by how little they are bothered by being on the receiving end and whether they get in on the joke or not. The most points are awarded for clever responses that increase the amusement of the observers.

True, some Marines are poor judges of that line. And when someone goes too far, you are considered within your rights to put them firmly back in place.

"Women are fucking stupid. They're nowhere near as smart as men," Sparky said, staring owlishly at me as he swayed gently with intoxication.

I put my drink down on the countertop and returned his gaze. We were drinking that night in a bar off-base in Wilmington, North Carolina, celebrating the last few weeks in 2008 before we were slated to deploy to Iraq in January. Midnight was approaching, and Sparky was already several rounds in. Our friend Mike, sitting on my other side, laughed and said, "Oh boy, here we go." The bartender, Nina, merely shrugged as if she accepted this statement as true and wouldn't contest it. For a bartender, this is strictly a professional decision.

Sparky's real name was Simmons. He was a staff sergeant like me, and he looked like any other white bro-dude frat boy drinking in a college-town pub. The cheap masculinity oozed from every pore. Nonetheless, I knew he expected an outraged squawk of protest from me so he could start mocking and provoking me for his own amusement. This was a regular thing with Sparky. He'd get a few drinks in him and decide to cause a scene by being as much of a jackass as he could manage. I wasn't about to let him lead me around by the emotions.

Naw, son. This is my party.

"Okay, tell you what. You bring the most intellectual, smartest topic you know about. I mean, top-tier game here. If I can't keep up or I get lost and am outmatched, I'll buy your drinks for the rest of the night. Don't care, you can drink top shelf all night, and I'll pick up the tab, tips too."

"And if you win?" he asked.

"You have nothing I want and are capable of nothing that interests me." I smiled as if I hadn't just insulted his existence, so, naturally, he took my words at face value, which in his eyes was nothing.

"Deal!" He smirked, brimming with unearned self-satisfaction.

"Okay, go for it." I tried to be visibly relaxed and self-assured, although internally I wondered if I could afford to pay the kind of bar tab this professional drunk would likely rack up in the event of my loss.

He looked me in the eye, trying to work up to a commanding tone, and said, "Psychology and sociology. You can't master both."

I was floored, I'll admit it, but not for the reasons Sparky was expecting. As a statement, it made no sense. It was most definitely not true. I was not sure he even knew what the hell he meant by it. But his strategy was made crystal clear when the female bartender who had been setting up our round suddenly threw her hands in the air in surrender.

"Oh my God, he said words that end in -ology. I'm done already." She walked off to the other end of the bar and left me standing there in shocked disappointment.

"Come on, I'm fighting for all of our gender here!" I shouted as she departed. Then I turned back to Sparky. "What? What do you mean? Why should they be exclusive to each other?"

He looked delighted by the question, thinking he already had me on the ropes.

"My parents are both professors. One teaches sociology and the other psychology. So I know they can't both be done!" He took a swig of his beer and waited for me to tap out right then and there. To be frank, I was more upset that he was wasting my time with this lame shit instead of giving me a real challenge. That was almost more insulting than the remark that started this. Hurr, durr, you can't study two social sciences. What kind of idiotic statement is that?

"Psychology studies the behaviors of a person, as in their individual mind and behavior," I began. "Sociology studies the behavior of societies as a whole—their culture, their values, and their community. Since societies are made up of people, you are basically studying the organism as a whole rather than its components—that is, individual human beings. Psychology handles that aspect. Therefore, studying both psychology and sociology makes sense. Psychology is the microcosm, and sociology is the macrocosm. The two fields most definitely overlap."

I took a pull from my cocktail and waited for his rebuttal. I wasn't clear about whether I was right but was sure he would come back with a solid, informed counterargument, and then I'd get to stretch my mental muscles. Right? *Right?*

He looked baffled, by which I mean he looked like a man who has just unwittingly fucked himself and could feel it. In a bid for time, he ordered another beer while he groped for a way out of this.

"I have to take a piss," he grumbled and stood to find the restroom.

"Wait! I really want to hear your argument, please. Am I answering your specific question? Is there some nuance I've overlooked?"

But Sparky ignored me and walked away.

I turned to Mike. "He doesn't have a reply, does he?"

Mike sniggered and shook his head, taking a pull from his beer.

Ten minutes later—quite a piss, that—Sparky returned and plopped back on his bar stool.

"All right, you won that one. But even if you *were* smarter than me, I'm still right because you're just not normal. Women are less intelligent than—"

I finished off my drink and interrupted him.

"Shhh, shhh. Be quiet, Sparky. You're much prettier when you don't talk."

PART SEVEN:

AL ANBAR PROVINCE, IRAQ

38.

DON'T CRY OVER
UN-SPILT TEA

About a month after I arrived in Al-Anbar Province, Iraq, with 2/10 Civil Affairs Group, I was settling in as an interpreter. Secretly, I was very worried about my Arabic skills. Modern Standard Arabic—or *fus-ha*, as it was called—is not widely spoken in the Middle East. Of the twenty-two countries that have Arabic as an official language, the Arabic spoken in Bahrain was about the closest I could get without losing comprehension. Iraqi dialect was a struggle for me. For instance, I had been taught the phrase "*Kefa halik?*" as "How are you?" Iraqis instead said "*Shlonitch?*" That phrase sounded like "What color are you?" to a *fus-ha* speaker like me, so I got confused pretty quickly when speaking with locals.

But I persevered because the last thing I wanted was to be labelled as a shitty translator. I'd only had two years of training in the language, so I often relied on other *muterjima*, or interpreters, to guide me through not only the vocabulary but also the proper etiquette in each situation. I had stacks of books and dictionaries in my quarters (called a "can" because it was a converted metal box and not an actual building), which I spent at least an hour each day poring over to improve as fast as I could. I managed the thirty-something other interpreters assigned to Civil Affairs teams, handling their pay issues, leave, and team assignments as need arose. My job was not only to "terp" for my commander but also to make sure every team far afield had access to language resources.

Despite my best efforts, I still got it wrong from time to time. When I got it wrong, it was for the most part no more than mildly embarrassing.

Occasionally, however, I did manage to humiliate myself. Badly.

My commander, Maj Simons, had an event scheduled on-base at which he was to meet with LtCol Abdullah of the Iraqi army. I tried to advise him, but he did not welcome guidance from a staff sergeant, and he despised my attempts to provide tips. Of particular note was the protocol for starting and ending the meeting. Refreshments should be served, especially tea, and the conversation needed to follow the rules of politeness that involved a lot of small talk before getting to the point. Maj Simons's exit also needed to be precisely laid out to avoid giving offense. The plan was that the commander would excuse himself, citing another meeting—with Col Love, who headed RCT 8 (our umbrella command, under which we were subordinate). That way, the Iraqi lieutenant colonel would not feel slighted by preemption for a meeting with a junior American officer.

My role in all this was to arrive and serve tea and pastries to the visiting Iraqis, which included LtCol Abdullah and his entourage. Then I was to sit and listen to the conversation, take notes, and speak only when spoken to. This was fine with me because I was scared spitless that I would get lost in the conversation very quickly.

On the appointed day, LtCol Abdullah arrived with his subordinates and his own translator, a gentleman named Michael. Terps often went by first names only, so keeping them straight got a bit hairy at times. I had scrambled to find an appropriately attractive glass tea set from the protocol office, tasty-looking pastries from the DFAC (chow hall run by civilians), and, of course, hot tea. I set everything up in the conference area, which was actually a small, makeshift auditorium, placing each danish and croissant on doilies on a wooden serving tray I'd located through the generosity of the RCT gunner (the name we had for a CWO5 that wore a bursting bomb on his collar instead of just the usual chief warrant officer bars).

As the Iraqis took their seats, I scurried around, carrying the tray to each visitor, asking in my heavily formal Arabic if they would like tea or sweets. The first person I served was LtCol Abdullah. As I poured his tea, I remembered that putting honey in tea was a common practice in Iraq, so I left a little bit of room in the cup so that he might add sweetener without suffering the embarrassment of his cup spilling over. I moved on through the rest of the attendees, remembering that Maj Simons hated sweet tea and therefore filling his cup to the brim accordingly. Then I took my seat and listened.

Their conversation sounded and felt like both Maj Simons and LtCol Abdullah were reading from a prepared script that they hated. They were polite, but it just felt awkward. As things moved on, my mind started to drift. I was half listening when suddenly Michael the terp called out to me.

"You speak Arabic, Staff Sergeant?" He smiled warmly. He was bespectacled, a swarthy man with a slight build, and looked like he would be an accountant if not for this pesky war. I stood and swallowed to wet my mouth. Then I mentally grabbed at the prepared phrases I had been practicing for just this moment.

I replied in *fus-ha*, "Yes, I studied Arabic language at the Defense Language Institute in California. But I don't know any dialects."

To my delight, this made everyone smile at me, like I'd just performed a clever trick.

Michael nodded. "LtCol Abdullah has a question for you, then."

He looked amused as I walked up to the table and stood as respectfully as I knew how before the Iraqi officer. With everyone staring at me, I did everything in my power to be innocuous. I asked in Arabic how I could help him, suppressing the urge to tremble. *Don't fuck this up, don't fuck this up, don't fuck this up . . .*

LtCol Abdullah asked me something in Iraqi Arabic and gestured to his untouched teacup. To my horror, I had no idea what he said. I glanced hopefully at Michael while the officer repeated his question. I asked in Arabic if there was something wrong with his tea and said I'd be happy to replace it for him if so. But he just looked annoyed and gestured to Michael to straighten this out. Michael laughed and said in *fus-ha*, "He wants to know why you gave him less tea than your commander."

My eyes were wide as I replied, "So he would have room for honey without spilling!"

That came out in English. Michael rattled it back in Iraqi Arabic, and everyone laughed. Michael explained to me in English that giving a guest less tea than everyone else was an insult in Iraqi culture. I gasped as if I'd been stung by a scorpion and covered my mouth. *Damn, damn, damn!* The most important mission I had as a linguist so far, and I just fucked it up royally.

I apologized profusely to LtCol Abdullah in *fus-ha*, explaining that I had no idea I had insulted him and I was very sorry, adding that I was only a student and still learning.

To my extreme relief, he laughed heartily and smiled at me, reassuring me in Arabic that I could understand that he was not offended but rather amused at my misguided error. I apologized once more and thanked him for his forgiveness, then backed away from the table.

Maj Simons then delivered his prepared excuses to depart and stood to shake hands with LtCol Abdullah. The major departed on his own while the junior American officers stayed behind until LtCol Abdullah and his team left. I stood by the door as they exited and thanked each person for coming. When I thanked LtCol Abdullah, he gave me the most intense eye contact and put his hand over his heart, nodding before exiting the building. Once everyone was gone, I breathed all the tension out in one long exhale. I began gathering up the debris and counting cups to make sure I returned the gunner's tea set intact. Once everything was restored to its normal state, I went back to my can and covered my face with my hands. *Goddamnit.*

Just when I'd gotten good and deep into beating myself up for my ignorant oversight, there was a knock at the door of my can. *Oh God, here we go. Here comes the ass-chewing.* I mentally prepared and went to answer the door.

There stood Lt Nelson, the Navy officer who was serving as Maj Simons's XO (executive officer). I greeted him and then stood by in silence. *Let's just get this over with.*

"Hey, Salz, I just wanted to stop by and tell you that was a great job you just did. LtCol Abdullah was very impressed with you, as we all were. Well done. I appreciate it." He smiled. "Thanks. We'll see you back at the shop after chow, okay?"

"Yes, sir. Thank you, sir."

Well. So, that just happened. Guess I'll skip my planned crying session and go eat lunch instead.

39.

HOSPITALS AND HUMMERS

Word had gotten around that Civil Affairs had a Marine Arabic interpreter, and I was requested to support other subordinate units within RCT 8. This was great, as far as I was concerned, because it meant I got to go "over the wire," out in town and to ceremonies and such, instead of being locked down on-base.

My first two times over the wire, I was attached to the medical officer's team. Our mission took us to the village hospital in Hit, which was peaceful and safe for the most part. We were tasked to find out what medicines, equipment, and other needs they might have that we could provide. We rode on a convoy into the village and stopped about half a mile from the hospital. Once we exited the armored personnel carriers, we formed up in a staggered line and patrolled to the hospital. I was paired up with a colonel from the Army, a small, round woman with bright-red hair who looked like everybody's aunt. A doctor who served in the Army Reserve and had been activated for this mission, she was a delightful change from the grouchy Marines I normally worked with. She talked about her grandchildren and how the armor plate carriers they made her wear just chaffed so bad.

The rest of the group were infantry Marines. Our escorts and protectors, they were kitted out like the Marines you see in movies. Every possible type of weaponry that could be attached to their body armor was on display. They had the dark sunglasses, gloves, Kevlar helmets, ear protection, magazines full of ammo, K-bar knives, the works. Then there was the colonel and me, the "noncombatants," wearing body armor and carrying only 9 mm pistols on leg holsters.

The colonel threw me for a protocol loop when she jovially told me to just call her Anne. The disciplined Marine in me would have rather chewed my tongue out than call a colonel by her first name, so I settled on the good ol' "Ma'am" (which sort of rhymes).

The hospital was thronged with people. This was not like a hospital in the States, where the movements of families, patients, doctors, nurses, and other staff were all regulated by zones. This was the kind of hospital that doubled as a community center. Everyone in the village seemed to be hanging out there, regardless of the state of their health. The courtyard leading to the main doors had men, women, kids, whole families for generations just enjoying the sun and catching up on the latest gossip.

The appearance of the US military there didn't even cause comment. The grunts who accompanied us had been to this village so often over the last couple years that most of them knew Iraqi Arabic and had favorite villagers they chatted with when they came to town. The grunts peeled off and went to their own waiting area, except for two who accompanied us on our tour of the hospital. Ma'am and I stripped off our armor inside the hospital director's office because we didn't want to give a poor impression of why we were there. Our first planned stop was the women's ward. Strict social rules dictated that only Ma'am and I could enter, so the grunts posted up outside the ward's doors, and we went in.

In preparation for the trip, I had shoved a handful of Beanie Babies in my pack. Those little stuffed toys were all the rage back in the United States, and the company had provided miniature versions of their toys for us to hand out when kids were around to help calm the scene at times. As I trailed behind Ma'am, relaying her questions to the staff in Arabic, I occasionally bent down and smiled at the numerous small children there with their mothers. I knelt to hand a small white bunny to a little girl of about three, saying in Arabic, "Aren't you pretty!" She looked at me warily but seized the toy anyway, obviously bored out of her little mind from waiting around in the ward. A female relative covered from head to toe in black cloth scolded me in Iraqi Arabic, but since I didn't understand a thing she said, it failed to register much. I just lowered my head and went back to following Ma'am.

Most of the hospital staff spoke English, so my services were only called upon from time to time. One male doctor of very junior status (I knew this because every time the chief surgeon dropped his finished cigarettes on the floor in the hall, it was this man who scrambled to pick them up and throw them away) quietly asked me on an aside for more medicine to treat bedsores. I nodded and scribbled a note in my notebook. He followed that up by saying, "*Arabetich muu zain*," which translates to "Your Arabic sucks." I rolled my eyes and replied, "*Thanks for that*, Lateef," also in Arabic. He avoided me for the rest of the visit.

When we departed the women's ward, we were met by the hospital's chief surgeon. He was probably about sixty years old, chain-smoked the whole time we walked the hospital (except in the operating theater, thank God), and spoke a gleeful, lilting English with perfection. This met with Ma'am's approval since it freed her from her dependence on me. She was now in her comfort zone, speaking English with another medical professional of high rank, and the chief surgeon took to her right away. This freed me up to coo happily over the adorable little kids that several Iraqi grandfathers introduced me to along the way. I babbled and handed out toys, having some actual fun in the process.

After an hour of wandering this labyrinth full of Iraqis giving us bored looks, the chief surgeon decided he couldn't hold back his excitement anymore and escorted us out to the back courtyard where his most prized possession waited in the noonday sun: a brand-new, deep-blue H3 Hummer SUV. It was very shiny, and he beamed with such pride that you'd think it was his firstborn son. Being the wet blanket that I am, all I could think about was how the hell someone even got that vehicle out here, undamaged, to begin with. I wasn't brave enough to wonder how he had afforded it. Those cars were boatloads of money in the United States, for Chrissake. Considering that Civil Affairs was pumping something like $5,000,000 into Al-Anbar Province, I had some ideas anyway.

The visit wrapped up with a luncheon hosted by the director of the hospital. Iraqi custom was to eat with the hands, but we had just strolled through every sick wing of a hospital, so there was the matter of hygiene to address. The director looked a bit confused about why we wanted to wash our hands before eating but offered us the use of his private restroom for the purpose. I went in expecting a sink and a mirror, maybe a toilet or even a shower.

Nope. No sink, no soap, only a tiled wall and floor with a hole in it. Because flushing was occasionally required to remove waste, a green garden hose dangled from a hook on the wall with the spout on the floor close to the hole. I turned around immediately and excused myself to the courtyard. I found the grunts clustered in the shade of a large tree, smoking and eating kabobs that one of them had procured from a shop across the street. I asked in a horrified whisper if any of them had hand sanitizer to get me through this moment of polite crisis. The grunts thought this was the funniest shit, but one had soap, and I used the water from my canteen to make up the rest. When I returned to lunch, I was stealthy in grabbing only the pieces of chicken I knew no one had come anywhere near. Stomach upsets suck, but stomach upsets when you are looking at a three-hour-plus convoy home take on a whole new terror.

We finally departed back for Al-Asad Air Base as the sun started dropping lower. Being out after dark was too great a security risk. Upon returning to my shop, I dropped all my body armor and felt fatigue creep in quickly. I was sticky, sweaty, and covered in dirt and probably chicken grease. My hair was an absolute disaster from wearing a Kevlar for six damn hours.

"Where the hell have *you* been?" Lt Nelson emerged from the building and came toward me while I cleared my weapon and removed the magazine, checking to make sure the gun was still on "safe." Accidentally discharging your weapon was a great way to lose all your rank and career hopes, and I'm not about that life.

"We . . . just got back, sir?" I didn't know how that wasn't obvious, but apparently that had to be said. All around us, grunts were dismounting and going through their post-convoy procedures. Most of us still had our Kevlars on.

"We have a meeting starting at 1800, like we do every day. You're late." Lt Nelson sniffed in disdain for my poor timekeeping. The meeting he referenced was merely four or five of us in Civil Affairs talking about the day and then concluding with a game of dominoes. "Major Simons doesn't like being held up by a staff sergeant."

His audacity astonished me. I knew he was Navy and not a Marine, but I was pretty sure he was aware that the timetable for our operation that day was handled far above my pay grade.

"Sorry, sir. Next time I'll tell the convoy commander to pick up the pace." I made sure that while the words were clear-cut sarcasm, my tone was not. Ma'am was a full-bird colonel who could've put Lt Nelson's dick in the dirt if she wanted to. I could see why he chose a softer target while loathing him for it.

"Just get inside. We're sick of waiting." He turned on his heel and went back to the office. Since everything about his indignation was ridiculous, I jettisoned the whole conversation and finished the work of disarming. What a prick.

40.

MUSIC SOOTHES THE SAVAGE VAGINA

One aspect of being female that has caused problems for ages is the menstrual cycle. Fighting has always involved a certain willingness to spill blood, but spilling your own blood on a regular schedule is somehow disgusting. Men who would happily pee on the entire landscape have long found the notion of bleeding from your reproductive system inexplicably repulsive. On the one hand, disease has been a terrible problem for armies throughout history, and part of a fighting force gushing blood from time to time without visible violence can cause sicknesses to spread. On the other hand, with some effort on the part of the wounded party, the hygiene issues can be controlled and dealt with in an appropriate, clean manner. So long as I kept an eye on the calendar, I could appear no different from the males. I made sure that the coming and going of my cycle went unnoticed by everyone but me.

Ultimately, there was no escaping it. The facts of the menstrual cycle did hinder my deployment capabilities. I needed to be near facilities like a shower at least once every three or four days, so while the males could be sent to the far-flung reaches of the province and then forgotten, referred to as "fire and forget," there was great care taken to ensure I never ventured far from civilization. It cost me, reputation-wise, because I never got the assignments that gave a Marine real credibility. I was escorted anytime I visited an outpost or FOB,[42] and then ushered back before anyone could come to harm. No one ever articulated this potential harm. It was just

---

42   Forward operating base

expected that everyone understood *why* I shouldn't be allowed to go on normal patrols, and that hinderance, in turn, meant it was easier for commanders to just leave me sitting on a shelf at times. If I didn't speak Arabic, I don't think I would have been allowed on a deployment. There were plenty of male data Marines—whose hygiene needs were considered far less complicated—ready to be sent anywhere and left there for about a year.

We female Marines occasionally commiserated, groaning about our cramps or about how the unit run had been especially rough this week. We quietly polled each other for suggestions on how much Motrin[43] would make a three- or four-mile run more bearable and which products would best support our boring but demanding lives.

In Iraq, this aspect of female existence crept into my work as well. The United States saw fit to ship entire CONNEX boxes full of feminine products to Al-Anbar, and we were to somehow get these things to the Iraqi women without the Iraqi men having to see or deal with the aspect of the female body they found eternally abhorrent. Eventually, we gave up on the task and just buried the whole delivery in the desert. Somewhere, in a land far away, an entire shipment of maxi pads molders away for future archaeologists to marvel over.

One day, I was sitting in the courtyard of our building, smoking a cigarette and waiting for the next mealtime, a marker that now served as the entire structural principle of my days. Life was pretty lonely as a staff sergeant. Considered too high ranking to talk to the sergeants and below,[44] I was also too young, at twenty-nine, to talk with the other staff NCOs. The gunnery sergeants were all thirty-seven or older, with at least one ex-wife they passionately hated and a pile of worries about retirement. I was not at that point in my life, so we didn't connect.

On that day, Cpl Harrison wandered out to the courtyard, groaning, and plopped down on the concrete bench opposite me. A tattooed Latina who had just turned thirty, she had that blend of raw strength and chaos that marked out many female Marines. We worked out in the gym together, and while I was running on the treadmill, Cpl Harrison would

---

43   Vitamin M, as we called it, because of the frequency and ease with which the Navy corpsmen handed it out

44   One odd exception to the rule was Cpl Yi (not her real name), who was my age and female. Despite the difference in rank, she and I could talk and hang out and go to the gym without inspiring too much malicious gossip.

do dead lifts and bodybuilding things. Today she looked as fed up as most of us felt daily.

I ashed my cigarette and gave her a wry smile. "Day going that good, Yee?"

Through the precarious rules of protocol, I was allowed to address her without rank due to my seniority but not allowed to use her first name. Only officers did that kind of thing. Nicknames, however, were permitted without being considered undue familiarity, so I called her "Yee," short for Yvonne. Yee looked at me, her frustration plain on her face.

"Oh my fucking GOD, my period is killing me today! I feel like I'm being punched in the vag. This is bullshit!" Yee took another drag of her cigarette, exhaling a big cloud and closing her eyes. She pulled her feet up onto the bench and set her chin on her knees. She was shorter than I, barely five and half feet tall, so when she curled up in her desert cammies, she resembled a small, angry sandbag.

"Did you take any vitamin M? Drank water, all the usual stuff?"

She shot me a look like I was stupid for asking, closing her eyes again and nodding slowly.

"Yes. Nothing fucking works. They should be allowed to give us something stronger than that."

I chuckled. "Whiskey would be nice right about now. Nothing sorts out muscle pain like a big ol' dose of drunkenness." I sighed wistfully. I didn't drink much back in the United States, but as soon as I got here, where even beer was hard to come by and strictly forbidden in any case, I suddenly craved a bottle of wine or something.

Yee continued, "My vagina is pissed I'm not making a baby, and it's trying to kill me. I hate this."

Smirking, I asked, "Maybe try playing music to it. Music soothes pain; I read that somewhere."

Yee groaned. "Yes, let me just drag my laptop out here and crank some jazz. Maybe if I sit on the speakers, that'll do the trick." She winced as a new cramp squeezed her momentary humor from her face.

I hated to see her hurting. The only thing I could do was try to make her laugh. "Better idea! I can sing to your vagina and maybe get it to calm down!" We both snorted and laughed, the preposterous idea taking her mind off the pain for a second. She took it one step further.

"Yep, lemme just spread my legs so it can hear you!" She leaned back in the seat and, in a display that would be vulgar anywhere else, put her knees in different time zones, grinning at me as we both giggled. But I was not going to be one-upped.

I leaned in until my face was almost level with, and between, her knees. Then, in my legendarily bad singing voice, I began to belt out "I Will Always Love You" like Whitney Houston would have done. (Spoiler alert: I am not Whitney Houston.)

"If I should stay, I would only be in your way. So I'll go, but I know I'll think of you every step of the waaaaay!" I crooned.

Yee cackled as I got to the chorus, holding her legs in the air and laughing hysterically.

"And I-iiiiiiiiii-eeeye will always [deep breath] loooove yooouuuuuu ooh ooh oh!" I kept cracking my lines as I tried not to laugh while singing.

Then, out of nowhere, we were not alone anymore.

"What. The. Actual. Fuck!"

The male voice caught us both off guard, and we turned to look at the doorway to the courtyard. Sgt Tietje stood there, an unlit cigarette hanging forgotten from his fingers, staring at us like we were both completely mad. I felt my face rush with blood. Yee dropped her knees, cracking up like this was the funniest shit she'd seen all day. Her background made her far less prone to embarrassment, so she just picked her cigarette back up and returned to her normal position like nothing had happened. I leaned back and straightened my posture, hoping like hell Sgt Tietje would forget what he had seen and heard.

Oh my God. I'm going to die of embarrassment.

"Hi, Sergeant!" Yee called to him. "My period's killing me, so Staff Sergeant was just helping me out!" Yee refused to feel shame about anything, and her honesty was occasionally more upsetting than the reality. Sgt Tietje nodded slowly.

"Okay. Wow. Um, I'm going to go to the head. Uh . . . yeah."

Sgt Tietje escaped the courtyard to find the port-o-potties. Yee winked at me, and we both burst out laughing. Putting out her smoke, she stood, stretched, smiled, and prepared to head back toward the building.

"Oh, before I forget! It's Latin Dance Night at the RCT classroom. You coming?" Yee leered at me. She knew damn well I had less rhythm than a concussed camel.

Latin Dance Night had been one of my deployment's bigger surprises. Shortly after we arrived to Al-Asad, a lot of us first-timers were nervous and anxious, not knowing what to expect in a war zone. The Latinx

Marines, on the other hand, knew *exactly* what to do. Someone found a couple strands of Christmas lights, another Marine had a laptop and some high-quality speakers, and several Marines compiled a killer playlist from the morale server.[45] Almost as soon as we touched down, the Marines had obtained permission to use the empty RCT classroom where units were briefed during the day, and they converted it to a field night club every Friday evening. Wearing regulation green PT gear, Marines would turn up, set their weapons off to one side of the dance floor, and proceed to boogie to reggaeton music. Yee's dance specialty was the bachata.

"Maybe," I replied, "but you know I can't dance."

"Who cares? Just come and hang out, have some pizza." Yee shimmied a bit. "Besides, I could always teach you, *blanchita*." With that final thought, Yee left.

I sat for a minute longer before following suit. *Well,* I thought, *maybe I can't dance, but that would still be less awkward than handing maxi pads to Iraqi women. Free pizza is free pizza.*

---

45   A morale server was an enormous, shared repository of music, movies, and television shows that were 100 percent pirated and continued to accrue content as each unit came and went. It was an entertainment lifeline that would've been totally illegal in the States.

41.

CATCH-ALL RULE 134

Lounging in the smoke pit a few weeks later, I flipped through books on my Kindle, alternating with paperwork assigned to me by MSgt Fox and soaking up the heat. Deployment had enough wall-to-wall boredom to stress a three-toed sloth. Despite the daytime heat, I preferred to sit outside so I could smoke while I worked.

I was on one of the three concrete benches in the courtyard when Cpl Yi burst into the smoke pit and began storming around as she tried to light her cigarette. She was muttering under her breath and getting more agitated each time the lighter failed to work. Finally, after managing to light the cigarette, she lost it and threw the lighter hard against the back wall of the courtyard.

"Fucking HELL!" Cpl Yi took a trembling drag from her cigarette. "Staff Sergeant, what the fuck is wrong with these guys!" It was almost a growl.

"Hey, Yi, how's it going? You okay?" It always pays to start with the dumb questions first. Her face contorted with her anger.

"These fucking PIGS," Cpl Yi snapped. "I just found out who's been spreading rumors about me. Argh, I just want smash them for this shit! Why do they even *need* to whisper about me in the first place?"

I yawned. "Yi, you know these guys. They gossip like crazy, and female Marines are always in season when the haters need someone to hate on. This can't be the first time you've had to deal with this." I flipped a few of the pages laid out on the bench next to me.

"It sure as fuck isn't, but I really didn't want to have to deal with this right now." Flicking the cigarette butt into a discarded ammo can, Yi finally sat, stewing in her resentment. "This PFC is going around telling everyone I'm cheating on my husband and that I'm easy."

"Does he have any proof? Like pictures or videos?" I scribbled over an inventory item on my spreadsheet. I was only kind of paying attention. *Where the fuck did my highlighter go? It was right freaking there!* I shuffled my papers.

"No, *of course* he doesn't! It's hard enough to be an NCO in the first place, but this asshole is undermining my authority and destroying my reputation!" Cpl Yi lit a new cigarette and exhaled a huge cloud of smoke. "I guess I'm a whore now."

Her obvious pain and frustration started to pull my mind away from paperwork.

We had both been targets of whisper campaigns before. It's one of those trial-by-fire things all women Marines go through once they join their first command. Of the utmost concern to curious Marines is always the major question: "Who are you having sex with?" Thus fueled, the rumor mill turns day after day, growing increasingly hysterical about all the genitals until it finds the critical answer. If a female Marine is seen walking with a male, they are now officially having sex. By that count, I'd had more lovers than Aphrodite.

"Wait, you said that the PFC admits he doesn't have any hard evidence to back up his gossiping, right?" I muttered, shuffling printouts for the fifty-sixth time today.

"Yes, *of course* he has no evidence!" Yi flicked her cigarette. "But why does that fucking matter when the rumors are already damaging me? Why do these diseased dickholes need to discuss *my* love life?"

I put my pencil in my mouth to help me think. "Why don't you just write him up? You know who the culprit is. You're a corporal, and he's not. Just give that dude a counseling or page 11 for disrespect. Hell, maybe what he's saying is worse than we think—"

"Counseling? Page 11? Do you think anyone in the entire command will back me up if I try to discipline a grunt PFC? Please." Cpl Yi sneered and took a drag from her cigarette. "I wouldn't know which articles of the UCMJ applied to this to start with. I just want to make him stop doing what he's still doing to this day."

"So, charge him with slander." I examined the work roster for the next two weeks. "That should shut him up a bit, or at least quiet him down. I mean, every single female Marine has had to contend with all the rumors, the ghastly gossip, and out-of-control folklore that haunts their steps the entire way."

After a few minutes passed, I looked up to find her silently staring at me.

"You okay, Yi?"

Cpl Yi regarded me as if rainbows had suddenly burst out of my skull.

"Say that again, Staff Sergeant? Please, one more time and a bit slower."

"Charge him with slandering you." I shrugged. "Why?"

Cpl Yi's entire demeanor changed. She approached me and asked, "Which article of the UCMJ would I base the charges on?"

"You can always just go with UCMJ article 134." *Great, now I've lost the black pen. Ugh.* "Article 134 gives you all the power you could want."

Without another word, Cpl Yi turned and went straight back to our offices. I tried to figure out if I had said or done something dumb, but nothing came to mind, so I returned to my monotonous tasks. *She probably won't do anything really radical.*

That evening at the shop, Cpl Yi finally reappeared, looking very satisfied with herself. When she stopped in the doorway to my office she whispered, "Hey, Staff Sergeant! Hey! Let's go smoke. I've got to tell you what happened!"

Like a lot of people, I got a small, happy thrill at being effective.

"What's up? What did ya do?" I grabbed my tobacco and followed her back to the place where it all began. Before either of us had lit the first cigarette, Cpl Yi burst out with the story.

"I did what you suggested and confronted PFC Rumormill. His staff sergeant was also there when the conversation kicked off. You'll never guess what happened next. I told PFC Rumormill I was going to charge him with slandering me and undermining my authority." She paused. "He looked directly at his own staff sergeant for help and asked him if this was possible. Like he couldn't believe his lies have consequences. His staff sergeant backed me up that slander charges are absolutely a real thing. PFC Rumormill is now closed for business."

"Makes sense to me. I mean, you could not get away with vulgar speculation about MSgt Fox or MSgt Wysocki's love lives. You can't go around whispering that they're super hardcore into ice cream and wild goat porn. That wouldn't be allowed to stand at all. They'd find you and whoop your ass."

Cpl Yi performed a brief happy dance. "I had no idea that there were rules that I could use to fight back! I thought we just had to put up with the bullshit and hope like hell they'd get bored and take a hint."

"I'm surprised too, Yi. Truth be told, I had no idea that it would work at all."

I laughed, but I worried that I might have given a powerful tool to someone whose leadership abilities I barely knew. On the other hand, it felt great to finally have an option, a weapon, to deal with the frequent, vicious, caustic attacks on our character.

42.

THE GIRL AND THE FOX

Many people I worked with in Iraq could be described as idiosyncratic, but no one could out-idiosyncrasy Master Sergeant Fox.[46] Whereas most master sergeants stomped and prowled, MSgt Fox just sort of smoothly materialized in rooms and meetings. Other senior enlisted Marines scowled, used tobacco, planned their retirement, and bitched viciously about their ex-wives, but not MSgt Fox. Most times, he sat quietly and stayed focused on his computer screen, not saying much of anything.

He was a slender Black man of medium height and sharp intellect. Marines usually carry on conversations loudly and with all sorts of crude remarks thrown in for good measure, but MSgt Fox didn't say anything for an entire hour sometimes. When he wasn't unnerving everyone by keeping his thoughts to himself, he was off playing basketball (every day at 10:45 sharp, come hell or high water) or getting a game of dominoes going. He was intimidating not because he towered over others with a fierce expression but because he gave them his *full attention*. Most Marines never give anyone or anything their *full attention*, so it could really rattle a person when MSgt Fox simply stared at them like he already knew what they were about to say and was just waiting to see how they were going to screw this up.

Deployment forces people into close quarters for up to thirteen months or more. MSgt Fox was 2/10's comm chief and therefore oversaw the data shops and was in charge of me while I was on Al Asad. The other members of

---

46 Not his real name

our team respected him, and the CO, Major Simons,[47] wanted to be friends with him. I tried pretty hard to stay quiet in the office we shared and not upset him. I could never tell what was going on in his head.

After a few weeks, I decided to see if I could figure out his angle. The months of silence ahead of me if we never spoke was too terrible to contemplate. But when I ventured the occasional witty or amusing remark, he just gave me a look and then went back to his own world. The look seemed to say, "You're trying to be funny. Don't try again."

One very warm afternoon, we were sitting in our office, and I was reading. The offices were not fancy in RCT 8. Sandy concrete floors, plain white walls, a window air conditioner that worked only sometimes, and a wooden door no one had bothered to sand or finish made up the accommodation. The desks were solid wood but very worn and old. Our laptops looked like they had spent more time in Iraq than the Iraqis had. The chairs had been retconned from some much better funded shop, so we had that going for us. To complete the room was an old couch that had also been relocated from a more luxurious place. A desk fan or two really tied the place together. We'd rigged some 550 cord and a full water bottle to the door so that it shut itself anytime we went in or out, to protect the small amount of environmental control we managed to achieve.

That was it. The silence of the fans and the oppressive heat of the afternoon filled every available square millimeter of the office. My rifle, which I despised having to carry everywhere I went and otherwise loathed with every fiber of my being, was propped in the corner behind my desk. I previously had a pistol which I loved because it was light, easy to carry in a thigh holster, and far more manageable overall, but our lieutenant felt that *he'd* much rather have a pistol (like all the cool officers had) than a rifle, so he ordered me to trade weapons with him so he wouldn't have a heavier burden.

It was ridiculous and petty of him, but he knew he could bully me into submission, whereas the other pistol-carrying gunnery sergeants he'd tried to swap with had almost choked laughing in his face. Stripping *me* of my sidearm was far easier because he knew Maj Simons, who hungered for the approval of the more senior enlisted men and could not have cared less about me in any way, would back him up and I'd have no support. Still, I tried everything short of outright saying "Fuck you," but I lost the fight. Adding

---

47   Major Simons was normally a Cobra pilot, so this enlisted ground-side world was
     alien and he hated it.

negligent insult to injury, Lt Nelson had not bothered to secure ammunition or magazines for the rifle before forcing the exchange, having turned in his own to the armory. Since I was routinely going over the wire, unlike him, I had to use connections within the unit to fix that little oversight on his part so I wouldn't be completely helpless on the next convoy.[48]

I sipped water and turned the pages on my Kindle, trying to ignore the sweat trickling from my neck. I had no idea what day it was anymore.

MSgt Fox suddenly locked his laptop, rose from his desk, and jogged out the door and down the hall. *Maybe the major summoned him,* I thought. Moments later, he returned with the tiniest smile on his face, holding several printed-out photos. I decided this was a good time to try to start up a conversation.

"Everything all right, Master Sergeant? Anything I can help with?"

MSgt Fox shook his head slowly while admiring whatever was on the paper. Grunting quietly with self-satisfaction, he set the documents on his desk and left the office again. I was bored and nosy, so I stood to see more clearly what was on the page. *Intel briefings,* I thought. *Graphics for convoy routes maybe.*

It was Angelina Jolie—a full-page-size photo of Angelina Jolie, licking her finger seductively while giving the camera the kind of smoldering, come-hither gaze most of us never receive in real life. In large white letters, outlined in black, the text across the bottom of the photo said, *IF YOU WASH YOUR HANDS, I'LL LICK YOUR FINGERS.* I was utterly perplexed. What kind of new kink was this?

MSgt Fox returned and caught me staring at the pictures. He smirked and finally spoke, his voice deep and quiet. "The guys here are disgusting. They don't wash their hands after they use the head, and it grosses me out. I'm going to put these up on the mirrors above the sinks."

He stared into space, clearly envisioning the reaction he would get and enjoying the vision. Then he scooped up the papers and, with a roll of tape, marched off. After the door closed, he peeked back through and said, "Oh, and . . . I'm going to the head."

Several weeks later, I was performing yet another mundane task that needed doing but that I completely hated: gear inventory. The CO wanted me to personally sign for gear that was scattered across all of Al Anbar

---

48   I remain very, very salty about this little episode.

Province—counting everything I could not physically find or see. Why? So that he wouldn't have to. That way, if anything went missing, it was only a staff sergeant that got burned.

It was no joke. Gear inventories were the death of many careers, and Maj Simons wasn't about to lose his over some stupid crypto. After being at loggerheads over signing my own (career) death warrant, MSgt Fox stepped in and agreed to oversee the inventory, breaking the stalemate.

I sat with several piles of gear, going through a printout of a spreadsheet of zillions of serial numbers. As I matched each piece with its spreadsheet entry, I made a mark and then moved it to another pile. One piece was giving me trouble, however. I double-checked the list: one monocular, unit of issue one each, no calibration required, etc. But there was no monocular anywhere in the pile. A monocular was pretty much just binoculars, for those who might wonder, but, you know, mono. I dug through the crate in front of me and couldn't find the damn thing. Finally, I gave up and went to tell MSgt Fox that something was missing.

MSgt Fox was in the room next to our office, which served as a sort of conference room and place for checking high-side emails containing situation reports from all over Iraq. Like everything else, it was a hasty construction of crappy wood furniture, old desks, and yet more sand. MSgt Fox's compatriot, MSgt Wysocki, was leaning way back in a chair in the far corner, pretending to huff canned air (no one in their right mind does this), and then muttering phrases like "Iwo Jima!"

In stark contrast to MSgt Fox, MSgt Wysocki was a giant of a Polish dude with the spiky, short haircut of someone who is just barely in regulations. MSgt Fox stood on the other side of the room, peering at MSgt Wysocki through the monocular. He frowned, took it away from his eye, flipped down the red lens filter, and then looked through it again, trying to adjust some part of the visual. Finally, he gave a frustrated sigh and said, "Marine, do you know you're ugly?"

Welp, I guess I found my monocular. I coughed and asked, "Excuse me, Master Sergeant, could I have that piece of gear for a moment? I need to verify the serial number."

Without taking his eyes off the corner of the room, he tossed it to me. "Sure, go nuts."

He left the conference room, and I went back to our office. After concluding the inspection, MSgt Fox signed off on the paperwork, and I could finally get back to doing my real job.

43.

HOLY MARINE CORPS ORDERS AND OTHER MYSTERIES OF CHAOS THEORY

Marines who are deployed have a different set of rules from Marines who are back on-base in the United States. The Marines with whom I deployed had to grapple with such restrictions as no alcohol,[49] no fornicating of any kind, and no leave back to the United States unless it had been scheduled months in advance. While leave is considered a right and not a privilege, because Iraq was still technically a combat theater in 2009, commanders had an unusual degree of latitude to deny leave requests.

The only impetus that could get a Marine leave to go home at a moment's notice was the dreaded Red Cross message (RCM). RCMs work like this: If a Marine's family back home suffers some tremendous loss such as the death of a parent, sibling, or grandparent, then the family can send a Red Cross message to the Marine Corps. Hospitals and affiliated institutions like law enforcement are equipped to send these messages as needed. Once the news of tragedy via RCM is routed to Headquarters Marine Corps, they track down the recipient and get word to his or her unit ASAP. By their very nature, RCMs trigger certain procedures and protocols that absolutely have to be obeyed, or else the offending commander might face a court-martial or worse. Think *Saving Private Ryan*, except with a lot less heroism.

After the Marine is notified, the unit begins to process that person

---

49   Regardless of Iraq being a "dry country," the prohibition was enforced because drunk Marines carrying an M16 A2 with eight full magazines of live ammo each equals *no*.

for emergency leave, set to begin within twenty-four to forty-eight hours. Travel to their home state is arranged, and leave is granted for two weeks.

One evening, as I was heading to the chow hall, I saw Sgt Tietje. We stopped to chat, and Tietje gave me the heads-up that an RCM was coming down for Sgt Porter.

"I just found out from admin. They're trying to get ahold of Maj Simons." Sgt Tietje served as the CO's clerk, so naturally he knew things first, and Sgt Porter was his roommate. "Porter already knows. His best friend and cousin, I guess, got into a serious car accident. He was calling them when I left for chow, but I gathered that the cousin didn't make it."

"Damn, that's a kick in the dick. Is he okay?"

Tietje scrunched his face. "He seems okay, but maybe he's still in shock. He said he was going to the office to use the computers and check his email."

"Okay, I'm going to go look for him after I eat. Thanks, Tietje."

Thirty minutes later, I walked over to the beige concrete block that served as our offices. Poking my head into each room, I finally located Sgt Porter sitting in the clerk's office by himself. Before I could step in the room to talk with him, MSgt Fox called for me from the conference room at the end of the hall.

Inside, Maj Simons, Lt Nelson, and MSgt Fox were all discussing what they should do about Sgt Porter. Not what they *could* do to help the Marine, but rather how little they could do and still meet the minimum requirements in the Marine Corps order. Disgusted, I sat silently on one of the tables and just listened.

"There's no way in hell I'm giving him two weeks leave right now." Major Simons always did have a soft heart. "Our manpower numbers won't look good. Besides, it's a pain in the ass to make those arrangements, and then we'll be short one person for half the month."

Lt Nelson never missed a chance to toady up to his boss, so he chimed in, "I don't see what the big deal is. It's not like his mom died. It was just some cousin or something. If we let Porter take leave for a distant cousin, then we'll end up having every Marine trying to use that as an excuse to get some leave. We've got to hold the line."

Inside, I seethed. This was the main concern of our leadership? Preventing Marines from "abusing" Red Cross messages? This was extra-special stupid because the Red Cross always verifies the tragedy before they agree to send the message. The death or life-threatening illness is confirmed by a doctor. Devaluing the loss of life because you "don't see what the big deal is" is utter bullshit, in my not-so-humble opinion. Besides, we weren't doing shit day in and day out. For months, we'd basically stared at the ceiling and taken turns running to the coffee shop or the gym. Porter's absence would have a net zero effect on the unit.

"Excuse me, *gentlemen*," I growled, "but has anyone arranged for Sgt Porter to see the chaplain? I mean, maybe it's just me and I'm stupid, but refusing to grant emergency leave to a distraught Marine and then sending him back to his can with a weapon and six magazines of live ammo is probably a very poor idea. Did any of you call to see if we can at least get him to someone he can talk to?"

Both officers froze, jaws slack. Of course they hadn't considered it. When the only thing they were paying attention to was themselves and their own inconvenience, the Marine's well-being came in dead last. Lt Nelson sealed my contempt for him by replying, "Yeah, why don't *you* take care of that, Staff Sergeant."

He smirked. Maj Simons stood and put his hands in his pockets. "His leave is denied. He'll just have to make do here. I'm not giving up a single Marine for a cousin's death. Forget it."

With that, Maj Simons turned back to the real concerns on his plate. "Hey, MSgt Fox, wanna set up the dominos? I could go for a game or two right about now."

I excused myself and went out to the smoke pit. I wasn't just pissed; I was fucking raging inside. This was completely wrong.

I didn't even bother to light a cigarette. I went right back inside my office and pulled up my web browser to look up the specific orders and stipulations relating to Red Cross messages. I read it twice and grabbed a sticky note, jotting down the exact order, paragraph, and subparagraph. I was not about to let them pull this shit unchallenged, and now I had the orders to back me up. No one outranks the Holy Marine Corps orders. This was the law.

This little subparagraph stated that the same rules applied if the relationship between the Marine and the person who died or was injured was considered the same as if they were siblings, regardless of actual blood ties. Sgt Porter was entitled to emergency leave after all.

I couldn't get actively involved in this. Maj Simons and I were already locked in several ongoing disagreements, and if he thought I was trying to undermine his authority with Sgt Porter, he was in his rights to punish me. But there are ways and then there are *ways*.

I went back to the office where I'd last seen Porter, and he was still there, sitting in the back corner, reading a book with his rifle slung across his chest. When I walked in this time, he put the book down. "Good evening, Staff Sergeant. How are you?"

"I was just about to ask you the same thing. You okay?"

Sgt Porter let his bearing slip by a fraction of an inch. "I'm okay. I really wish I could go home at least for the funeral. They're burying him in two days and—" He choked up for a second and took a few deep breaths. "Oh well. This blows."

I sat in a chair opposite him and then subjected the ceiling of our office to some intense scrutiny. "Sgt Porter, I was thinking that when people suffer a major loss, they often find great comfort in scriptures."

I paused and saw the puzzled expression on Porter's face. No one in the unit knew me to be a devout Christian, and this wasn't like me.

"Whenever I'm going through a hard time, I take solace in reading Marine Corps orders. They can be very enlightening. I suggest you give it a try. Here's a good starting point."

Not looking at the desk, I pressed the sticky note onto the wooden surface and stood, feigning nonchalance the whole time. "Just a thought, Sergeant."

As the door shut behind me, I caught a glimpse of Porter's befuddled expression. It was as far as I was willing to go. Sgt Porter would have to decide what he wanted to happen next.

After lunch the next day, I went back to my office and pored over a spreadsheet listing all our interpreters and which units had whom. It was silent in the office except for the sounds of MSgt Fox typing, so we both heard Maj Simons making his way down the hall, coming in hot. He shoved the door open and stood staring at Master Sergeant and me. Then he spun to face me directly, clutching a sheaf of papers that someone had highlighted with an orange marker.

"Was it you that gave him this idea? Did you fucking put him up to this?"

He was so angry his nostrils flared with every breath.

"What, sir? What happened? I haven't heard anything. What are you talking about?"

My reaction was genuine. After I left the night before, Sgt Porter hadn't told me anything about his next move. But if I had to hazard a guess, the naval message printout Maj Simons was waving like a club was probably the same scripture I had recommended to Porter.

"This motherfucker is requesting MAST! Somehow, he got it in his head that he rates leave! Now I *have* to grant it to him or else! Are you fucking satisfied?"

Well, yes, actually. But before I could say that, or anything like it, out loud, MSgt Fox spoke up. "Sir, Sgt Porter's a smart kid, and he knows how to use a computer. He most likely looked it up himself. It's not exactly hard." He gave a small shrug.

Maj Simons stared at MSgt Fox. He respected and liked MSgt Fox, so he wasn't inclined to bitch him out for the correction. Little by little, Maj Simons deflated.

"Well, fine. I'm headed over to the command post to get his leave approved, but this all your doing, Salz. No matter what anyone else says, I know you had a hand in this."

He turned on heel and left, simmering. When we sat back down following his departure, MSgt Fox made a happy grunting noise in his throat. "You've done it this time, Marine. He won't forgive that one."

"How in hell can anyone say I told Porter to request MAST? I did not, and it's not exactly esoteric knowledge that things can be looked up on the interwebs. Geezus."

"That's not going to matter to him. He thinks you're starting shit, and that's all that matters, right or wrong."

"To be honest, Master Sergeant, I don't even care anymore. Besides, I really want to hear him argue that I was being inappropriate by telling a junior Marine to read the damn orders. Can't have staff NCOs going around and making Marines educate themselves on the orders. That flies in the face of professionalism, that does."

Sgt Porter departed for Texas that night. He made it to the funeral.

44.

THE UNEXPLODED FEMALE

When I was slated to return to the United States from Iraq, I was separated from 2/10 and attached to 3rd Tank Battalion, who, because accountability is king, were now responsible for getting me home to the States. They were the only unit making this movement at the time I was scheduled to depart, so that was the only option.

Third Tanks was yet another all-male unit. Most combat arms were, at the time. I trudged with my seabag and my other stuff into the makeshift airport on Al-Asad and saw a huge group of lounging, sleeping, very sandy-looking Marines in the waiting area. Here, for a few weeks, was my new unit. I sighed and made my way to the edge of the group. I would have to go through the process of convincing them all I wasn't a threat to their existence while we were stuck together, just like I did every single time I showed up to a shop. It could be exhausting, but the heat of summer in bloom in Iraq made it feel impossible. The little airport was air-conditioned, but since they had to keep various doors open to move gear, Marines, and supplies around, it felt barely one or two degrees cooler than outside in the sun.

I selected my seat carefully. *Don't wade into the masses of tank Marines,* I thought, *but be close enough to hear when word gets passed.* None of them knew who I was. I set my shit down on a seat at the outer ring of the group and then wandered off to check my emails on an open desktop computer in the very small lounge. When I returned, GySgt Pakton, whom everyone referred to as "Big Money Gunny," was shouting out the instructions for what we were supposed to do when the flight line opened up for us to move to the C-130. GySgt Pakton was bald and short (barely my height), but he was as broad as he was tall and had a face like he breakfasted on lemons and whiskey. In true Marine gunny style, he spoke to the herd like he suspected every single one of us to be unspeakable shitbirds but didn't quite have the evidence yet. It was kind of comforting. If that's how he spoke to his own troops, I couldn't imagine he would treat me differently.

After he got done haranguing the group on not fucking up this simple task, he stomped off to his own perch in the waiting room. The giant group of Marines awaiting movement, all wearing desert cammies, resembled a pride of lions at rest. They weren't attacking anything, but sullen menace radiated from them anyway. Impatience to get the fuck home and be done with this deployment arose from every single man like steam. I decided I might as well introduce myself to someone, and since GySgt Pakton obviously hated the whole world, it might as well be him. I was pretty sure I couldn't make him *more* upset.

I double-checked myself to make sure nothing was out of place that he could fixate on and chew me out for. The worst start to this trip would be for me to get reamed out in front of my new unit. After verifying I had two chevrons, one on each collar tab, my hair was in regs (for females, our hair can betray us at the worst possible moment if we don't take precautions), and there was nothing dirty about me beyond the normal level of grime that pervaded everything in Iraq, I made my way to GySgt Pakton.

"Pardon me, Gunnery Sergeant, but may I ask a question?"

I wasn't going to parade rest because we were both SNCOs, but he was higher ranking, and I didn't know what his particulars were yet, so I stood straight, clasped my hands in front of me, and made a very serious but meek face. He glanced up from digging in his backpack and gave me a look as though I were yet another responsibility he didn't want.

"Yes, Staff Sergeant, what do you want?" he snapped.

It didn't feel like specially directed malice—more like he'd prefer if I asked whatever stupid, obviously unimportant question I had and then moved the fuck on.

"I'm Staff Sergeant Salzgeber. I'm making movement with your shop back to the States. I just wanted to ask what is going on so I don't get lost." I swallowed and hastily reconsidered my words. *Damn, that sounded like I don't know my own ass from breakfast time. Damn, damn, damn.*

Now that he knew I was going with them, I saw all sorts of unwelcome possibilities cloud his mind. He sat all the way back and subjected me to a long, cool glare. His eyes flicked from my boots back to my face. "You're with *us*?"

"Yes, Gunnery Sergeant." *Don't say one word more than protocol demands, and you might get out of this with minimal damage.*

Gunny Pakton muttered a "fuck" under his breath. "Well, Staff Sergeant, we're scheduled to depart at 2000. There isn't shit to do. Find somewhere to sit in the meantime, and don't make me come fucking find you when it's time to go."

I nodded, and he seemed satisfied. This was off to an auspicious start.

The key to approaching all-male units was to be as quiet and unassuming as I could. The quickest way to arouse their ire was to come in and try to flex like my staff sergeant rank meant something. They would give me the space and courtesy due my rank, but if I tried to act like I was the equal of their own staff NCOs, trouble would find me very quickly. It was not so much about my femaleness—although that definitely weighed against me; I was a POG.

POGs are "personnel other than grunts." We were Marines, but the combat arms MOSs viewed that as a technicality. We weren't trigger pullers, gun bunnies, bullet sponges, or snake eaters,[50] so we were considered "support," which sometimes felt like a nicer way of saying "the help." As an interpreter, I was considered one of the scholarly types who was too soft to be of real use in combat, but so long as I didn't put on airs, they'd tolerate me, and we'd all pretend I wasn't a liability.

Rah.

---

50   All nicknames for different combat arms Marines based on their weapons and duties.

I got the occasional worried glance, and some of the Marines shifted their belongings ever so slightly to pull away from me. Because, despite everything I just said about my sub-status, there was an undercurrent of real discomfort. Combat arms Marines knew one or two bits of lore about female Marines, and those bits were disquieting to them: We were all out to accuse men of sexual harassment. We could end a man's entire career with a word to the commander. We hated the male Marines and were inclined to seek revenge if they made any mistake where we could see it. These guys had braved the deserts along the Iraq–Syria border for over a year, but now the human equivalent of a viper was in their bedroll. It's very difficult to get comfortable with that.

In an effort to make myself seem harmless, I pulled a book out of my bag and skootched down against my seabag, ready to read and pretend like I wasn't causing problems already. After a couple hours of boredom and no one getting court-martialed since my arrival, the next phase began, in which I was deliberately ignored. *Good, that works for both parties*, I thought. We could all ignore each other all the way home. *That's fine.*

I couldn't fall asleep on the cheap plastic seats, and my seabag felt like I'd stuffed it with building materials, but I lay back on it anyway and stared up at the ceiling, trying to figure out what I'd do once I arrived back in Camp Lejeune. With my eyes safely averted, the Marines now whispered curiously.

"Who is she? Why is she sitting so near to us? Is she lost?"

I groaned internally and rolled to my side, closing my eyes to fake sleep. *Get it out of your system, lads. It'll all be better once we get through this.*

I dozed off a bit in the heat and was startled awake by the sounds of hundreds of Marines getting to their feet. I looked around with bleary eyes, trying to figure out how fast I needed to get my shit together. It turned out to be a false alarm. Someone thought they'd heard it was time to march, only to realize the plane wasn't ready yet. After a couple more of these, the real deal finally came down.

It was night; planes preferred to take off and land under the natural cover of darkness. Everything had been loaded by the embarkers, and we could board the plane at last. I grabbed my bags and found GySgt Pakton again so he'd know I was there and not off doing my hair or something. When I left 2/10, they took all my weapons back to the armory, so, unlike every other poor sod in my new unit, I didn't have to manage an M16 and all my body armor as well as my bags. I was traveling as light as a Marine ever does. I stood nearby so Gunny could see me, but stayed out of the way and stared at the floor, waiting. We finally boarded the aircraft and began the first leg of a very long journey home.

C-130s are usually cold. No one bothers to insulate the plane much for human comfort because human comfort is as far down the list of military priorities as up-armored llamas. I have no idea why we tried to sleep on those flights in and out of the Middle East. The pilots enjoyed messing with us by doing unnecessary swooping in the name of "combat landings and takeoffs," even though no one had taken serious shots at a C-130 in nearly a year. Between the cold, the numbness in my butt from seats that were clearly designed by aliens with no thought for human anatomy, and the surprising peaks and troughs of altitude, you didn't surrender to sleep so much as forced yourself into it. Unfortunately, with roughly one hundred other Marines on board, no one else was interested in rest at that moment. With my head back and eyes closed, I still heard the stupid loud and clear over the ear-clogging noise of the plane's engines.

"So, what I am saying is, if zombies do attack, you can't use fire to kill them because fire takes fuel, right? And who can carry all the fuel around with their flamethrower while running from zombies?"

"Certainly not you, Mr. Fall the fuck out as soon we hit mile two."

"Go fuck yourself. I was hungover. Listen, though, my point is all those zombies got the virus from sleeping with your whore of a mother in the first place."

"Really? I always thought they were the children you and your sister had."

"Oh? Well, you just lost the game, fuckface."

Oh, the Game. Dear reader, if you read this, *you* have lost the Game. It might be the most vapid and awful idea ever to crawl out of a boredom cesspit. The Game is not to think about the Game. You lose as soon as you even think about it, and in a turn of events like unto suicide bombings, people will make themselves lose the Game just to remind YOU about it so that you lose. Do not try to comprehend it. It's a lot like the platypus. It exists, there is no reason, just accept it. The Game is perverse in the extreme, and enlisted Marines are connoisseurs of perversity.

And why shouldn't they be? Deployment shares many of the hallmarks of prison. No sex, no drugs, no alcohol; there's some TV if you're lucky, the housing and hygiene situations are pretty dodgy at times, no visitors, lots of guards, weird food, and boredom. So. Much. Boredom. There are no days off because what is there to even do if you have a day off? There's a gym so you can get into peak physical condition. That way, when you're bored, you're at least bored with a resting heart rate of fifty-five beats per minute. Privacy is attained probably only in a port-a-potty, and the idea of being in one of those longer than absolutely required is repugnant. The smell alone cures all desire for alone time.

Hours later, we touched down in Kuwait. Camp Arifjan was pretty comfortable by Marine standards, and, as a female, I found it even better. Whereas my brothers-in-arms would be quartered for the night in a giant, squad bay–like structure, with dozens of them in each building, I got a building to myself. Females were given separate living space, and there were rarely more than three of us at any one time passing through Kuwait. I'd get a cot, air-conditioning, and blessed silence for one or two nights while the next part of the trip waited to execute.

It was nice and cool outside because it was roughly three in the morning, and I dropped my stuff in the female quarters and walked to the smoke pit. There I could work my diplomacy into meeting my new comrades. I found the pit closest to 3rd Tanks' quarters and pulled out my pack, feigning fixation on selecting a smoke and finding my lighter as I approached. Several men were in the smoke pit. When I arrived, the susurration of conversation died down briefly. I nodded to them as I picked a part of the gazebo to lean against.

"Good evening, gentlemen."

One person coughed, and then, after I didn't seem to be leaving, they shrugged and started talking again. One particular lance corporal was the center of attention. LCpl Allan[51] talked nonstop. He said nothing at all, like a politician with no platform, but he carried on as if he had done all the stimulants before disembarking the plane.

"You guys wanna take bets on who gets married first when we get back? Hahahaha, I bet there'll be like three weddings and ten pregnancies, hahahaha! Hey, hey, Johnson! You just lost the GAME, fuckface!" Allan sounded like this was more of a party than a burden. The one who answered to Johnson punched LCpl Allan in the chest, and everyone laughed.

I shook my head very slightly. *Do they even hear themselves?* I ashed my cigarette and took in the scene. There were maybe six in total, but

51 Not his real name

that number ebbed and flowed with Marines coming to the smoke pit and leaving for bed or chow. I got lost in my own thoughts and didn't even notice until I heard my name called. *Who in this group even knows my name?* I snapped my gaze to the source and saw GySgt Pakton standing with a couple other gruff-looking men.

"Hey, Staff Sergeant, we're headed to chow. Want to join us?" He sounded like he couldn't possibly care less if I came or not, but the invitation itself was a sort of peace offering. I was dead tired, though.

"Thank you, Gunnery Sergeant, but I'm exhausted. I'm going to hit the rack."

I gave him a smile and bobbed my head as I left. He looked crestfallen for a second and then turned and left with the group. I probably should have gone with them, fatigue be damned. It was an opening to introduce myself, but I just couldn't be bothered right then. I went to bed.

The next morning, I awoke, and it was glorious. There was no sound in the whole room. It was cold. It was dark because there were no windows. I had nowhere to be, and no one wanted anything from me. It was as close to heaven as I had been in a long time. So what that I was in a temporary structure with concrete floors and sand for inches and miles around? For a few moments, I had peace! I giggled. Peace in the Middle East! I'd found it!

I got up and rummaged for my hygiene stuff. There was a trailer with showers a mere sixty feet behind my building, and I wasn't going to pass up a chance to wash off Iraq. After a quick trip to the showers, I strolled back in my T-shirt and shorts, humming and feeling good about the universe in general. I looked at my watch. The chow hall opened for lunch in an hour, and I could sample all the delicacies a grill and a deep fryer could provide. Yay!

I ate in solitary bliss, taking in one of my favorite books on my Kindle as I chewed through some salad. After that, a brief smoke, and then I decided to catch some rays and finish the book. I found a slab of T-wall[52] near my quarters and propped myself up with my backpack, pulling my cover down to shade my eyes. I lay back, crossed my legs, and flicked to the last page I'd read.

I soon became aware that I wasn't the only person out there. I tried to block it out, but the other people were murmuring and whispering. I looked over the top of my book, and the noise stopped. No one was there.

---

52 The giant concrete barriers erected all around building areas that prevented who-knows-what from happening.

I frowned and went back to my book. Moments later, the same noises arose again. This time, I just ignored it. It wasn't any of my business. A bit more time passed, and I clearly heard a male voice say, "Just go!" And then my peace was disrupted.

LCpl Allan walked up, smiling and waving. "Hi, Staff Sergeant!"

I nodded and said hello back, but my guard was up. Lance corporals don't just wander up to staff NCOs unless they have something on their minds. He sat on the T-wall right next to my feet. I scowled at the intrusion into my personal force field but didn't say anything. I was going to make him either spit it out or leave out of discomfort. My book was calling me.

Allan had a deep tan, although whether that was circumstantial or genetic, I had no idea. He had very close-cropped dark hair, big brown eyes, a dopey grin, and he was lanky. But he moved like someone who could go from dopey to vicious, so I was wary. I waited for him to say something. He gulped and looked at his feet. *Please don't hit on me, please don't hit on me*, I thought.

"Hey, Staff Sergeant! Wanna play a game?" He flashed a huge grin. "The game is you gotta get married as soon as you get back! First one wins!"

I was dumbfounded. Despite myself, I answered, "But . . . I'm technically married anyway. Do I win automatically?"

"No, no, no, no. You gotta get divorced and then get married as soon as you're back home!" Allan nodded eagerly. I was about to tell him to fuck off when I spotted the source of the previous noises. Three other Marines were peeking out from behind another T-wall, watching the whole conversation with worried expressions. One of them was GySgt Pakton.

This was a test. They'd sent LCpl Allan over because he was entirely unafraid, and now they wanted to see if he would set me off. This was explosive ordnance disposal on human beings. *Okay, guys, I'm onto you.*

"Naw, thanks, Allan. I don't have the time to file for divorce before we fly."

I started to raise my book back up to reading level, and Allan saw his chance slipping away.

"Okay, well, there's another game we can play! The game is not to think about the game or mention the game or speak about it. Or else you lost the game! I just lost it six times, so you can play too!" There was the head bob again, and he looked so eager for me to respond.

"LCpl Allan, what the fuck are you even talking about? No. Thank you anyway. I think I'm probably not good at games. I can read aloud to you if you want."

His manic grin froze for a second. Being read at didn't sound like fun, not even in the thick of desert boredom.

"Why are you with us, Staff Sergeant?" After all the gibbering, the straight-shot question was unexpected and caught me off guard. I figured that whatever I told him would go out to the masses pretty quickly. *Let's get this right the first round.*

"I'm done with 2/10. They don't need me anymore. So, I'm attached to you to make movement home. That's all."

"They don't need you? What is your MOS?"

"I'm an Arabic linguist." I wasn't about to bring up being a data Marine as well. Saying out loud that you fix computers will fill your free time with personal requests to fix individual Marines' laptops and email issues. After the things I'd seen on Marines' laptops, I was not opening that door again.

"You speak Arabic? I know some Arabic! What does this mean, Staff Sergeant? *Kussitch kabeera!*"

He looked suspiciously innocent, but the phrase translates into "Your pussy is big."

"*La, zoobik saagheer,*" I shot back. (No, your dick is small.)

He laughed in delight. I smirked. He stood and waved again.

"See ya, Staff Sergeant!" He departed in the direction of the stealthy observers, and I figured he'd probably give a pretty good account of me. *Your move, Gunny.*

45.

THE SLOWEST LEAVING
EVER DONE

It was dark outside in the empty desert of Kuwait. The generic government transport disguised unconvincingly as an old tour bus sat there, lit only by the lights of a nearby airstrip where several aircraft awaited clearance to begin boarding. Tired, dirty Marines lay around inside the bus like discarded clothes, draped in impossible positions over packs, seats, weapons, and other miscellany as they somehow managed to sleep with their bodies contorted in ways that would give a cat cramps. A few muted conversations took place among those with insomnia.

After a year of deployment in the Middle East, sand had become as ubiquitous in their lives as air and unbearable heat. Sand was in everything. It got in their hair, their eyes, their underclothes, their dreams. Night traded positions with the day and brought with it a stunning chill that ate through clothes designed for temperatures of forty degrees centigrade and up. In the vast nothingness of sand, twenty-five degrees Celsius felt like winter.

They were waiting. It seemed as though waiting was all we did: waiting to catch a flight, waiting to move between bases, waiting for something to happen, waiting to return home. Thirteen months of waiting could take a toll on even the most stable person, and while young, enlisted Marines have many sterling qualities, patience and fortitude in the face of unending boredom are not among them.

But here we were, waiting for the plane to let us board. Again. Waiting to take off. Again. Waiting and waiting, so much that Purgatory became a real place, and we were in it. This time the delay was supposedly because our airplane was stuck behind a different airplane and the pilots were nowhere to be found. The only reward I'd been promised for all this waiting was a seat in the first-class area of the plane with all the other SNCOs and officers. Rank does have its privileges. But none of that mattered much right now. I was uncomfortable, tired, and I'd had sand under my eyelids for the past forty-eight hours, which made everything in the whole world suck balls.

One particular lieutenant was strolling up and down the aisle of the bus, wearing all his body armor and stopping to talk shit with the Marines. I could tell they'd all spent too much time together because the trading of barbs crossed my far-more-uptight sensibilities. I was a protocol princess compared to these guys. The lieutenant was getting all kinds of flak about how his wife would probably waterboard him when he got home (later I learned it was because she was an intelligence officer) and how useless he was. Swaggering past me, he clapped back at the Marines by saying, "Y'all just mad you aren't sexy like me."

Suddenly, Marines were leaping on him from every direction. I slunk down in my seat and watched in horror as he was taken to the floor of the bus, and all I could hear was shouting from a press of bodies. I scrambled out of my seat and backed toward the driver, looking to get off the bus. I could always come back when they got this sorted out, right?

GySgt Gonzalez burst through the door of the bus, pushing past me.

"What's happening! What's happening?!" he demanded of me.

"They're beating their lieutenant! I think," I sputtered.

GySgt Gonzalez deflated. "Oh. Shit, I thought it was serious."

I stared at him like he was crazy. Or I was. Someone was. That part was certain.

He sighed and got to the pile.

"All right, ALL RIGHT! That's enough! Get off of him." GySgt Gonzalez untangled everyone and helped the lieutenant up. "You're not supposed to cause fights, sir."

That got a laugh out of everyone.

"What did he say this time, huh?" he queried the group as a whole.

"He said we weren't sexy! And a girl heard him!" shouted one corporal from the back.

Everyone laughed again, and I shook my head. *These guys are nuts.* I turned and climbed off the bus to find the smokers. They weren't likely to do anything weirder than discuss how much money, exactly, it would take to get one of them to suck someone else's dick. For a "straight" group, they sure loved talking about gay sex a lot. I could hang with that.

PART EIGHT:

CAMP LEJEUNE, NORTH CAROLINA

PART II

46.

THE HOMECOMING KINGS

F inally back in the United States a few days later, we were all tired. A sea of desert-colored camouflage uniforms had one particularly homogeneous quality aside from color: I was fed up with looking at it. The Marines, the endless beige, the unending delays after days and days of patience-trying inanity. We were all so very sick of everything and each other. But even though we were back in North Carolina, we still weren't free to go.

We were attending a safety standdown, which, for the uninitiated, is an exercise in boredom threshold expansion. Three hundred Marines were crammed into an auditorium with only the scant air-conditioning the facilities maintenance provided. The walls were boring white, the stage was plain, aging wood, and the screen for the projector was slightly warped and not nearly large enough to be clearly visible in the back seats. The room smelled of the sweat of tightly packed human beings and the remains of lunch.

Slideshow after slideshow, we were inundated with lessons on not beating our spouses, not drinking excessively, and not engaging in unprotected intimacy. The speakers were uncomfortable with the material and the concept of public speaking, droning and pausing like a poorly maintained ride at the county fair. The fold-up theater seats creaked every time someone's ass became too numb to withstand another moment. None of us were models of patience to begin with, and this little episode, scheduled to go all day until 1600, was the capstone on a solid week of delays meant to cool us off.

The grueling process was designed to ease us back slowly into society with a minimum of bad results. They weren't hoping for good outcomes, just fewer disastrous ones involving the local police. The briefs had been written by people whose primary qualification was having the time and computer know-how to make a presentation. The information was out of date and horribly inaccurate in places, but that didn't matter because no one was listening. We were all going through the motions so we could get out of there and celebrate our return to the United States properly. That celebration was a point of serious trepidation for the unit commander. Marines are not famed for their polite manners when they're partying.

The current brief was the high point of the tension. This was the "Sexual Assault Brief." The speaker was fumbling through an admonition to the general effect that we should not rape anyone. It was insulting from the jump, and the wording just made things worse. SSgt Smith clutched his briefing papers in sweaty hands and licked his lips, clearly torn between duty and being the focus of 300 angry Marines who were not on board with his message.

The room was definitely developing an atmosphere. I felt the hostility rising and the impact of the occasional hostile glance. From time to time, the guys realized that one of the female enemy, all of whom were out to take their money and destroy their careers, was in their midst. I was seated more than halfway toward the rear of the auditorium, so it was noticeable when Marines spotted me, nudged their neighbor, and indicated my presence with a head nod. This led to people turning in their seats to glare at me and then turning back. I could tell they wanted to protest the brief, but with me there they were worried that if they said anything indelicate, they would be called out and maybe even reprimanded. Guys who would face down gunfights on the battlefield wanted nothing to do with me.

Their grumbling became positively audible when the staff sergeant reached the legal slide.

"Sexual assault is defined by Marine Corps order as 'non-consensual penile penetration,' and that includes oral, anal, or vaginal. It is punishable under the UCMJ by brig time, loss of rank, and loss of pay."

A wave of groans issued from the assembled Marines. I stifled a laugh because these men, who used obscenity as their default mode of communications, were offended by such sterile words as "penile."

But wait a minute. That legal definition struck me as highly unequal, even though it slanted in what would be perceived as *my* favor.

"Excuse me!"

Suddenly, I noticed that my hand was raised and I had spoken. *Where did* that *come from?*

My feminine voice made the whole room turn. Once upon a time, hundreds of people staring at me would have caused me an instant panic attack. Now, I shrugged it off. If they wanted to kill me, it would not be with mean looks.

Like one rudely awakened, SSgt Smith had gone wide eyed.

"Oh! My apologies, ma'am. I didn't see you there."

Well, no shit. That's the whole point of wearing cammies, isn't it?

He flashed a nervous smile. "What is your question?"

"That definition. Does that mean it's impossible for me to rape someone? As someone with no 'penile' appendage, I mean?" I realize now that there were lots of ways things could go wrong, but give me a break. I was improvising on the spot. I needed to do something to lighten the mood because I felt myself becoming more of an outsider by the second.

"Uh . . . uh, yes, ma'am. According to that wording, you can't actually be punished under that, uh, statute. Um . . ."

I turned and pointed to the Marine two seats away from me, GySgt Puller (a friend by this point), and yelled, "I've got roofies and a switchblade. I'm coming for your ass!"

To my enormous relief, the room roared with laughter, and Marines turned back around, except GySgt Puller, who gave me a mixed expression of horror and, because he's still a Marine, possible interest.

Only later did I kick myself at the realization that part of the room, the literal-minded part, read that as my announced intention to get GySgt Puller in my bed. But the ambiguity was worth it; my outburst instantly diminished the hostility coming my way. The rest of the brief was far more comfortable for me, if no more interesting. The staff sergeant seemed to breathe out, and then, cringing, stumbled his way through the rest of the slides for the remaining fifteen minutes.

Afterward, I stood and went into the bathroom during break so I could get my shaking under control. I covered my face and did some deep breathing. I didn't know why yet, but the whole situation had been unnerving. Actually, everything was a bit more upsetting now than before. But more on that later.

47.

JUST A LI'L NIP/TUCK

When Marines came back from Iraq after a year of deployment, they often had a lot of money in their pockets. Like thirty grand or more in some cases, and I was no different. While many of them spent it on the usual good things like beer, women, and cars, I spent mine on getting a place to live and furnishing it in the hopes of my daughters coming back to live with me. Putting together a home from scratch was daunting.

But one very popular expense was rather unexpected. It was perfectly legal, but it was not something I had ever associated with grizzled warfighters.

Liposuction.

"What, really?" I asked GySgt Puller.

We were lounging in the auditorium, waiting on our final safety brief, and after the weeks-long effort of returning to the United States together, GySgt Puller now found me acceptable enough to talk to honestly.

"Yep! The captain and I are both getting it done. MSgt Ski from the unit we relieved said he got it done when he came back. There's this doctor in Wilmington that's supposed to be pretty good. He said it took like six inches off his waist, and he finally looks shredded with all the two-a-day workouts."

I didn't know what to say. I'd never thought of having plastic surgery before. I mean, I'd heard from other females that we could get free boob jobs so long as we told medical that our current breasts were negatively impacting our self-esteem, but that seemed outlandish. None of my bras would fit then, and it added complications to running that I didn't need.

But GySgt Puller was casually flipping through pictures on his phone while talking about girdles and recovery time.

"But, I mean . . . why? Like, isn't it all just diet? Wouldn't you rather buy a BMW?"

I actually had no idea if he was in the market for a car, but E-7 pay, tax free, for thirteen months (plus hazard pay) could probably score at least a base-model Beamer.

"Already got a BMW," he replied. "No wife, no kids. I can take all the time I need to heal. Since the captain is getting it done too, he can waiver my PFT until I'm good. Besides, Salz, I'm getting older. Fat doesn't melt off me like it does the young kids. Gotta take steps now before they start calling me fat and I end up on the body-composition program."

BCP was where you were sent if you were fat or weak, according to most Marines. They thinned you out and toughened you up, or else processed you out of the Marine Corps and back to civilian life. It held real terrors for us all, should you gain too much weight or fail a physical fitness test.

These men with whom I returned from Iraq, who had just spent a year sitting in the desert, eating MREs and such, were coming back to the United States and giving their cash to plastic surgeons. The reasons for this were obvious once someone actually pointed them out to me. Career and reputation required a certain look, and that look was worth tens of thousands of dollars to these guys. In other words, there was social pressure to look like the Marines in the recruiting posters. That was enormously difficult as they aged, and they were crazy self-conscious about their physiques; they were willing to go through a lot. There were the meds they had to take, and a six-month recovery where they had to keep running and working out instead of healing quietly in their homes. It wasn't just liposuction, either. Some Marines were getting other cosmetic surgeries, and all of it was totally mystifying to me.

Everybody says our society's standards for women are unrealistic. Well, take care not to get mowed down under the desert boots of very rugged, masculine, gun-toting, one-shot-one-kill, penile-equipped Marines rushing to appointments at a plastic surgeon near you.

The final briefer walked in and took center stage. Everyone shifted in their seats and got quiet, ready to get this last hurdle out of the way. As the Marine began to speak, I felt my chest tighten. Confused, I tried to take deep breaths, but it wasn't working, and I gripped the arms of my seat. GySgt Puller shot me a glance and, without saying a word, opened an app on his phone of a koi fish swimming lazily in a pond. He set the phone on the arm between us and tapped the screen, causing ripples as if it were water. The visual was soothing.

Slowly, I exhaled and surreptitiously tapped his phone screen again. The fish moved toward my finger. I watched it in delight. The alien stress that had grabbed me melted away. GySgt Puller pretended not to notice.

48.

IT ALL FALLS DOWN

I clenched the edge of my desk, gritting my teeth and waiting for the moment to pass. But it wasn't passing. Hot tears ran off my chin, staining the PowerPoint slides I'd printed out. I had no idea what they said. Trying to read them was like viewing them through warped glass. My chest refused to expand. I'd forgotten how to breathe. I sat frozen, nose burning, mind racing, feeling every heartbeat push the blood through my ears.

You have to breathe, I thought. *You must inhale, or you'll die.*

Compared to my current situation, dying sounded like a relief. The lights were way too bright, and the sound of Gunny Nunez typing was like elephants crushing aluminum cans. The colors were awful, the whole room was crushing the life out of my mind, and I wished for my body to follow suit. When the purple spots started flashing through my watery vision, I finally inhaled. The loud, ragged sound being pulled from my throat was my sanity being dragged across a saw blade.

I'm not okay. I don't know what do.

I was always the one who knew what to do next; I always had clever answers or saw solutions others missed. But not here, not now. Now I couldn't think of the future because even five minutes from now was as distant as the beginning of the universe. Everything was actively participating in my destruction. With escape as my only goal, I shoved my chair backwards and groped for the door. I fled to the bathroom, found a stall, rushed in, and slammed the door shut behind me.

There was no one else in the bathroom, so I released my stifled sobs at long last. I heaved, trying to accomplish respiration and expulsion of stomach contents at the same time. I braced myself over the toilets and wretched, the tears now cascading into the toilet along with bile and spit. I hadn't eaten for three or four days now, only drinking coffee and taking diet pills, so there was nothing for me to expel. I convulsed with shivers and collapsed to my knees, clutching the unimaginably disgusting surface of the toilet seat like a life preserver.

You're okay, you're okay, you're not dying, I repeated in the shrieking storm of my own psyche. The ghastly beige tiles under my knees were comforting in their blandness.

This will pass. It's okay. No one is trying to kill you. No one is torturing you. You are strong enough to get through this. It's going to be okay.

The thought stream started to slow, and my breathing began to regulate once more. I closed my eyes and kept taking deep breaths. *You're safe. No one will come into the bathroom and bother you for the moment. It's okay.*

As calm spread her blanket over my screaming head, I struggled back to my feet. I finally achieved some semblance of normality, wiped my drool off the seat, and flushed the toilet. Exiting the stall, I checked whether anyone else had come in while I had been freaking out. It was still blessedly devoid of other human beings.

I took a deep, calming breath and went to the sink to clean up. No matter how intense my distress, it would never come to the point of touching my own face after touching a toilet in a Marine Corps head. I wasn't *that* crazy yet.

I splashed cold water on my face as I had seen a thousand times in movies, but it was hardly effective. I was red and blotchy in the cheeks, my nose glowed enough to guide several sleighs through a winter's night, and the rings under my eyes proclaimed to the world my sleeplessness. Even as I examined my own face, I avoided eye contact. I didn't want to see what I already knew was there.

I was broken.

This had been building since I returned from Iraq. I couldn't go to stores because the people enraged me by the way they slouched on their carts as if their bodies had become too rotund to support themselves any longer. Everyone was in my way, no one seemed to know what they were there for; the aggressive redness of every single aspect of the store, the lights that felt like searchlights, the enraging, unmelodious music, the nonstop invasion of my personal space—it all made any trip to the store mental torture and almost impossible to deal with while maintaining my composure. It pressed me harder and harder until I had to get out of there as fast as I could. I started going without all kinds of things for the simple reason that getting them and driving home were monumental tasks I couldn't complete.

I'd lost nearly thirty pounds, and I still didn't want to eat. The sensation of taste was too powerful for my fragile state to endure. I hated my existence and everything it entailed. My marriage had dissipated before the deployment thanks to our mutual career ambitions taking priority over each other. My children had only been able to live with me off and on for years now, and when I sent them to live with their grandmother while I was overwhelmed with Marine Corps duties, a rift had opened between my parents and me. Every single day, I awoke to the feeling that I was the worst human being alive. I was a terrible mother who would never raise her own children because I was a pile of bullshit that couldn't handle basic responsibilities. I was a terrible Marine who never seemed to be able to do what GySgt Nunez wanted, and his wife provided the only daycare services I could find on-base. So long as I depended on Jessica to watch my daughters, GySgt Nunez was free to treat me however his moods took him.

My career, which had been so glorious to me when I traveled to Iraq, was now in shambles, thanks to a dispute over the validity of my third reenlistment contract, which had gone all the way to my home state's US senator. Everything that had seemed solidly built was collapsing, and I could not do anything about it. I had failed, and I suffered more ridicule for "trying to get out of things" because even Jessica didn't want to watch my daughters from 0200 to 2000 so I could go on hikes and field ops. My life, in short, was a fucking mess.

This was all my fault. I could have gotten out and stayed home and raised my children instead of subjecting them to whatever vagaries my own mother doled out as her capricious mind vacillated between kindness and sadism. I could have been an officer's wife. Jens had completed pilot training and was now headed to Futenma in Okinawa to fly big CH-46 Sea Knight helicopters. But no, I had been so in love with my own ambitions that I enrolled in DLI, deployed, and then crashed back here, on Camp Lejeune, working for Base G-6 and ready to die of loneliness and self-loathing.

That was how I felt every day now.

After I had restored a modicum of composure, I walked out of the head, and instead of going back to my desk, where I would likely put myself through this whole thing all over again, I set off for the battalion aid station (BAS) down the hall. Passing through the front offices, which were spacious, pleasant, and decorated with wood furniture, sparkling tile floors, and pleasant, unaggressive sailors of varying rank, I suddenly doubted if I needed help. This could just be a mood. After all, Marines I knew had been in real live firefights, had been blown up on convoys in Afghanistan by IEDs, and had been made to deal with the corpses of innocent Iraqis rotting in the sun because the local resistance fighters threatened to kill anyone who tried to bury them. Compared to that, my own terror seemed unearned and undeserved.

Just as I was about to turn around and suck it the fuck up, I saw a Marine gunnery sergeant walking in the opposite direction and felt my stomach clench so hard I almost dry heaved.

No, Tracy, it's time to admit that you are having a major malfunction.

I kept going until I reached the little clinic in the back.

It was a simple clinic, and the Navy medical officer (MO) was a stranger to me. I took a chair by the door to wait until he had time to see me. His corpsman assistant brought me paperwork to fill out. The room was very basic. There were a desk, a window, a privacy divider, a little adjustable exam table, and a locker for medicine and tools. That was it. The corpsman nodded in time to some rap music playing on an MP3 player in the exam area. It was surprisingly soothing. I made a note to myself to check out 50 Cent's other music. He'd probably be surprised to find out his tunes might prevent panic attacks.

When the medical officer, a lieutenant (junior grade),[53] came to the front desk, I started to reach a better place. I trusted him for irrational reasons. His black hair was cropped in a short yet wildly out-of-regulations-for-Marines style that looked far less military than most. He had very dark eyes, pale skin, and a relaxed, easy bearing that I associated with people who definitely knew what kind of job they would do after leaving active duty. He picked up the clipboard with my information on it, reviewed it, set it back down, and flashed a warm smile.

"How can I help you, Staff Sergeant?"

Here it was. The moment of truth. Telling an officer that you think you may be losing your mind and that you are on the verge of becoming

---

53   Curse the entire Navy rank system for being utterly arcane and incomprehensible without study.

crippled by madness does not seem, on the whole, a winning strategy. Marines of all ranks treat any sort of mental distress as a kind of invisible herpes. Even if the others never see it for themselves, once rumor gets out that a person isn't feeling okay in the head, he or she can expect to be ostracized and be made the object of a whispering campaign. It isn't crazy to sneak a goat into the barracks (yes, this really happened), but if a person has an emotional breakdown, they will exist on the fringes after that. I needed to communicate my desire for help but in such a manner that I didn't lose my security clearance (those are excruciatingly hard to get and easier to lose than a set of car keys), my job, and my reputation.

"I . . . can't sleep. It's affecting my work. I can't sleep, I can't eat, and I can't think straight as a result. I don't know what to do. I'm so sorry for troubling you. This is probably stupid."

The angry hordes of embarrassment marched up my neck, burning everything as they went. My blush was incandescent. I wanted to unsay that. I wanted to laugh this all off. *I'm an idiot, I'm weak, I'm—*

I slapped my hand over my mouth as my tummy lurched once more, threatening me with even worse disaster if I tried to back out of this. Once my salivary glands had eased the nausea, I took my hand down, staring wide eyed at the medical officer. *Yep, he totally saw that.*

The MO frowned with genuine concern, and internally I was pathetically grateful. I lived alone except for my daughters occasionally staying with me, so there were no other sympathetic adults in my social sphere. Seeing the MO look more worried than judgmental made me want to burst into tears and tell him how fucking horrible my own mind was being and how I wanted nothing more than to lie down and never start breathing again.

I didn't.

The MO returned to my chart, looking for certain details.

"You just got back from Iraq a month ago. Was everything okay with your tour?"

"Yes. There wasn't any violence. I was fine." I used very small sentences to stop from blurting out anything that might get away from me. I couldn't just go around trusting people.

The MO stared hard at me. "Staff Sergeant, you haven't looked me in my face since we started talking. How bad is this sleeplessness really?"

"Bad," I whispered, feeling the stinging in my sinuses that portended tears.

He nodded, turned, and began writing out two different scripts. A few silent minutes passed before he handed me both of them.

"The first one on top there, take to the pharmacy. It's medicine to help you get a good night's rest. The second one is a referral. Go to Deployment Health. I'll draw you a quick map of where it's at. Ask them to make you an appointment."

With a final, encouraging smile, he stood, signaling my visit was at an end.

"In the meantime, if you experience anything troubling, please come back. Have a good day, Staff Sergeant."

I thanked him and left the clinic, clutching my two papers. No matter what, I didn't want Gunny to see them. If he started telling people in the shop that I was taking "crazy pills," that'd be the death of me. Never mind that I had no idea what the medication written on the chit was. The MO was a standout exemplar of the Illegible School of Prescription Writing. Paranoia had kept me out of trouble this far. I wasn't going to give in to reason now.

At Deployment Health, they gave me an appointment for a week later—a week of being hauled across broken glass and salt. By the time I arrived on the appointed day and hour, I was in complete disarray.

The Deployment Health clinic looked like the regular clinic but with small, important upgrades that spoke of a separate and plumper budget. There were actual magazines in the waiting room that had been printed in the last ninety days, the nurses doing check-in were civilians and very professional, and the chairs had cushioning that wasn't filled with lumpy concrete. There were even potted plants not confected of plastic. Deployment Health also had a dress code quite different from a regular BAS. Everyone coming in was instructed to wear civilian clothing and not their uniform.

The day I arrived, the clinic had four other people in the luxurious waiting room. I avoided eye contact with every single one of them. Using peripheral vision to guide myself, I went to the front desk and checked in. The only way I could keep it together anymore was by just not looking at things. I became a world-class champion at floor staring. I could tell you what color tiles were in every building I visited. I looked up only when I was driving. Therefore, I have no idea what the nurses looked like or what their names were. I knew only that they were female and sounded tired.

After verifying my appointment on the slow, obsolescent computer at her desk, a nurse slid a clipboard across the counter and told me to fill everything out before my appointment could begin. I took the clipboard, struggling with a rather unreasonable emotional response to what seemed a vast burden she had just loaded upon me. Did I *look* like a person capable of filling in forms right now? Gritting my teeth as I did when GySgt Nunez gave me some asinine task, I grabbed a pen from the jar and trudged to an open seat.

I took a deep breath and looked at the first blank. Name. *Why the fuck do I need to write my name? It's in the computer. This is such bullshit.* Next was "age." *Goddamnit, my date of birth is in the computer too! Why are they punishing me?* I scanned ahead to see what other unbelievable demands this form was going to make of me.

"Chief Complaint"? How should I fucking know? I don't know what's wrong with me! That's the whole reason I'm here!

By the end of page one of at least half a dozen pages, I was furious and wanted to scream at them for handing me this. *Just let me see the goddamn doctor, for fuck sake!* I stormed back up to the counter, drawing a few curious glances from the other waiters that I interpreted as judgmental, and dropped the clipboard on the counter. Still not making eye contact, I announced, "I can't do this." The form was far too much to expect from me, and I accepted whatever the consequences of my failure were.

The nurse gave me a look like I had just told her the screaming cockroaches in my head said no. Slowly, gently, she took the clipboard back from me. She said that was fine and assured me that I could fill out the forms after the appointment.

Pleased with my small victory over the forces of oppressive paperwork, I returned to my seat. I did not know why, but the anger kept me seething over every remembered slight and insult throughout my entire life. An unfortunate side effect of having a good memory is that my mind had a defense contractor's arsenal worth of material to go over when boredom and a lack of overt provocation presented themselves.

At length, another nurse I couldn't look at called my name and led me down a very quiet hallway to the doctor's office. She asked me in soft, soothing tones to please have a seat, and she shut the door as she left. After her departure, I seized on the moment to evaluate who my opponent—I mean, doctor—was. The very impressive diploma on the wall, decorated with all the curly bits and shiny seals a true professional could ever desire, declared my doctor to be Dr. Timothy Van Dyke. The diploma was issued by Johns Hopkins, and I was impressed in spite of my mood. Maybe this guy could actually help. Deployment Health had different reporting requirements than BAS, and HIPPA was taken extremely seriously. Here, at least, my privacy would be inviolate unless I did something truly drastic and self-destructive.

When Dr. Van Dyke arrived, I saw out of my peripherals that he was a very respectable-looking gentlemen of probably sixty years with silver hair, blue eyes, and a very calming demeanor. Every word and gesture he made as he introduced himself and went to his desk made me feel far less attacked and threatened than I had in months. God bless him, he didn't even bring up the subject of my intense staring at the bookshelf while we talked. After stating unequivocally and out loud that I had no intention of harming myself or others, I finally let everything come out to this patient, attentive human being.

I told him that not seeing my children for months or years at a time was killing me. That the constant, suffocating fear that someone around me would decide to destroy my career and rob me of my ability to provide for those children made every day terrifying. That hiding all this because of the scorn with which these needs were met was so painful that I would rather suffer the loss of my family than invite destruction for my weakness.

The tears came back for a few encores, but I controlled my voice and never took my eyes off the bookshelf. It was all falling apart. I couldn't remember why I had chosen to put us all through this in the first place. I hated everything. I hated myself.

Dr. Van Dyke would be the one who talked me down out of the tree of despair I'd gotten marooned in. I will never be able to thank him enough for saving my life.

49.

DESPAIR TURNS TO RAGE

Shortly after I started seeing Dr. Van Dyke, I was afforded another occasion to witness the ugly changes taking place in my mind. A young female sergeant in my shop, who had spent almost her entire enlistment on light duty,[54] countermanded a lawful order I gave to a PFC.

I had instructed PFC Smith to take a quick trip over to the regimental headquarters and help out the commanding officer with a password reset. After I walked away, Sgt Dawn told the PFC to ignore my instructions because "that's not how we do things here."

The Marine Corps has a rule of going with the last word passed, so of course the PFC obeyed her. When I came back to the office and he still hadn't left, I demanded to know what the holdup was. PFC Smith replied that Sgt Dawn had ordered him to disregard my orders. Worse, Sgt Dawn hadn't even attempted to speak with me first to explain herself. She just cancelled my orders and went back to surfing the internet while waiting for her medical-separation paperwork to process.

Fuming and not entirely sure of my self-control, I went to address this insubordination directly. I found her limping on crutches back from the head, and I ordered her to step into the office with me and close the door. This was so I wouldn't lose my bearing in front of the troops and destroy her limited authority in the process.

After she closed the door, I took a seat on the couch while Sgt Dawn

---

54 A status given to someone who has a medical "reason" to avoid physical training and/or standing duty

sat one seat over. I demanded to know in what fucking plane of existence she thought she could order someone to disregard a lawful order from me.

Sgt Dawn sighed as if explaining this was taxing but she'd do me the favor.

"I know you are new here, Staff Sergeant, but we don't make trouble calls for anyone who is not a VIP or a general. Therefore, I told the PFC not to obey you because you were in the wrong."

This malingering idiot was referring to the regimental commander, a full-bird colonel who had deployed to combat theaters while this moron girl hid behind her supposed injury to avoid that fate. And yet this sergeant, who had always dodged PT, duty, and any other responsibility for over a year now and set a terrible example by her inability to be good at anything, including her job (her tech skills sucked so badly that she was considered useless and a liability in the unit), had the obscene audacity to think HE wasn't important enough to warrant her attention? She thought so much of herself that she would openly disrespect me like that and think she'd get away unscathed? Especially over something as minor as providing help-desk support!

Sgt Dawn babbled on in an unpleasant, condescending manner that deepened my hatred of her with every passing second. She spoke to me as an inferior who did not know her place, and she was merely taking pity on me. Sgt Dawn sincerely thought that this was a winning strategy.

By the time she finished her speech, I was being boiled alive from the inside out by the gas jets of indignation. *How* DARE *she? Hit her. Hit Her! HIT HER!*

I took a deep breath, hoping this would restore my composure. I started to say that from here forward, if she had an issue with the orders I gave, she would come directly to me about it. But Sgt Dawn cut me off to say that, actually, she didn't have to.

I snapped.

Grabbing the edge of the glass coffee table in front of the couch with both hands, I flipped it with all my upper-body strength as I rose. The noise was tremendous, the glass instantly spiderwebbed with cracks, and Sgt Dawn froze, at last realizing she had gone way too far by half. With the most guttural fury I could summon and at the maximum lung capacity I could achieve, I lost my shit.

"YOU WILL FUCKING DO WHAT YOU ARE GODDAMN ORDERED TO DO OR I WILL SEE TO IT YOU ARE PUNISHED

TO THE FULLEST EXTENT OF MY ABILITY FOR THE REST OF YOUR ENLISTMENT!!!"

This wasn't the high or squeaky sounds of an angry woman. This was the sound of an animal out to cause as much pain as possible. As I stood over her, I fought my hardest to get the angry genie back in the bottle, because it was telling me to say all manner of unkind things that would probably terrify the girl for life. I was shaking. I wanted to hit her over and over as hard as I could until I got tired. I despised her with every fiber of my being. I wanted to crush her utterly so that she would never, ever again think to challenge me on anything ever for any reason.

"DON'T YOU EVEN FUCKING THINK OF SAYING ANYTHING BUT YES, STAFF SERGEANT! I SWEAR TO GOD I WILL FUCKING DESTROY YOU IF YOU EVER DISRESPECT ME AGAIN! YOU ARE A FUCKING BROKE-DICK SERGEANT AND NOTHING MORE. DON'T YOU EVER STEP TO ME LIKE THAT EVER AGAIN. DO YOU FUCKING UNDERSTAND?"

My vision was clouded with a red mist, and I became only slightly aware that my voice was reaching the levels of physical blows. (Thanks, Mom, for teaching me that little trick.) I sucked air through my teeth, chest heaving, and stared at her face. Strange how eye contact was taboo for me except in cases of outrage. I remembered the face I had seen on animals mere moments from killing their prey, and I suffused that into my own features. I wanted her to fear me in her soul. A perverse part of me sincerely hoped she was too stupid to take the not-so-subtle hint and would provoke me further. I'd been dying to get some aggression out, and boxing at the gym wasn't cutting it anymore.

But Sgt Dawn was now pressing herself as far back into the couch as she could get, her crutches sprawled on the floor from the table's impact. Her face was white as a bedsheet, and her eyes were huge. She mumbled an apology, careful not to make any sudden moves. I wasn't in the right frame of mind to hear any argument from her.

I exhaled a little more slowly and said, in deep, low tones at a much quieter volume, "Get the fuck out of my office right the fuck now. Get. Out."

I watched her pathetic scrabble for the crutches and offered no help. I didn't want to get too close to her. I knew myself to be nonviolent, but right now my dark-red hindbrain was screaming at me that it would feel damn good to just let it all out on someone.

I will not become that, I repeated over and over. *I will not be that person.*

Once Sgt Dawn had escaped, I sat again on the couch, staring at the shattered glass. *Shit. This table is probably going to take some explaining,* I thought. Oh well, better the furniture than the human being. I could afford to replace a table, but I wasn't about to nearly kill someone with my bare hands *again*.

50.

A COMMUNICATIONS COMPANY

Within a few months, I was transferred to Comm Company, a subordinate command of Headquarters Battalion. There was more need there for a staff sergeant, and with most of the unit still in Afghanistan, I would have lots of downtime to repair myself. The assignment was a gift from LtCol Vrable, who had noticed that I was going through something but respected the barriers between commanders and underlings by not asking what. He knew I needed some time, and he'd found a way to provide it. To Comm Company I went.

It was a small shop in a separate building from all other units, about a mile and a half down the road on Camp Lejeune from where I had worked for LtCol Vrable. Despite knowing that this was the best thing for everyone, I still felt ashamed of having been sent there. A whisper in my head told me I had really failed if I was being reassigned. I tried to squash it.

I figured everyone would be happy with this arrangement, but thanks to some severe personal disagreements with GySgt Nunez, I found out this was not so. GySgt Nunez had gotten wind of my reassignment and decided to make sure I received a proper welcome by calling ahead and telling anyone who would listen that I was a complete shitbag, not to be trusted with any task or believed on any front. I've never been sure what I did to that man, but he hated me with gusto. When I arrived and began the process of presenting myself to the chain of command, the look in their eyes said they were certain I'd be trouble. I flinched and kept quiet. Maybe I was trouble. I certainly wasn't doing myself any favors at this point.

My last stop was with the master gunnery sergeant in charge of admin, and he looked through my documentation. Finally, he put the papers down and leaned back in his chair.

"Staff Sergeant, you're going to Data Platoon. Currently, there's about four Marines in the platoon, while the rest of them are slated to come back in a month. You'll be under GySgt Primack. Do as he says, don't cause any trouble, and we'll see where things go from that point. Understood?"

"Yes, Master Guns." I felt hollow and stared at the wall behind his head.

"Good. Here's your check-in sheet. Have a good day."

I took my papers and headed out the nearest exit. Lucky for me, that exit was directly across the hall from the entrance to Data Platoon's shop. I pushed open the door and took in my new home. It was a huge, cavernous expanse of a warehouse-style bay. There was enough room in the shop to park six or seven Humvees side by side. Although it was mostly empty, there were gear boxes—hard green plastic containers used for shipping computer gear to and fro—stacked against the walls and in corners. Bright fluorescent lights hummed far above, hanging among the girders in the ceiling. Because all the gear was in the field, there was no need to control the environment, and the heat of the North Carolina summer was let in via the open bay doors at the far back. Against the back wall was a giant whiteboard and a long table where several Marines were gathered, playing cards with their feet up.

Welcome to your new home, Salz. Don't fuck this up.

As luck would have it, the small group of data Marines were loudly discussing how much better off they were than their rivals down the hall, Radio Platoon.

"Well, it's true, dog. Look at Radio; they have like five female Marines, and they are *always* in trouble for something."

"Data doesn't have females," replied one guy as he flicked a card onto the table. From what I could tell, they were playing spades. That was always the game when there were four people.

"That's fucking right! Thank God for that. Data is too difficult for girls. They're not really cut out for computers anyway."

The others started chuckling and ribbing him, prompting the weak defense, "It's not sexist; it's just true."

"Damn, dude, don't say that too loud. You'll get charged with harassment or some shit." They all laughed.

The radio operator MOS did have more women than the data systems MOS, though I never knew why. There had only been two females, including myself, in my class at comm school in Twentynine Palms, California. Data systems school was difficult, but the difficulty I experienced was in learning things like how to subnet out a limited IP range so that I could get every device on the network without conflict or error. I have no idea what they learned in radio school, but it probably had to do with frequencies and antenna ranges. I didn't see what the situation in my trousers had to do with those skills, but since these guys were my platoon now, it'd probably be best to leave that whole conversation alone. I just wanted peace and quiet.

As they continued their complaint session about gender diversity, they were unaware that I had entered and was now waiting at the makeshift front desk/counter with my receiving paperwork, pretending as though I required assistance with it. I banged on the desk with my fist, which is the appropriate way of announcing a Marine's presence in a variety of situations. A Marine named Sgt Williams jumped up from the card game and approached the counter.

"Good afternoon, Staff Sergeant! What can I do for you today?"

"Hello, Sergeant! I need someone to sign my check-in sheet,[55] please. I'm joining the unit as your new data chief."

His face was a picture of discomfort as a few things dawned on him. First, Data Platoon was getting a female Marine. Turns out the guys had been a little premature in their celebration of an all-male clubhouse. (I've heard prematurity is a common condition for a lot of guys their age.) Second, I outranked and out-billeted him. Third, there was no way in hell that I hadn't heard their remarks clearly.

But I wasn't going to mention it. I didn't care anymore. Who knows, maybe they were right and I wasn't cut out for this like I thought I was.

The Marine took my paperwork and gestured to the small opening in the counter that allowed passage into the rest of the shop.

"Come on in, Staff Sergeant. Gunny's in the back. I'll take you to him."

I followed the sergeant to the rear of the shop, ignoring the curious stares from the other cardplayers. They'd figure out my presence soon enough. Hopefully, we could all just ignore each other in peace. We reached a door in the back, which I assumed led to a maintenance closet, and I was therefore surprised when Sgt Williams opened it to reveal a brightly lit office instead. Even sweeter, a blast of cold air told me that it

55 The paperwork process for new Marines upon arriving to a new unit

was an air-conditioned office. I now wanted to be in that office instead of standing behind the sergeant, growing stickier by the minute.

Sgt Williams cleared his throat.

"Excuse me, Gunny. There's a new staff sergeant here to see you."

I peered over Sgt Williams's shoulder to try to catch a glimpse of GySgt Primack. There was no point. He was wedged behind a shelf/desk combo that concealed his entire body except for the soles of his boots, which were propped up on the desk. The room smelled of reheated pizza.

"Hmm?"

Sgt Williams gave me an embarrassed smile. "Gunny, there's a new person here."

"Oh." The feet fell off the desk with an unceremonious *thunk*. After some unfolding, GySgt Primack appeared from behind the shelves. He was tall, bespectacled, and looked tired of everything. He shoved his glasses up on his nose and took the proffered papers from the sergeant. "Thanks, I've got it."

I was taken aback. Unlike all the gunnery sergeants I'd known up to this point, GySgt Primack didn't seem to give a fuck about my rank or his. His whole slouched demeanor screamed, "I'm just waiting for retirement. Who cares about any of this shit?" Carefully, I tried to feel out his attitude so I could calibrate a response. I needn't have bothered.

Sgt Williams departed. As the door closed, the room fell deadly quiet. There were a grand total of three desks. A quick glance told me one was occupied by an officer, based on a spare pair of silver bars left beside a coffee mug. I wondered what I might have to do to get the third desk. It looked empty, with scattered detritus of office supplies, spare laptops, chargers, and the rest as its only occupant. Yes, I might be with striking distance of other people, but there was air-conditioning. That wasn't to be sneezed at.

"Salzburg? Salzgerber? What the fuck is your name?" GySgt Primack scowled at the papers.

"Salz-ge-ber," I responded in the tones of someone who has to do this all the time, every day. "Just call me Salz, Gunnery Sergeant."

"And just call me Gunny, for fuck sake. You're not a private."

"Aye, Gunny."

"Well, I don't know what to tell you. There isn't shit to do. Be here by 0830 for accountability, but otherwise, if you have appointments or movers or whatever the fuck going on, take care of it. I'm ninety days out until I retire, and I don't care to spend energy managing you. Manage yourself. The rest of the unit will be trickling in soon from Afghanistan, and then all of them will be on leave once they're back, so you have basically six months of nothing to look forward to. Welcome to Data Platoon. Do you smoke?"

I blinked. "Uh, yes, Gunnery—Gunny."

"Cool, we'll finish the rest of your brief in the smoke pit. I'm dying in here." He patted his pockets for his lighter before heading out the door. "Where you coming from?" The heat came back as we left office, all the more unwelcome for the contrast.

"Headquarters, H-1," I replied, citing the exact building I'd worked in. Everyone knew H-1 because the four-star general was housed there. That was a place to avoid, in the minds of most Marines.

"Gross." Gunny led the way to a gaggle of Marines under a light fog of cigarette smoke. As a sign of their hated status as smokers, the designated area was out in the sun, in the corner of the parking lot. Command probably figured shade would motivate Marines to spend even more time out there and so deprived them of it.

Thus began my time with Comm Company.

51.

ONE SHOT, ONE FILL

Urinalysis testing is commonplace in the Marines. At some point, someone decided it would be super if we all got randomly tested for substances we shouldn't ingest—yet another groan-inducing event that Marines walked into face-first when they arrived at the shop in the morning.

For obvious reasons, it was never announced ahead of time. It was always a gigantic pain-in-the-rectum operation, too, because Social Security numbers had to be verified, bottles of pee had to be handled properly without biohazard issues exceeding the normal threshold, and observers had to be located and secured before things could get underway in earnest.

The Substance Abuse Counseling Office (SACO) would notify command they were coming down, and then the scramble would begin to nail down staff NCOs before we got away. Observers at Comm Company, where I was now assigned, were almost always staff sergeants or gunnery sergeants. Our job, to put it as tastefully as possible, was to make sure that the human being filling the little plastic cup was not pulling any shenanigans while their pants were around their ankles. If there is one way to make the average Marine Corps workday worse than usual, it is by forcing people to stand very close to other people and stare at their junk while they urinate. Not trying to kink-shame anyone who is into that sort of thing, but, suffice to say, it could make my mornings really *stink*.

I arrived at work one Monday after receiving a phone call from GySgt Crosby telling me to skip my bullshit gym session and get my ass to the shop ASAP. It didn't matter what I actually did for PT; to GySgt Crosby it was all bullshit because the man considered anything short of a triathlon a waste of time. The plot twist was that I hadn't even gotten out of bed yet when he called, so I had to pretend he ruined my morning. He had done just that, of course. I just didn't know it yet.

I dragged my ass into the dark-brown, brick building and, stifling a yawn, reached for the glass doors by the front office. Just as I was about to stumble through (I'm not a morning person, and no amount of beatings changed that), I realized there were sheets of paper taped to the glass. Blinking until my eyes focused, I saw what it was and groaned.

It was the dreaded list of names.

The list was every Marine in the unit who had been randomly selected to come fill a cup for SACO. Approximately 80 percent of the list was of no concern to me because those were male Marines and therefore not my problem, as far as being an observer went. It was the surprising number of female names that made me want to hit my head against the wall. *Great.* As I was the only female SNCO on deck (at that time; others came and went in the surrounding weeks), every single female would require my "personal" attention. I heaved a deep sigh and then went to find GySgt Crosby.

He was sitting in the shared room that served as our office along with 1stLt Smith's.[56] Gunny crouched over his laptop, staring at the screen as though it had been cheeky to him. Ever since returning from Afghanistan, he'd been what I can only describe as "spiky." I didn't ask why. I mostly waited for him to speak and otherwise kept to myself. I could probably say nice things about Gunny Crosby, but that might offend him.

He grunted at me as I dumped my backpack in my desk chair and tried to log in to my own computer. Without taking his eyes off his screen, he snapped, "About fucking time there, Staff Sergeant. Piss test starts in ten minutes."

"Good morning, Gunnery Sergeant. I saw that."

GySgt Crosby was that rare type of man who was tall and skinny while also managing to hulk and loom. He stood and stretched, looking about enthusiastic as I felt. He glowered at me.

"You look like shit. Didn't sleep? Out drinking all night?"

"No, Gunnery Sergeant. I didn't get any coffee this morning, that's all. Or even soda."

---

56   That IS his real name. What's the point in changing it?

In a rare moment of magnanimity, he gestured toward the small refrigerator we all stored our lunches in behind the door.

"There's some fucking Diet Dr. Pepper in there, if you want one, Staff Sergeant.[57]"

Before I could stop myself, I mumbled, "I don't want your old-man soda, Gunny." We all teased him for drinking diet soda by the case, especially when it was a rubbish soda to begin with.

"You shut your whore mouth!" he snapped back.

We stared at each other in shock for a moment, and then I burst out laughing. Holy shit, neither of us were morning people! All the tiredness and stress kept me laughing longer than the moment really called for, and Gunny relaxed a bit, clear that he hadn't crossed a line and neither had I. He threw open the door to head to the testing check-in area, and I trailed behind him, not entirely ready to do my bathroom duties. I tried thinking up a few ways to lessen the awkwardness while obeying the rules, but my imagination rebelled against such a vulgar task.

Out in the hallway, I leaned against the wall behind the testing tables and stifled a yawn. Marines began arriving and reporting in for their piss test. Down at the other end of the long tables, I heard GySgt Crosby haranguing a male Marine for signing on the wrong line. Slowly, my eyes started to close.

"Morning, Staff Sergeant!"

"Yes, unfortunately it is."

My eyes snapped open to see LCpl Harris searching the taped printout for her name.

"Congratulations, you're my first customer."

LCpl Harris smirked, signed under her name, and then turned and took off her cammie blouse.[58] Folding it neatly and setting it against the wall where it wouldn't get walked on, she straightened and waited for her plastic cup. I found the garbage bag under the table, pulled out a generic plastic cup, and tossed it to her. I yawned again and came out from behind the table to follow her to the restroom.

"Um, Staff Sergeant . . ." Harris shifted her weight and gave me an awkward look. "The . . . other cup? Please?"

"Oh. Yes. Sorry. Fuck. Let me find those." I went back to my station

---

57 This quirk of his, wherein my entire rank was used instead of a name, continued my entire tenure under his leadership.

58 No, she didn't just go topless. We wear T-shirts under our cammies.

and looked for the *other* bag of plastic cups. They were bigger than the normal ones because, well, there's no way around it: females can't hit a small target with their urine very well. I couldn't figure out why they didn't just buy big cups exclusively and be done with it instead of two different ones, but hey, that's why I'm only getting paid $2.76 an hour.[59]

I tossed the bigger cup to her, and we proceeded down the hall to the head.

LCpl Harris walked in front of me so I could make sure she wasn't, I don't know, pulling some clean pee out of her pocket and putting it in the cup before I'd notice. She carried the cup at shoulder height in one hand, trading barbs with the males shuttling back to the tables with their full cups and the occasional worried expression. As we reached the door, LCpl Harris pushed it open with her hip, and we entered the spartan bathroom.

It was a very military head. The tiles were the same color as pea soup, the stalls looked like they'd done more service in the Marine Corps than our sergeant major, and the toilets were white porcelain with black seats. LCpl Harris set both cups on the aluminum counter just below cheap mirrors the size of a notebook and began washing her hands. I crossed my arms and watched, pretending not to monitor such a mundane task. Once she had dried off, she picked up the big cup and went into a stall.

I pushed the stall door open, and while Harris undid her trousers, I made conversation.

"What did you guys do for PT this morning?" I asked, feeling like a weirdo as she dropped trou.

"We played football, Staff Sergeant. The grass was really slick, though, so we didn't play for as long as we wanted." Harris finally got into the seated position and then locked eyes on the toilet paper dispenser and tried to carry on like no one was staring at her. I risked a quick glance to see that her, um, bits were the place where the urine sample was coming from and then stared at the wall behind her head. *Geezus, this is weird.*

Once there was enough in the big cup to complete the rest of the operation, she set it on the toilet paper dispenser and finished up. With the cup set to one side, I had something to stare at that wasn't another human being, so I watched it carefully in case it showed signs of wanting to leave the situation as badly as I did. Harris stood and did up her pants

---

59   If a Marine is a Marine 24/7, then technically, after some clever math, this was in fact my hourly wage.

and then emerged back to the sinks. Carefully, so neither of us would have to do this a second time, she poured the pee from the big cup into the small cup and then threw the big cup in the trash can. She sealed the small cup and washed her hands again, this time more thoroughly. I hummed a tuneless melody to myself and waited.

She picked up the small cup, once again holding it over her shoulder, and we returned to the tables. There, she took a small strip of red tamper tape and placed it across the lid, initialed it with a black sharpie, and placed it in the cardboard box that was to be its home until the SACO pulled it for testing. I leaned over the list, found her name, and signed under it to indicate I'd observed her providing the sample.

"All right, you're good to go. Thanks, Harris."

"No worries, Staff Sergeant." She flashed me a brief grin and then disappeared into the throng of Marines now surrounding the table. The next female came up, and away we went.

"Good morning, Marines! One shot, one fill! Step right up for your clear plastic cup!" Snark was my only way of reducing a nasty job to a tolerable one.

After an hour or so of repeating this process, I'd seen the most eclectic collection of female undergarments outside of a fetishistic catalogue. Some of the ladies had even worn male undergarments instead because boxers were far less awkward in their opinion. Two hours later, all the females were done, and any appetite I'd had for lunch was ruined. Scanning the crowd and double-checking the list, I was pleased to discover that all the paperwork was correct, and I was off the hook now. I sighed with relief, sealed the box that contained our specimens, and then returned to the office. I didn't have any work to do, but there was internet access in there and some sweet, sweet air-conditioning, so it was my haven.

A while later, GySgt Crosby stormed in, slamming the door back and tossing something in the middle of the floor. I looked up from my screen and stared at him.

"Everything all right, Gunnery Sergeant?"

"These nasty, cheating FUCKS!" he barked.

"Huh?"

GySgt Crosby pointed at the thing on the floor.

"Can you fucking *believe that shit?!*"

I glanced down, and once I saw it, my eyes widened in disgust and horror.

It was a, well, a . . . strap-on. With bright-white cloth straps that, thanks to an internet search, I knew were for going around the legs and waist of a human being. There was a clear plastic bladder that was still moist from whatever had been in it. And a flaccid, flesh-colored penis on what I assume was the front.

What the fuck?

"Gunny, I'm not sure that's e-okay," I remarked while refusing to crack a smile.

He growled and kicked it under the lieutenant's desk.

"I caught one of the nasty little fuckers wearing that! He was using it to piss!"

GySgt Crosby pulled out and screwed together a rifle cleaning rod, and then used it to fetch the thing out from the dark recesses under the lieutenant's desk. Holding it at the pole's length, he turned and carried it back out the door.

"I'm going to First Sergeant's office, Staff Sergeant. Don't fucking come looking for me."

"Why would I—"

The door slammed shut behind him. He had left.

For few minutes, I just stared in shock at the wall. I mean, it was gross and obviously against the rules, but I was amazed by the audacity and ingenuity of such a device. Someone really, *really* wanted to use recreational substances unhindered to go to those lengths. My horrified imagination started to picture what the female equivalent would be, and I squashed the whole train of thought before it ended in a fiery cataclysm.

That's enough for one day. I locked my computer and decided that now was a good time to hit the gym. Nothing cleared my head like focusing intently on how much I loathed running, and right now, I needed that. But first, a quick trip to the head.

PART NINE:

THE PENTAGON, WASHINGTON, DC

52.

SGT GARGANO PUNCHED A COP?!

The Marines taught me cold calculation in a lot of ways. You wouldn't expect the Marine Corps to teach deep, careful thinking, but there's a large difference between the schoolroom and the actual live environment. The schoolroom is all about teaching habits that will keep you alive when shit becomes chaotic. I may not have any clue about what is happening or why, but I damn well know how to keep my weapon on safe until I'm ready to shoot something and keep my finger straight and off the trigger until I am ready to fire.

The real world throws curve balls and exceptions all the time, and that's when the ability to let go of emotion and actually think comes into play. Thinking requires the knowledge of how to think (that's actually a skill), and that requires knowing how to ask questions. For example, when someone comes running to tell me that three of my Marines were just caught with a goat in a govvy (government vehicle), I need to let the question-asking kick in before the reacting begins.

"Where were they caught?"

"By whom?"

"Was the goat intact and alive?"

"How long had it been since chow?"

You'd be absolutely correct if you thought that my first impulse was to go immediately to where the Marines, the goat, and the vehicle were located, but when it comes to Marines, it pays to ask questions first. The answers are not always what you assume. And, sometimes, they are exactly what you assume.

I often found that asking questions could defuse situations faster than yelling. For starters, as a female Marine, yelling was not my go-to. The men took it wrong. When they got yelled at by a large, angry gunnery sergeant of the male persuasion, they'd walk away afterward going, "Damn, we just got our asses chewed." When a female Marine yelled at them, they'd grumble about being "bitched at." If I was going to yell, I wanted it to be seen for the ass-chewing I intended it to be.

So, I asked questions instead.

"Where were you?"

"How much did you drink?"

"Who was with you?"

"When did you get there?"

"What exactly happened?"

"Why is *that* what happened?"

"For the love of GOD, why did you choose to do THAT?"

Later on, I was told this was far more intimidating.

As I learned from the counterintelligence Marines, people tend to stumble far faster when they are getting rapid-fire questions and their answers are being paid attention to very closely. Even better was the trick of repeating a question I'd already asked and then watching their faces as they tried to remember the answer previously given. I was surprised at how often their answers fell apart when they were asked a second time. New information came out, or facts changed. On rare occasions, the story stayed exactly the same. Sometimes I interrogated them just to buy myself time to process what was happening while looking like I was actively engaging with the problem.

I was asleep at home one evening, peacefully blowing slobber bubbles into my pillow, when my cell phone rang. It rang for almost a minute before I realized what I was hearing. I fumbled for it, still half asleep, and blinked blearily at the screen: 2 a.m. *Who could possibly be calling me at two in the morning?* After a few false starts, I made out the name on the screen. It was Sgt Winklevoss, my platoon sergeant. *Oh no. If he's calling me now, shit has gone sideways.*

I groaned and tapped the answer button.

"What?" I grumbled, rubbing my face.

"Staff Sergeant? It's Sgt Wink. Um, we have a problem."

Sgt Winklevoss was very polite, respectful, and conscientious. These qualities made him extremely dependable. He was also great at analyzing situations and their possible outcomes, which meant that he always called to let me know if things were about to go up the chain of command. I was quietly grateful for every time Sgt Winklevoss had saved me from getting blindsided by senior Marines with bad news.

"Yes, Wink, I imagine we do. Mind telling me what it is?"

"Um, Sgt Gargano has been arrested. They're saying he punched a cop in the face."

I groaned. What the *hell?* This was not good. This was *not* good. *Okay, okay, let's calm down and think.* Marines sometimes make things sound a bit more dramatic than they actually are. But I couldn't think of a single way this could be less bad than it sounded. It was time to get some facts.

"Where is Gargano being held?"

"Are you there with him?"

"Who told you this?"

Those were the first things I needed to know. If I was getting dragged out of bed, I wanted to know where I was going, who was there, and what kind of situation I was walking into.

"He's at the barracks," Wink replied.

I paused, wondering if I'd heard him correctly.

"What? I thought you said he's been arrested! By police? They've let him go?"

"Yes, um . . . he was arrested Friday. I just found out about it."

I could hear Sgt Winklevoss cringing through the phone line.

"He fucking WHAT?" I sat up, fully, unpleasantly aware now. It was two in the morning, as in MONDAY morning. *How the hell did no one think to tell me this days ago?* I was rapidly becoming furious, not a difficult feat after such a rude awakening.

"Wink, tell me what happened." I couldn't even think of the right questions at the moment.

Sgt Winklevoss explained that he'd been at the barracks, playing video games in his room, and one of the troops playing on his team mentioned that Sgt Gargano had gotten arrested on Friday. When the Marines played video games together, like *Call of Duty*, they often used voice communication to coordinate their movements in-game. In between rounds, they usually had casual conversations in the virtual lobby about what they'd been up to all weekend outside of the game. Sgt Gargano was a regular player, so when the team noticed his absence online, the story came out. Sgt Winklevoss had listened carefully and then told them he needed a bathroom break, stepped outside, and called me. He only knew what had been said online, so he couldn't answer many more questions without arousing suspicion among his teammates.

To someone outside Marine culture, this probably sounds insane, but there's very well-established codes of conduct that are unspoken among the lower enlisted. When I was a lance corporal, we always had the freshest information about the battalion, company, or shop. Colonels might think they run things, but the Lance Corporal Underground is an intelligence network built on the people who actually file the paperwork, process the expense reports, and do the grunt work. The lofty high-and-mighty Marines make choices, but it's always we minions who execute their plans.

On one occasion, I embarrassed my major when I came to tell Master Sergeant (and, by proxy, the major) that our travel was delayed until the next day because a senior officer had usurped our vehicles. The corporal working in embark had told me so. The major snapped at me that I was wrong and that the colonel had told *him* that we were leaving today. Then, moments later, the colonel called the officers to a meeting, where he passed word that we were now delayed by one day. The major had come back furious with me. Sorry, sir, but the Lance Corporal Underground knows better.

If you want to be plugged in and get the scoop before the word comes down officially, the rule is that you do NOT go outside the underground and snitch. Sgt Winklevoss was plugged in enough that if the other junior Marines found out he was sliding me the occasional heads-up, he might be left out of future information sharing. That would be bad for him and me both. Therefore, there was a limit on how much of my cat's-paw he could be in this situation. I needed to think of a way he could help out without betraying the connections he used for the intel.

"Okay, Wink, here's the plan. Go to Gargano's room and ask him what the hell happened. Just sergeant to sergeant. See if you can convince him to call me so we can get a strategy together before MSgt Thomas finds out. We both know that man will go straight up the chain of command if he thinks he can burn Gargano. He freaking hates him. I imagine that if the DC police let him go home for the weekend, there's more to this story than 'punched a cop.' Cops don't let you go home after you 'punch a cop.'"

After all, Sgt Gargano was known to be impetuous and rash, but not straight-up stupid.

As the staff NCO in charge at the shop, I technically should have immediately called the gunnery sergeant and reported everything. As a Marine, however, I should handle everything at my level if that was at all possible. As a human being, I felt that I just didn't have anywhere near enough information to make decisions on next steps yet.

I decided to go back to bed for the few hours I had left before work. I had accounted for the whereabouts of my Marines and their status. Sgt Winklevoss said everyone was in the barracks, and there were no other reported (or discovered) issues. Everything else would still be messed up at 0900. Might as well have a clear head to take whatever was coming.

When I arrived at the shop several hours later, I snatched up Sgt Gargano the moment I saw him. "Hey, Gargano. Come with me. I need coffee," I muttered.

Sgt Gargano sighed and followed me out of the office and into the Pentagon's long, labyrinthian hallways. At first glance, it was easy to believe Gargano had punched *someone*. He had the face of an amateur boxer and the square build of a man who could easily give and take when it came to trading blows. He also had chips on both shoulders, hated everything about being stationed at the Pentagon, and really wanted to go anywhere else in the Marine Corps.

"Okay, spill it. What the fuck is this I hear about you punching a cop? You look in pretty good shape for a man fighting the law."

We were weaving our way to the Pentagon's food court where the coffee shop was. The line there was always insane, so we'd have lots of time to chat.

"I didn't punch a cop! This other guy did, and they thought it was me. They let me go after we got that figured out." Sgt Gargano looked annoyed at having to explain anything to me.

"What, like you just told the officers it wasn't you, and they apologized and let you go on your way? Wait, no. WHY were you in any position to be suspected of punching the cop? Why did anyone anywhere punch a cop Friday night?"

I was struggling to back him into a corner, and I was getting a bit angry.

"I didn't do anything," he grumbled. He crossed his arms and fell silent.

It was my turn to sigh. "Look, Gargano. I know you hate me and the Marine Corps and the Pentagon specifically. But Master Sergeant knows about this now. He used to *be* a cop. He's going to get about a mile deep in your ass when we get back from coffee. So, use this time to figure out what you're going to say, all right? Because I don't care enough to do paperwork on you." Gargano didn't respond to kindness, so I'd try cruelty if I had to.

"Some guys outside a club in Adams Morgan shoved into me, and the cops tried to break up the fight. One of them swung and hit the cop accidentally, but since all of us were in the group, the cops thought it was me. Once they saw I didn't have a black eye, 'cause, like, the cop swung back at the guy, they let me go. That's all, Staff Sergeant. That's all that happened. Like, it wasn't nothing, okay?"

"Cool. Then we have nothing to worry about. Who else was with you? Because you know they're getting dragged into the office too. Master Sergeant spreads the love."

"Sgt Emerson and Sgt Hathaway."

"Great. Thank you. Want a coffee?"

We had finally made it to the front of the line, and I felt a lot better about things. Turns out all the questions were finally giving me results, and, stunningly, no one was getting in trouble.

53.

FAN MAIL AND THE FALLEN FLY

A t the Pentagon, I had the unusual experience of seeing the highest echelons of Marine Corps leadership more often than the average Devil Dog. The commandant was based there, and that meant the sergeant major of the Marine Corps was too. While they spent a lot of time traveling around the Corps, giving talks at different units and bases to keep in touch with Marines at many levels, when they were home in DC, they also held "all-hands." These are giant gatherings at which the CMC and the sergeant major of the Marine Corps brief the troops on impending policy changes and reinforce changes that have already come, talk about issues and solutions, training, and so on. Attendance is not optional.

That year, the CMC announced a change to uniform wear that specifically mandated the sleeves on all cammies to be worn down all year round. Like other changes, that was incredibly unpopular. Marines prided themselves on their tightly rolled sleeves—to the point of rolling them so smoothly and tightly that circulation was impaired to the lower part of their extremities. What made the edict even more upsetting was that we had all been hounded to pieces about having tattoos. For reasons above my paygrade, we were forbidden from having tattoos that were visible in uniform. But Marines go with tattoos like sailors do. It's part of the culture, right up there with drinking and hitting things really hard. Now, with sleeves down, the rule seemed increasingly arbitrary, and therefore an all-hands was scheduled where we thought we'd get an explanation—not the kind of explanation where something is explained, but more along the lines of "Because we fucking say so."

At the appointed day and hour, I walked to the auditorium. Like most Marines, I rarely wanted to travel between points alone because if two or more of us were lost, there was far less chance we would get excoriated for skipping out. Today, I went along with SSgt Jones, a Marine from my shop who seemed completely content with anything and everything so long as the gym was open and his chow was uninterrupted. SSgt Jones had the kind of demeanor that goes really well with the Marines. He didn't mind, so it didn't matter.

"Jones, look at me real quick. Am I jacked up? Before we go in there, I want to know I'm not jacked up. Am I? Jones? JONES!"

SSgt Jones shoved his protein snack bar back in his cargo pocket, resigned to having to wait until the event ended. He gave me a cursory glance, checking for any gross violation of regulations that might get me eaten alive by the ambitious and obsequious officers trying to curry the CMC's favor by showing their dedication to being motivated and hard-assed.

"You're good. See anything wrong with me?"

"No."

As usual, SSgt Jones looked ready for a recruiting poster. It was sickening.

We followed the throngs of Marines in. Normally, at all-hands events, all the Marines tried to get seats in the back rows. This was as routine as the meetings themselves. Command would call an all-hands "formation," and everyone would try to cram into the seats farthest away from the presenters and speakers. Then someone who was really bucking for promotion would stand up, bark at all of us to cover down on the front rows, and then the private pecking order would force the lower ranks and billets to obey while the higher-ups trickled in after them, thereby keeping a sort of back-row privilege. We all knew the drill, and we never tried to preempt it. You knew where you stood by how long you could hold out before having to sit down.

But since this was the CMC and sergeant major of the MC, everyone cut the shit and sat in the first available chair. Shortly after we were all seated, we were called to attention, and with much ceremony, the commandant came to the stage. We stood at attention until he gave the order to be seated again. This sitting-standing-sitting thing reminded me of what I'd seen of Catholic Mass, and the rituals carried a similar purpose.

When he began to speak, everyone was completely silent. You did not want to be the one who took even one eyeball off the CMC. Even coughing would get you in trouble—later.

"Good afternoon, Marines!" the commandant boomed.

The entire room replied as one voice, loud to a point approaching the auditory threshold of pain. After a few motivated platitudes, the CMC got right down to business. This was not about uniform regs. The issues of the day were the scandals that had erupted from Marine misbehavior in combat theaters. The CMC was trying to control the political fallout from some very bad headlines that went all the way up to Congress and had inspired congressional hearings. In short, he was displeased.

As he talked, Jones and I watched with the kind of shocked expressions people wear when it's not *their* misdeeds causing trouble. As we listened intently, the CMC showed slides of the offenders and explained why they were horrible people. I got a bit of a thrill from being so close to what the head of the entire Marine Corps was thinking, even though what he was thinking was, *What the fuck is wrong with you people?*

Unfortunately, some of those thoughts were a bit garbled by his preoccupation with the bad scenario overall. I'm not sure what the sentence was supposed to be, but what I heard as the CMC paced the stage, looking tired and stressed, was this: "Marines aren't all lily white, and I'm trying to turn you into axe murderers . . ."

Without moving my head, I shot a sideways look at Jones's face to see if I was losing my mind. His confused expression confirmed that he'd heard it too. *What the hell?*

The CMC continued without any more exciting misspeak, and when he finally ran out of things to say, we were all called to attention once more, and he departed. As he left, I saw his shoulders sag ever so slightly. Poor guy, he probably expected being CMC to be a lot easier than this.

Now came the fun stuff. Sergeant Major wasn't bound by the same protocols as the CMC. He could speak a bit more freely and way more coarsely. He strutted back and forth across the stage with the barely contained energy of a motivational life coach, speaking encouragingly about how Marines could overcome anything and that a couple of shitheads giving us a bad name was something we ourselves could police and prevent. Every Marine was critical to protecting the legacy of the Marine Corps.

It was a fantastic speech, and I perked up in spite of myself. Then he completely floored me.

"If the Marine Corps is going to be at its strongest, we need to embrace our female Marines. We need to realize that everyone who earned the title of Marine is valuable, and we are stronger together. Every unit I've visited with the commandant has been outstanding, and the females are contributing to that equally. Marines are Marines. Enough said!"

Holy . . . For the very first time in my entire career, I felt myself fighting back emotion at an all-hands. He . . . spoke . . . to *me*. I felt seen.

I never, ever thought I'd hear that from any sergeant major, let alone a man as powerful as "The Sergeant Major" of the Marine Corps. His saying it was just wow. If he said it here, to *these* people, that meant real change could be happening. I became a fan of his right then and there.

Once the all-hands concluded, Jones and I wandered back to our shop, stopping to get some coffee in the food court. We both got a kick out of that off-the-wall axe-murderer remark.

"I don't think I have the time in my schedule to become an axe murderer. That's easily six to eight hours or more a week. I'd have to give up video games."

Jones shook his head. "Me neither. I don't have space in my apartment for my workout gear, let alone corpses."

"Of course you have a home gym. Why didn't I realize that before?" I poked his bicep.

"All I know is, if he adds an axe-throwing portion to the PFT, I'm going to have to retool my workouts."

Returning to my desk, I stared at my computer screen and grappled with my newfound respect for the sergeant major of the Marine Corps. I mean, of course I respected him before. But that was the kind of chilly respect I have for successful people residing on some mountaintop far away, who I will never meet and will never notice me. But now I respected him on a personal level, and that was a new experience. I decided I should tell him so.

A big benefit of being a data Marine was that I had email access everywhere I went, and by the nature of my responsibilities, I had the power to email anyone in the Marine Corps. Of course, I was never so stupid as to email outside my rank range unless protocol and chain of command demanded otherwise. Written evidence of undue familiarity was not on the list of mistakes I was keen to make.

Now I laced my fingers together and stretched. *Let's write an email to the sergeant major of the Marine Corps!*

I began.

"Good morning, Sergeant Major!"

I hit backspace and then deleted it. *It's afternoon, you moron. Screw up the proper greeting of the day, and you're going to get your ass chewed. Oo-kay. Let's start over.*

"Good afternoon, Sergeant Major!"

Wait, is that his proper formal title? Do I type out "of the Marine Corps"? What if that's disrespect? I agonized for a bit. What if my status as a mere staff sergeant meant that any email at all, regardless of the words, was disrespect? *No. Be bold!* He was the most senior enlisted person in the entire Corps, and a fan letter would be welcome so long as I was strictly professional, polite, and kept my message streamlined. He was a busy man.

After twenty minutes of going back and forth, I finally had a neat paragraph that seemed harmless enough. I thanked him for his wisdom (flattery was a good tactic with higher-ups so long as no one else saw you do it), and said I appreciated his inclusion of female Marines in his message. I stopped before I expressed any other opinions, and I wrapped up with a neat conclusion and signature.

Then I stared at the screen, feeling like I was making a major life choice.

Fuck it. You're getting out in like eleven months. Do it.

I clicked *Send* and went for a couple laps around the E-ring of the Pentagon to burn off my nervous energy. *What am I even doing right now? Salz, you don't know your limits. Whee!*

The next day, I came into the office feeling the Sword of Damocles hanging over my head. I put my stuff down, checked in with the watch officer, said hi to Gunny Moore, and went to get coffee—all to avoid opening my email and seeing whatever disaster I had invited with that message.

I argued with myself.

You idiot, Salz. You could've just kept your giddiness to yourself, but oh no, that wouldn't do.

I have the responsibility to encourage leadership to keep including us. If no one ever tells them that the effort is being heard, they might stop talking about us altogether.

Who do you think you are, Salz? You're losing it.

Finally, I sat down and stared at the email icon on my desktop.

Do it. Click on it. You can always run to Gunny Moore and ask for help.

There's nothing he can do, but still . . .

I clicked. There, in my inbox, was a reply. From the sergeant major of the Marine Corps. To me. *Oh my God.*

I opened it. The message was simple and direct, but it was not what I was expecting:

> Ooh-Rah SSgt! Thank you for your email. I am a proponent of an inclusive Marine Corps and I am excited to share the Commandant's message that all Marines matter.
>
> I'd like to invite you to my office on Friday at 1300 to discuss it further. I'm always happy to meet motivated Marines! See you then.

The message was signed and certified. I stared at it. *Did he just order me to come to his office? Wait. I don't know what to say to him! I'll say something stupid! Argh!*

Feeling and doubtless looking a bit concussed, I wandered over to GySgt Moore's desk a few feet away. I stood staring at him, goggle-eyed, for a moment before he looked up. When you might have gotten in over your head, it helps to ask for backup.

"What, Staff Sergeant?"

"Gunny . . . I did a thing."

GySgt Moore looked smug. He knew I was probably up to something, and I was born with a face that made me look guilty anyway, so hearing me sound like I had screwed up hard pleased him. It's nice to be right about someone.

"Who'd you piss off this time?"

I paused. "No one. Maybe? Possibly the sergeant major of the Marine Corps?"

That got his full attention. "You *WHAT*?"

"I may have sent him an email. A nice email. He doesn't seem mad. Um. He wants me to come to his office."

Contradictory expressions fought for control of GySgt Moore's features. Horror and curiosity were in a three-way tie with a bit of envy. I didn't know which way he'd go, but I did know that GySgt Moore really liked meeting important people, and this was an invitation he'd enjoy being a part of. I decided I could use a friend when I went to report in and played to that.

"Would you come with me? Just to see that I don't accidentally make our shop look bad?"

Yeah, I know, it's a bit slimy and playing to type, but my crushing social anxiety made meeting complete strangers kind of brutal. I was sincere in my desire for help. I also didn't want this absolutely enormous jump in the chain of command to fall entirely on my shoulders. I was in uncharted territory.

GySgt Moore puffed up with pride and smiled. "Sure, Marine. I'll inspect your uniform before we go so you don't embarrass me. When did he tell you to come up?" Our office was on the second floor. The sergeant major's office was on the fourth.

"Tomorrow at 1300. I don't know what to say to him."

"Forward me his email."

The next day, I was really nervous. I skipped chow, and at precisely 1230, GySgt Moore and I started making our way to Sergeant Major's office. As I've mentioned before, in the Marines, if you aren't *at least* fifteen minutes early to any appointment, you are late. The whole distance, I just babbled to GySgt Moore, who was rather amused by the whole thing.

"You wrote him. You were all brave hitting that send button and now you're getting cold feet? What did you think was going to happen?"

"I dunno! I thought he'd probably ignore me! Or tell me to fuck off. I didn't think he'd be like, 'Hey, let's meet!' I don't talk to people like him. *They* talk at me and I say, 'Roger that.' Or something."

"Look, it'll be fine. I read his email. He just wants to shake hands or whatever. Just smile and nod. If it gets awkward, I'll take over, okay?"

"Okay. Okay. That's better."

By 1240, we were at the door. GySgt Moore pounded on the hatch and stood with me as I hovered slightly behind him and to the right. In a space like this one, every petty little detail of protocol is important. The door opened, and a female sergeant greeted us, inviting us into the reception area. Once I was through the door, I was taken in by the luxury of the room. Most Marine Corps facilities cannot be described as beautiful by even the most generous liar. But this room had new furniture, lush blue carpet, hardwood bookshelves, brand-new computers, decorations on every wall, the works. There were pictures of Marines doing everything from handstands while surfing to charging across a battlefield in the desert. The young sergeant who served as the sergeant major's secretary went back behind her desk and retrieved a very expensive-looking digital camera.

Setting it neatly on the desk, she said she would let Sergeant Major know we had arrived.

Within minutes, Sergeant Major came bursting through the door between his office and the reception room, radiating a field of sheer Marine Corps motivation that probably knocked down children and pets wherever he went. He wasn't wearing a uniform. Instead, he had on a gray suit with a lavender tie, but no matter what kind of cloth might be covering him, he was undeniably a sergeant major in every sense of the title.

What really set him apart from any other sergeant major I'd ever known was the glowing smile plastered across his face. He beamed at us with pride as we got to our feet and GySgt Moore greeted him formally. I repeated the greeting and took in the scene while Sergeant Major vigorously shook GySgt Moore's hand, saying things like, "Oo-rah! Motivate! Outstanding to meet you!" He was the first person I'd ever met that I could describe by the word *dynamo* with zero inaccuracy.

However, because I'd taken my eyes off his face, I now saw a looming disaster.

Oh no.

His fly was down. Not like halfway down; not like just needs a little tug to fix it. Completely unzipped, and the gap was gaping. When he shifted his weight, it threatened to yawn. I yanked my gaze back to his face and stared at him like he was imparting the secrets of the universe. *Oh my God. How do I tell the sergeant major of the Marine Corps his fly is down?*

He was going full steam with GySgt Moore, preaching the gospel of an almost legendary Corps that generated heroes the way Hershey made chocolates. GySgt Moore somehow kept pace with him, making the right sounds between emphatic statements of true love for the Marines he represented. I bit my lip. *I can't interrupt him when he's talking about the warrior spirit. How do I say this?* I wanted to ignore the fly situation, but part of me is still in middle school and wanted to giggle like an idiot.

Okay, get it together. You're a professional. Just keep your eyes on his face.

GySgt Moore, may all the gods of wardrobe issues bless him, kept Sergeant Major happily going while I started to relax.

Okay, you got this. No big deal. I started to chime in to the flow of gold and crimson permeating the conversation. It had only been five minutes, but my internal struggle made it seem longer. As they were winding down, Sergeant Major turned to me and said, "Let's get a picture together!" He shouted out the door, "Sergeant! Get the camera!"

He firmly ushered me to a pair of highbacked chairs on one side of his office and indicated the one on the left. I sat as ordered.

No. Noooo . . .

He sat in the one on the right, set his legs firmly shoulder width apart, and leaned forward, giving me the most encouraging yet serious look I'd ever encountered. I stared at his face, smiling the way I did when I was seconds away from losing my bearing, and the sergeant obediently took the picture. I stood and backed away with relief, letting GySgt Moore take his turn.

After the sergeant left the room with her camera, the gentlemen talked a bit longer, and then we said goodbye. I don't think I uttered more than two sentences the whole visit.

On our way out, the sergeant stopped us and handed us large, eight-by-ten color copies of each of the photos in a neatly embossed black folder. They were both signed by the sergeant major of the Marine Corps in gold sharpie. We thanked her and left.

Back out in the hallway, once we were clear of everyone else, I paused and leaned against the wall, staring wide eyed at the smooth tile floor. GySgt Moore seemed very pleased about the whole affair and tried to buck me up.

"See, Staff Sergeant, you didn't do anything stupid, and he was really cool. All good, right?"

I looked up at him.

"Gunny . . . even his underwear is Marine Corps red!"

54.

BEING A MARINE IS LIT

Life in the operations center could get a bit slow at times. TVs mounted on the walls played the news channels, and we had a modest amount of internet access, but being Marines, our primary entertainment was talking shit to each other.

One afternoon, I was leaning against a desk, chatting with the sergeant who was leading that shift's watch, Sgt Owens. We were trading barbs that culminated in my saying something that caused Sgt Owens to grab a big handful of fast-food napkins and hurl the whole lot at me. As napkins rained around me, Sgt Pierce and Sgt Schulte cackled and hooted. I raced to think of how to assert my dominance without crossing the line into an actual clash, and thus I grabbed a bottle of hand sanitizer off the desk. Slamming the pump with my hand, I squirted hand sanitizer all over Owens's cammies. A Marine with fewer bacteria wasn't a bad thing, in my opinion.

Sgt Owens laughed and protested that I had in fact just made him extremely flammable.

Shit, he's right.

I knew he smoked, so I suggested he dry off before he went to smoke again. But Sgt Pierce wasn't about to wait that long. As I turned my back to collect the napkins off the floor, Pierce scooped up a can of cleaning spray from a nearby locker and pulled out a lighter. When I went to put the napkins back on the desk, a burst of flame shot past me, startling me. The flame had been directed toward Sgt Owens, and I slapped the can of cleaning spray out of Pierce's hand.

"What the FUCK ARE YOU DOING?!"

Pierce looked surprised.

"Seeing if he really was flammable, Staff Sergeant."

"WHY??"

"But . . . it's your fault he's flammable!" Pierce seemed to feel this was adequate justification for making Marine en flambé. Not his fault. Mine.

Sgt Owens was mercifully unharmed. After a quick assessment showed no one had been hurt and no property had been damaged, I shouted at Pierce a bit more, and that was the end of it. After I collected myself, I turned back to Owens.

"Wanna go smoke?"

55.

KARMA COMES FOR WINKLEVOSS

admired many Marines while I was on active duty, but the people who most impressed me were the Marines under me. As the sun set on my final contract, I had a young platoon sergeant who regularly amazed me. I didn't tell him so because confessing such things to a junior Marine is bad manners, but I tried to show my appreciation in small ways.

Sgt Winklevoss, whom I mentioned earlier, was consistently polite, positive, professional, and other words that start with P. When a Marine injured himself on a run, Sgt Winklevoss took him to the hospital and stayed with him for hours to make sure he got back to base okay. If someone's car stopped working, even at 0200, Sgt Winklevoss would answer his phone and come get them. If anyone ever needed help of any kind, Sgt Winklevoss might as well have had a mask and cape, so often did he come to save the day. I reminded myself never to take him for granted. That kind of selflessness is rare.

In August 2012, the Marine Corps was trimming the force hard. The bloat from two wars was becoming unsustainable, especially with drawdowns in both combat theaters. Measures included such unexpected moves as the Voluntary Early Release Program (VERP), which allowed Marines to cancel the final year of their contract and return to the civilian world ahead of schedule. That was unheard of, and I personally availed myself of it, trimming off a previous contract extension.

Additionally, the Marine Corps throttled reenlistments. For years, if a person reached the end of their contract and for some crazy reason wanted to remain in the Corps, it had been a fairly simple process. Unless you had gross misconduct on your record, you were generally accepted. Sometimes, they even paid bonuses to certain jobs if the needs of the Marine Corps were high enough. Now, though, they were closing out reenlistment spots by the hour. Those who got their paperwork in the very second they were eligible were still being turned away and forced out. You either changed your MOS or else started to learn what a resume looked like.

While I had decided to part ways with the Marine Corps, I watched my troops struggle with this situation. Sgt Valcourt, who had always been very forgiving toward me when I was in a foul temper and was reliable in all matters IT, could not reenlist. We came from the same places in Florida, so I felt particularly bad that he couldn't follow his original plan, but I couldn't do anything for him—or for Sgt Walker, Cpl Gadtke, Sgt Kelly, the list went on. One by one, Marines had to figure out their next steps, much sooner than they'd anticipated.

Sgt Winklevoss was one of the first ones to drop off his paperwork for reenlistment. When Marines do something like that, they usually have to find the first staff NCO in their chain of command, hand them the documents, and hope like hell that NCO gives enough of a rat's ass to process it up to command promptly. Being forced to rely on someone else to prioritize your needs and goals out of a sense of duty could give a rock anxiety. I tried to build up a reputation among the troops that, if nothing else, I'd handle their administrative needs consistently and with urgency.

I was sitting at my computer, reading over yet another stupid email I wasn't even sure pertained to me, when Sgt Winklevoss hurried up to the desk. He was actually wringing his hands and looked genuinely upset.

"Staff Sergeant?" Even his voice had a pleading note to it.

"Hey, Wink, what's up? You okay?" I frowned.

Sgt Winklevoss looked like he was the one who needed saving. That made me worry. What on earth had happened *this time*?

"Staff Sergeant, my reenlistment got denied! I took the request to MSgt Thomas, and he said that he'd help me out with finding a new MOS to lat move[60] into, but he's been on leave, and I don't know when he's coming back, and I don't know what to do!"

The whole thing came out in a rush. Winklevoss was panicking.

He wasn't wrong to panic, either. His future, his career, was hanging

---

60   Basically, change jobs

in the balance here, and every single minute, the window closed further still. Things were happening so fast that if he went to bed tonight without something major happening, tomorrow might be too late for him.

I blinked. Winklevoss had always had my back, always kept me in the loop, and watching his dreams drown was unbearable. The Marine Corps had taught me to wrestle giants (it's easy, actually, if you remember where the soft bits are), and this was one big bastard. Winklevoss was looking to me. I had to do something. He trusted me. He came to me because he really thought I could help, and if I disappointed him, what the hell was the point of even being a staff NCO?

"Give me your Social Security number.[61] Let me make a few phone calls. Don't leave the shop in case I need to find you very quickly, okay?"

Sgt Winklevoss breathed out and rattled off the number for me. He looked a little less terrified. I dismissed him and turned to my computer, looking up an old friend from 3rd Recon. MGySgt White was now a big player up at Manpower in Quantico. Marines and their duty station assignments, as well as the available seats in the MOS, were his field. If he couldn't help me, he probably knew someone who could. Not only was he a former Recon Marine and a data chief, but he was also a former scout sniper. The old man was an absolute beast.

I dialed him up, hoping against hope that he had yet another miracle up his sleeve. MGySgt White was practically magical in his ability to find solutions, and he was responsible in more ways than one for the entire shape of my own career. I'd never find a way to thank him enough, and here I was, about to ask for yet another favor.

"Be advised, this is an unsecure line. Good afternoon, sir or ma'am, MMEA-6, Master Gunnery Sergeant White speaking. How can I help you?" The gruff voice crackling on the landline was a very sweet sound right then. The likelihood he would be out running a marathon, or whatever he did on his lunch breaks, was pretty high.

"Good afternoon, Master Guns. It's Staff Sergeant Salzgeber. I'm having an issue with a Marine's reenlistment. Do you have a moment?" We might be friends, but I wasn't going to drop even one beat of proper form here. Good manners are of paramount importance when supplicating to the Manpower deities.

Master Guns didn't waste words. "What?"

---

61   Required for nearly every transaction in the entire military anywhere

"Sgt Winklevoss was trying to reenlist in our field. It's closed. Do you have any seats left in Intel? I'm trying to help him get a lat move."

"Social?"

I repeated the number Winklevoss had given me. I waited in dutiful silence while Master Guns performed whatever strange alchemy on his end decided these things. After a solid minute, he announced, "I have two openings left in imagery intel. Does he want it? His scores are good enough to qualify."

"Yes!" I answered, even without checking with Wink. I knew to say something immediately or else see the whole thing vanish like steam.

There was another long silence. Then Master Guns spoke again.

"Can you get to J-2? The Intel office in your building?"

"Yes, Master Guns, right away."

"Go. Ask for MSgt Bayless. Tell him who you've brought with you. They'll give your sergeant the test for qualification. If he scores well enough, we'll process his package today."

"Thank you, Master Gunnery Sergeant!"

"Rah." He hung up.

I leapt from my desk, banging my knee on the edge of it as I stood. Sgt Winklevoss was startled by the noise and stared as I charged over to his desk a few feet away.

"Wink, you down to do imagery intel?"

I spat the question with clear intention that he say "yes" or "no" only.

Sgt Winklevoss's other sterling characteristic was the ability to grasp urgent situations with alacrity. "Yes, Staff Sergeant."

"Grab your notebook and two black ink pens. We're going to J-2. Bring your ID and lock your computer."

Without a single word, Sgt Winklevoss obeyed. We walked through the halls with the kind of purpose and urgency that would bring a happy tear to the eye of the most rabid drill instructor. Within five minutes, we were at the door to J-2. We entered, signed in the logbook as required by security, and I asked for MSgt Bayless. He came out (no one is allowed in J-2 without heaps of procedure and paperwork, so it's easier to just wait outside for them instead) and looked at my name tapes.

"Staff Sergeant Salzgeber. This is your sergeant?"

He turned and looked at Sgt Winklevoss, who was rigid with anticipation.

"Yes, Master Sergeant. Can you help him out? He wants to join your ranks."

MSgt Bayless looked at Wink. Sgt Winklevoss was fit, tall, and superbly disciplined, and therefore MSgt Bayless saw no immediate red flags that disqualified him as a desirable candidate.

"Yes, although I have two sergeants who are taking the test for the last seats with him. If he outscores one of them, then we should be able to do something for him."

Wink shot me a worried look, but at time like this, I behaved as if I knew Sgt Winklevoss could steamroll any comers with no effort at all. If he was unsure about this, I'd have confidence enough for both of us.

"He will not disappoint you, Master Sergeant."

MSgt Bayless nodded and then verified Sgt Winklevoss had no cell phones or other prohibited devices. He gestured to a door off to one side of the reception area.

"Go in there and take a seat. The other guy hasn't shown up yet, so we'll give him another minute or two, and then we'll start." Master Sergeant turned to me and said, "You can go, Staff Sergeant. We'll send him back when it's over."

I bowed my head and thanked him before departing. *Welp, Wink, don't let us all down.*

An hour later, I got a call on my desk phone.

"Staff Sergeant Salzgeber, it's Master Sergeant Bayless. Your boy outscored everyone. We'll take him. I'll call MMEA-6 right now. Tell him to start the paperwork."

"Aye, Master Sergeant. Thank you so much!" I was elated. Internally screaming with joy like it was *my* dream coming true, I got up to see if Wink was back yet. Just as I reached the door handle, it turned, and Sgt Winklevoss emerged into the office.

"WINK, YOU FUCKING DID IT!" I bounced on my heels and then, realizing people were staring at me, regained my composure. "Uh . . . I mean, start the paperwork. You got the seat. You are going to be able to reenlist."

The look of gratitude and respect Sgt Winklevoss gave me right that moment will sustain me through whatever dark times may lie ahead. I was happy, I was proud, and I felt that for once, I'd really made a difference. It was all worth it.

When MSgt Thomas returned from leave several days later, he ordered Sgt Winklevoss to come to his office so they could talk about what he'd like to do about reenlisting. Sgt Winklevoss, oblivious to the ego play here, simply replied, "Oh, don't worry about it, Master Sergeant. SSgt Salzgeber already took care of me."

I heard through the grapevine that MSgt Thomas was absolutely furious with me over that. He was not pleased with the notion that I had that kind of influence, being notoriously vain about his rank and position. But I don't know how he planned on helping Wink in the first place.

Don't care. Still won. Wink, wherever you are now, brother, great work and Semper Fi.

56.

THE MOROCCAN DINNER NIGHT

A s my time in the Marine Corps wound down to the final few months, I decided that there was only one way to go out. I wanted to throw a party.

Not a kegger, not a rager, not a frat party with stumbling, drunk coeds all over the place. That's not my style. I wanted a party that would be linked indelibly with my own persona. I was not motivated by vanity as much as I wanted Marines to remember me—because I knew I'd always remember them. There were normal little lunches to send a Marine off, but those were dull, and Master Sergeant usually made them worse by watching everyone like a hawk and listening to every word spoken. Most of the time, going-away lunches became activities to escape at the first opportunity. I didn't want to go out like that.

At the Pentagon, morale was low. Marines who had been stationed there straight out of comm school often looked morose and disappointed. Most Marines looked that way after the first year or two, but these guys were like tigers bred in captivity. They weren't sure they were really Marines because they didn't even go to the rifle range annually for weapons qualification. They sat at their air-conditioned desks in windowless rooms with bright, awful fluorescent lights, staring at their uniforms and wondering if they weren't more like civilians with extra rules. As the Operations SNCOIC (read: manager of sorts, but Gunny takes all the credit), I felt for them.

The problem lies in the oxymoron of "mandatory fun." Marines at the staff-NCO level hold "functions," not parties. Parties are wild and involve alcohol. Mandatory fun functions involve forcing everyone into "appropriate civilian attire" and making them give up four hours of their normal time off to come to a specific location and eat bad BBQ and play "combat" frisbee. In short, no matter how good the intentions are, as soon as attendance becomes a requirement, it loses all appeal.

On top of that, there weren't facilities for my old standby of martial arts ground fighting, so as their staff sergeant, I wasn't sure how to go about lifting platoon spirits without breaking rules of propriety. Those rules were complex and required adherence if I didn't want to lose face with the troops. Basically, I could invite everyone to a gathering, provided that I invited everyone. I could not make distinctions between who I didn't mind and who I couldn't stand. All or nothing. I could NOT serve alcohol or facilitate the provision of alcohol—and bear in mind, alcohol-fueled misconduct was practically a stereotype of Marine gatherings. Conversely, sober gatherings weren't much of a draw. The usual resolution was to have the gathering at a restaurant where the restaurant, not the host, was responsible for serving alcohol and sorting out whom to cut off and when.

I also considered carefully what kind of burden the gathering would place on attendees, although any decent host in or out of the military makes this calculus. Marines weren't cash-rich people by and large, so throwing any sort of event where the participants had to pony up more than five dollars was frowned upon. Finally, it was up to the host to decide if the gathering was mandatory or not.

"Make it mandatory." GySgt Moore was having none of my bullshit today.

"Gunny, I want it to be voluntary! Come on, I'm paying for everything; I don't want to force attendance. It's just a dinner."

We both knew that if there is one thing Marines will turn up for, minus alcohol, it's free chow. I didn't see the need to make it mandatory if everyone was going to show up for a hot meal anyhow.

GySgt Moore sighed. "Really, Salz, if you do that, no one will come."

"No, Gunny, I already took an RSVP. Like, thirty people are coming!"

"A what?"

"An R-S-V—look, I asked who's coming, all right? They're coming. Even our civilian boss is coming, and he's bringing his lady friend. Everyone is coming. *You're* coming!"

"All right, but if your party sucks, it's your fault. I tried."

I scratched together my slush-fund savings and went into downtown

Washington, DC, to a local restaurant called Marrakesh. It was a lush place, yet strangely accepted cash only and required advance payment. Basically, I prepaid for my platoon to have a banquet.

I started a small but effective PR campaign to get everyone to come. A couple of the troops with whom I had rapport specifically talked about how it was going to be awesome. We'd all drive into downtown DC on a Wednesday night (so not to interfere with the Marines' personal plans for their off time), and we'd go to this unknown place, and it would be wild. The whole meal was paid for. All they had to do was show up! No one cared what they wore, so long as they didn't get arrested! There would be belly dancers. Half the guys had never even heard of belly dancers before. But of course, as someone who had studied Arabic and the Middle East, I'd heard of them, and I figured a Moroccan restaurant with belly dancers was just so me. More importantly, it was just so them. (Not that they knew it. Yet.)

There was one holdout. Sgt Quincy and I had never seen eye to eye. He thought I was stuck-up and treated some Marines better than others. I thought he whined and complained too often. Plus, I thought he was lazy. The result was that I just avoided him altogether, which is probably where he got the ideas he had about me. When I announced the dinner, Sgt Quincy immediately declined. He was very smug about it, positive that his example would lead others to decline and result in embarrassing me. He decided to stay home that night. It was now a contest of wills.

Wednesday night came, and at the rate of five people per car, we all crammed into vehicles and found the place, just off a side street with a tiny parking lot that didn't charge for customers. As Marines piled out, everyone got excited. We were dressed like normal twenty-somethings, and protocol for inter-rank behavior was relaxed. Some guys had brought their wives or girlfriends. Gunny was even going easy on the knife hands. There were nearly thirty people, and we all gaggled our way to the front door of the restaurant.

Marrakesh had thick wooden doors with studs all over them. There was no window. The exterior was decorated in stucco and blue-and-white-tiled Middle Eastern patterns. A single lamp by the front door cast dim light on the portal. I approached and, as required, knocked. A slot shot open at eye level, through which a swarthy man in a fez peered.

"Yes, *sa'eedati?*"

"Salzgeber party, sir. We're here."

The guys gawked over my shoulder at the strange door ritual. I smirked.

"Very good, *sa'eedati*."

He closed the slot and then opened the large door. When the port was completely open to allow us all entrance, the sight of the interior brought a hush over our group. Couches, cushions, and pillows were everywhere. Low tables were set in the middle of the lounging areas, arranged like a collection of small, brightly colored living rooms instead of a restaurant. There were low-lighting chandeliers, staff in traditional Moroccan garb, and chatter in Moroccan Arabic from a few tables near the large, restful-looking area that had been set aside for us. This was about as close to the Middle East as most of the Marines in my platoon had ever been. Even the ones who had gone to Iraq weren't used to scenery like this.

At our two tables, we broke into two groups, segregating comfortably along normal lines of rank. But it didn't take long for everyone to realize that rank wouldn't allow for even distribution. Plus, there were ladies present, and those ladies generally wished to accompany the person they came with, so in no time flat, we were all intermixed comfortably. SSgt Jones sat next to Cpl Milby and his wife, I lounged comfortably between Gunny Moore and Sgt Schulte, and our civilian boss, Brian, perched near the end of the couch with his lady friend. The lance corporals and privates were strewn about in between everybody.

Soon, the waiters arrived at the table to wash everyone's hands and take orders for drinks. Alcohol could be purchased from the establishment, so everyone sorted out their preferred liquid courage booster, and the night began.

As food was paraded to the tables and hefty baskets of bread offered, it dawned on the crew that we would be dining with our hands. After a few false starts, SSgt Jones broke the tension by scooping up some chicken and announcing, "This makes me feel like a BEAST!"

Everyone laughed, and Cpl Milby one-upped him by snapping a hollowed chicken bone and using it like a straw to siphon chicken juice off the tray. Almost an hour into our meal, things were getting raucous, albeit still within normal limits, when the lighting turned very low. The Marines paused, looked confused, and strained to see what was going on.

Then it happened.

A spotlight snapped on. There, on a rug, on a table being used as a stage, was the belly dancer. Several men pulled out drums and began to tap out a very Middle Eastern rhythm. One began playing the flute. As soon as the melody coalesced, the girl, clad in a bright-pink-and-gold bra top with sheer skirts of equally bright-pink, gauzy material, snapped her head back, sending her long black hair cascading down her back. Snapping her fingers, she started dancing, moving with a fluidity and grace that made me wonder if she had a different spine than I did. She strutted and skipped back and forth, going around the rug, balancing a sword on her head while swaying and winding to the beat, all without looking like any of this took the slightest effort. She wore a brilliant smile of private delight as she danced. She was beautiful.

Well, don't take my word for it. I took note of my guests' transfixed stares. Even we ladies were in awe. She was killing it with curves that would never have made it into a fashion magazine but were truly eye-opening in real life.

One young sergeant in particular sat with his mouth slack and his drink completely forgotten in a limp hand. His face was that of a man who had found what he had been missing all along. I giggled and drank from my wineglass. If nothing else, the dancing girl was winning me "party of the year" while all I had to do was eat, drink, and be merry. Well done indeed.

When the girl completed her routine and was whisked away (wrapped in a blanket to protect against indecency or whatever), the lights came on, and everyone turned back to the table. While we had been riveted, the waiters had swiftly cleared the area. Now baklava and tea sat before each of us, tempting us to further overindulgence. I kept elbowing Gunny as the night wound down.

"Glad I made it mandatory, huh, Gunny?"

"Oh, shut up. You got lucky."

"Just saying, all these people here—"

"Go RSVP yourself."

We finally cleared out by ten in the evening, and with a watchful eye to make sure no one got in a driver's seat drunk, we all went our separate ways. For some, the night was young, but I wanted to go home and sleep. That way, the whole party would stay perfect in my head. It had gone as flawlessly as a script. I was over the moon.

The next day when everyone trickled into work, there was Sgt Quincy. Marines were gossiping about the night before; the sergeant who'd fallen in love with the dancer said he'd met two other girls later that evening who professed to possess belly-dancing skills, and he was going to see them this weekend. Everyone told Sgt Quincy about it while he sat and fumed. Finally, because I can be a bit of a smug asshole at times, I went and leaned on the wall by his desk.

"Should've come, Quin. I'd have bought you dinner."

"Yeah, Staff Sergeant, everyone keeps saying that."

He got up, grumbling under his breath, and left the office. I laughed quietly and went back to work. It was the final victory before I left active duty a mere ninety days later.

57.

THE WORLD CHANGED, AND I DIDN'T FEEL A THING

E very Marine, and I do mean *every* Marine, daydreams about leaving the Marine Corps. Some of us start having that dream in boot camp. For others it takes a bit longer. But even those who stay to the very limit of what is allowed dream of the end: What will it feel like? What will I do first? Will I tell off the entire chain of command and storm out in a blaze of profane glory?

In October 2012,[62] I was about to experience it firsthand. The unimaginable day had arrived. I drove to Ft Myer in Arlington, Virginia, and made my way to Henderson Hall where the Marine Corps and I would conclude our business for good. As I walked through the doors, my brain froze over. When I left through these same doors, I would no longer be on active duty. I was no longer a Marine. I mean, yes, I know "Once a Marine, always a Marine." But I wouldn't be one of *them*. I entered the dark stone hallway decorated with motivational posters, a neat set of eight-by-ten pictures of the chain of command all the way to the president of the United States, and the Marine Corps flag majestically displaying every battle streamer that the unit had earned. I took a deep breath and headed up the stairs.

On the second floor was an office for our military IDs. I had an appointment at 1000. As I ascended the stairs, I moved for senior Marines bustling by, heading toward whatever duties they had at the moment.

---

62 Ironically, the date the Mayans supposedly predicted the world would end. Mine certainly did.

I no longer mattered in that regard. They didn't have anything for me, and I couldn't help. Feeling like I was operating someone else's body, I turned in to the office and stood rigid in front of the receiving desk. The woman behind the desk gave me a bored expression and mumbled, "Good morning."

"Good morning, ma'am. I'm here to, um, turn in my ID." My throat was tight. *This is what you wanted. You wanted to get out. You wanted to go live a normal life again—if you ever had one. Why are you feeling the beginnings of a panic attack?*

In my head, I wailed. Since joining as an overgrown child, this ID card had been in my life every minute of every day! It told the world who I was and who owned me. It gave me a different set of rules. Giving up my ID card was like . . . becoming no one. I know lots of religions out there espouse the peace and relief of becoming "no one," but right now, it felt like I'd just pop out of existence.

But the Marines taught courage in the face of certain oblivion, so I pulled the ID card from my wallet and set it on the desk. The lady glanced it like she'd seen this a million times and would see it a million more before the end of the day and, smacking her gum, turned to the computer and jammed some keys. I stood, waiting in numb disbelief. This was really happening. *No, something's going to go wrong. I'm going to get to the battalion commander's office, and he's going to chew my ass out for faking an EAS, and I'll get sent right back out of here with my ID and possibly a reprimand.*

The woman turned back to me. "Fill in your name and social on that sheet in front of you. Last four only." I nodded and scooped up the pen, saying nothing. At this point, my face must have looked some kind of way because she broke her bearing and asked, "You excited?"

No, not really. Angry, terrified, and about to throw up.

"Yes, it's a big move." I smiled.

She gave me the glimmerings of a smile and then looked back at her screen. From her desk drawer, she pulled a giant black sharpie that made the whole room smell when she took off the cap. Carefully, she drew a giant black *X* across my ID. Across the picture of my face.

Now I'm no one.

"All right, well, best of luck to you!"

One more brief smile, and she went back to her monitors, watching the news channel that was streaming on the internet.

I turned and left the office. Next stop was the career planner's office.

In a trance, I climbed the stairs to the third floor and found his room off to the side of the battalion's offices. I sat down. SSgt Crumbliss nodded at me but didn't say anything, his headphones blaring some sort of reggaeton music. He rummaged through a stack of big yellow envelopes until he found the one with my name on it. Tossing it across the desk, he dislodged one headphone and asked, "You ready to go see the CO?"

"Yep." I sounded far less shell shocked than I felt.

"Cool. Do us a favor, though, and don't start telling him all the ways you hate the Corps, okay? You're getting out. That's good enough."

"I'll . . . keep it together." I smirked. By this point, the idea of bitching out a colonel had lost its appeal. I wanted it to be over with already.

"You already seen Admin? They sign off your terminal leave and everything?"

"Yes, sir."

"Cool. Cool, cool, cool. All right, let's go." He stopped the music, removed the headphones, and squeezed around his desk to lead the way to the battalion commander's office. I followed, letting years of behavioral conditioning do the work of thinking and feeling. We reached the hatch, and SSgt Crumbliss pounded on it. It was open, he could have just leaned in the door, but hey, why skip the chance to punch a wall when protocol set one up for you?

"Come."

LtCol Billings had a huge dip in his mouth and his feet up on his desk. He was perusing some documents and occasionally moving his head to spit into an empty plastic bottle. We entered and stood at attention until given "At ease." LtCol Billings put down his papers and bottle and came around the desk to look at me. My body stiffened.

"So, you're leaving the Corps, eh? Why?"

"It's just time, sir."

That made him snort. He'd probably gotten some very wild answers to that question. But I had been drained of all the emotions I had about the Marine Corps by this time. Mostly, I just needed things to change, or I was going to be irretrievably broken.

"Good enough." He reached out to SSgt Crumbliss, who handed him the yellow envelope. LtCol Billings dug around in it for a moment and then signed on a line on the front.

"Well, Semper Fi, best wishes, and I hope you have great success." With his duty done, he turned and went back to his seat. "Drive safely,

Staff Sergeant."

"Thank you, sir." I took the yellow envelope from SSgt Crumbliss and retreated from the office. When we reached the hallway, the staff sergeant turned to go back to his own office, and I went left, heading for my final descent down the stairs.

"Good luck, Staff Sergeant!" he called, as his door was shutting.

I stared at the floor with a blank expression. *It's done. All there is now is for me to leave. I no longer belong here.* I walked out in a daze. My brain kept telling me to go places that I had habitually gone for years. *Go back to the shop. Go back to the gym. Time to get chow.*

It wasn't even noon yet. I stepped out into the sunlight, the glass doors closing behind me slowly. I blinked and walked to my car. I got in. I turned it on. I placed the envelope in the seat. I backed out of the parking spot.

When I exited the gates for the final time, something inside finally happened. I pulled over and sobbed. I cried until my whole face was red and glowing. I rocked back and forth in the driver's seat. Then a song came on the radio.

> *"Wished I had told, ooh was (the) only one (uh oh!)*
> *But it's too late, it's too late*
> *He's gone."*

Wiping my face, I put the car back in drive and headed out. Ms. Tracy Salzgeber took herself to lunch that day and didn't put on cammies ever again.

EPILOGUE

SOMETHING ENDS, SOMETHING BEGINS

The thrumming of the car engine lulled both of us into our private thoughts. On the radio, NPR discussed what were probably momentous events of the day. In 2020, momentous events were routine occurrences.

But our own momentous event was taking up all available personal bandwidth.

"Damn, dude. Use your blinkers!" I muttered, changing lanes as the other driver struggled to reach the exit.

"They make me really nervous." Taely hated the idea of driving, a sentiment that set her apart from the previous generation of teenagers, who swarmed the DMV as soon as they reached the age of permission. She sat wringing her hands, staring out the passenger window. Her hair had been clipped so short that it was nearly in male regulations for the Air Force. Otherwise, she was just another skinny girl worried about her future.

"It's all good, Pookie," I tried to soothe her.

She never rebuffed my childish nicknames for her. I felt that I should say something more, but I didn't want to make things worse. Finally, under self-inflicted pressure, I spoke up.

"I'm really proud of you for doing this. You're going to love it. I promise. You'll have your independence, your own income, your basic living expenses covered—"

"Yeah, and college paid for. I know, Mom." She sighed. I shut up and left her to her own thoughts. Sometimes good parenting is knowing when to leave well enough alone.

I pulled into our destination, and we got out of the car, standing on opposite sides. I waited while she dug around for her personal items and then shut the door. For a moment, neither of us moved.

"You ready?"

She gave a semi-shrug and then nodded. "Let's do this."

The beige, three-story office building looked mostly vacant, but the recruiters for all four branches of the military had set up shop on the first floor and did a brisk trade in Fairfax County. As we approached the door, a couple of soldiers emerged, their green-and-brown cammies setting them apart from their fellow service members. One of them stopped to hold the door as Taely went through, and I followed, thanking him. In the tiny lobby, Taely looked around. The doors weren't clearly marked, but she knew what she was looking for.

"Should I at least chat with the Marine Corps recruiter first?" She flashed a wry grin, knowing full well what my reply would be.

"Taely, do you really like the smell of ball sweat? Are you just dying to get yelled at a whole lot and clean rooms?"

It sounded like a rebuke of my *almus pater*,[63] but the truth is, Taely had an entirely different background. She liked asking "Why?" way too much for Marine Corps tastes. She got nervous whenever someone became aggressive. She'd never thrown a punch in her life.

Above all else, I couldn't bear the thought of giving her to the Corps.

---

63   Like an alma mater, except more fatherly. The Marine Corps loves its Latin, hence "Semper Fidelis."

Dedicated to Taely and Ava. Love you guys.

Super-duper thanks to my awesome team:
Maximilian Uriarte/Terminal Lance (Cover and Back Page Art)
Alan Axelrod (Editor and Mentor)
Phillip Schulte-Hordelhoff (Reader)

ABOUT THE AUTHOR

Tracy Salzgeber is a veteran of the US Marine Corps and served from 1999 to 2012.

Her military awards include Joint Service Commendation Medal, Joint Service Achievement Medal, Navy Marine Corps Achievement Medal, Rifle and Pistol Marksman badges, and brown belt martial arts rank.

Tracy continued to pursue her education and graduated from American University in 2017 with a master's degree in international relations. Tracy's off-duty activities include studying languages, playing video games, writing, and, when opportunity allows, travel.

'Rah.

CPSIA information can be obtained
at www.ICGtesting.com
Printed in the USA
LVHW110928290522
720029LV00005B/40